Q & A SERIES
REVENUE LAW

SECOND EDITION

Cavendish
Publishing
Limited

London • Sydney

First published in Great Britain 1996 by Cavendish Publishing Limited, The Glass House, Wharton Street, London WC1X 9PX, United Kingdom

Telephone: +44 (0) 171 278 8000   Facsimile: +44 (0) 171 278 8080

e-mail: info@cavendishpublishing.com

Visit our Home Page on http://www.cavendishpublishing.com

© Ramjohn, M   1999
First Edition   1996
Second Edition   1999

British Library Cataloguing in Publication Data

Ramjohn, Mohamed
Revenue law – 2nd ed
1. Internal revenue law – Great Britain
I. Title
343.4'1'036

ISBN 1 85941 412 5

Printed and bound in Great Britain

Q & A SERIES
REVENUE LAW

SECOND EDITION

M Ramjohn LLB, LLM, ATII, JP, Barrister

Principal Lecturer in Law
Thames Valley University

Cavendish
Publishing
Limited

London • Sydney

TITLES IN THE Q&A SERIES

BUSINESS LAW
CIVIL LIBERTIES
COMMERCIAL LAW
COMPANY LAW
CONFLICT OF LAWS
CONSTITUTIONAL & ADMINISTRATIVE LAW
CONTRACT LAW
CRIMINAL LAW
EMPLOYMENT LAW
ENGLISH LEGAL SYSTEM
EQUITY & TRUSTS
EUROPEAN UNION LAW
EVIDENCE
FAMILY LAW
INTELLECTUAL PROPERTY LAW
INTERNATIONAL TRADE LAW
JURISPRUDENCE
LAND LAW
PUBLIC INTERNATIONAL LAW
REVENUE LAW
SUCCESSION, WILLS &PROBATE
TORT LAW
'A' LEVEL LAW

ACKNOWLEDGMENTS

I would like to express my gratitude to Dr Abimbola Olowofoyeku, of Keele University, who, at relatively short notice, made a significant contribution to the section on inheritance tax.

I would also like to thank the staff at Cavendish Publishing for their continuing friendly support and ever-efficient work in compiling the tables of cases and statutes and the index.

CONTENTS

INTRODUCTION

The Chartered Institute of Taxation cites a former financial secretary's comments on a finance bill:

> I confess to the Hon Gentleman that I have studied the text of Note 2 to Table 2 for some time. I am not sure that it was clear to me precisely what it meant, either before the amendment that I am now moving or after it.

The tax codes have been branded by experts as too long and at times too complicated. The Chancellor of the Exchequer in his budget statement on Tuesday 28 November 1995 said:

> Tax law has become too long and complicated. Some experts have described it as incomprehensible. The Inland Revenue will shortly be publishing a report on tax simplification. We will propose that the revenue tax code is rewritten in plain English – a major task.

It seems that the codes are set for an overhaul which could take at least five years. This process has already been commenced, but some experts believe that putting the tax codes into plain English will not necessarily shorten them – an alleged ambition of Oliver Cromwell, who is said to have wanted to reduce the laws of England to the size of a pocket book. The conversion will probably increase the length of legislation, but, mercifully, will mean that that the average business person will be able to understand tax law.

Despite the 'doom and gloom' comments above, this book cannot take the slog out of revenue law, but it can take the fear away from the study of the subject. It is an immensely important, rewarding and fascinating subject. A book full of questions and answers could be the single most important purchase that you, as a student, make in preparing for your examination. Having experienced similar questions will give you a tremendous advantage before sitting down to write the examination. Having actually answered 50 questions on the same topics as those on which you are to be examined must give you a good chance of meeting the ambiguities and peculiarities of terminology that arise in an examination paper on revenue law.

The purpose of this book is to help the student in his or her revision of revenue law and to provide him or her with a means of gaining practical experience in the answering of examination questions. It is not designed to give a summary of the law on the subject and is not intended to be a substitute for one of the recognised standard textbooks.

I have endeavoured to state the law as at 1 December 1998.

M Ramjohn
London
December 1998

TABLE OF CASES

TAX TABLES

Income tax

	1997–98			1998–99	
	Rates			*Rates*	
Lower	20%	up to £4,100	Lower	20%	up to £4,300
Basic	23%	£4,101–£26,100	Basic	23%	£4,301–£27,100
Higher	40%	above £26,100	Higher	40%	above £27,100

Discretionary trusts are chargeable at 34%.

Tax credit on UK dividends is 20%. This is treated as satisfying the full liability of basic rate taxpayers. Higher rate taxpayers are required to pay an additional 20% and discretionary trusts an additional 15%.

Income tax allowances

	Age	*1997–98*	*% relief*	*1998–99*	*% relief*
Personal allowance					
	Age under 65	£4,045		£4,195	
	Age under 65	£5,220		£5,410	
	Age 75 and over	£5,400		£5,600	
Married couples					
	Age under 65	£1,830	15 Tax credit	£1,900	15 Tax credit
	Age 65–74	£3,185	15 Tax credit	£3,305	15 Tax credit
	Age 75 and over	£3,225	15 Tax credit	£3,345	15 Tax credit
Additional allowance for children		£1,830	15 Tax credit	£1,900	15 Tax credit
Widow's bereavement allowance		£1,830	15 Tax credit	£1,900	15 Tax credit
Blind person's allowance		£1,280	15 Tax credit	£1,330	15 Tax credit

Value added tax

The value has been and remains 17.5%. Registration threshold from 1 April 1998 is an annual turnover of £50,000.

Capital gains tax

Individuals pay tax on capital gains at their marginal rate of income tax – 20%, 23% or 40% as the case may be.

Companies pay corporation tax on their capital gains at their normal rates.

Corporation tax

	Financial year 1997	Financial year 1998
Standard rate	31%	31%
Small company's rate	21%	21%
where profits less than	£300,000	£300,000
profits up to:	£1,500,000	£1,500,000
Marginal relief fraction	1/40	1/40
Advance corporation tax	1/4	1/4

Inheritance tax

Mode of transfer	Rates	From 6 April 1997	From 6 April 1998
Lifetime or death	nil	up to £215,000	up to £223,000
Lifetime	20%	above £215,000	above £223,000
Death	40%	above £215,000	above £223,000

Taper relief is granted in respect of chargeable transfers made more than three but less than seven years before death.

SECTION I
INCOME TAX

CHAPTER 1

INCOME TAX: GENERAL PRINCIPLES

Introduction

Income tax was first introduced in 1799 and was repealed in 1816. In 1842, income tax was again introduced and formed the basis of the current system. The Income and Corporation Taxes Act 1988 (ICTA), as amended by subsequent Finance Acts, consolidated the provisions contained in the Income and Corporation Taxes Act 1970. ICTA does not purport to be a codifying statute, that is, the Act does not attempt to incorporate the results of decided cases or correct anomalies, but simply collects the current statutory rules and places them in one statute. Obviously, such an instrument requires regular amendment and has been regularly amended by subsequent Finance Acts. The Taxes Management Act 1970 (TMA) deals with administrative matters. The capital allowances legislation was first consolidated in the Capital Allowances Act 1968 and has again been recently consolidated in the Capital Allowances Act 1990.

The 'income tax year' (or year of assessment) commences from 6 April in one year and ends on 5 April in the following year.

Liability to tax exists if the taxpayer's activity falls within the provisions of the Acts in force. In interpreting the Taxes Act (the Income and Corporation Taxes Act 1988 (TA)), it is necessary to refer to the considerable volume of case law on the subject. It is a basic principle of tax law that if a person comes within the clear provisions of a taxing statute, he is liable to pay tax, however great the hardship may appear to be. Accordingly, it is legally permissible, within strict limits, for a person to arrange his affairs so as to minimise his liability to taxation. This is called *tax avoidance*. On the other hand, *evasion* of tax is unlawful and may result in heavy penalties (and even imprisonment).

Income is classified according to the source from which it is derived. The basis on which the amount of taxable income is measured or computed differs as between Schedules. The taxpayer is assessed on his *statutory* income, which is the aggregate income computed according to the rules of each Schedule. There are currently four Schedules which classify income. Income which is not classified within at least one of these Schedules is exempt from tax.

Question 1

Explain and discuss the scope of the 'Schedular system' of assessing income tax.

Answer plan

This is a standard 'book' question on the relationship between the Schedules as a means of assessing income tax. A good answer should discuss:

- the Schedules;
- source doctrine;
- income tax is one tax;
- mutually exclusive Schedules;
- Revenue choice within Cases.

Answer

Income tax is charged by reference to years of assessment in respect of income comprised in the Schedules A, D, E and F (s 1 of the Taxes Act 1988 (TA)). A year of assessment commences on 6 April during a calendar year and ends on 5 April following. The Schedules are outlined below.

Schedule A (s 15): this Schedule taxes the annual profits or gains arising in respect of rents, rentcharges and similar receipts from land in the UK.

Schedule D (s 18): this Schedule assesses income tax by reference to six Cases as follows:

Case I –   the annual profits or gains arising from a trade carried on in the UK or elsewhere;

Case II –   the annual profits or gains arising from a profession or vocation;

Case III – interest, annuities and other annual payments as well as discounts and public revenue dividends not charged under Schedule C;

Case IV –   income arising from securities outside the UK and not charged under Schedule C;

Case V –   income arising from possessions outside the UK, not being income consisting of emoluments of any office or employment;

Case VI –   the annual profits or gains not falling under any other Case of Schedule D and not charged under any other Schedule.

Schedule E (s 19): this Schedule is sub-divided into three Cases:

Case I –   the taxpayer who is both resident and ordinarily resident in the UK is liable to income tax on his emoluments derived from an office or employment, subject to s 192 in respect of foreign emoluments;

Case II –   applies to emoluments of those not resident (or if resident, then not ordinarily in the UK). The taxpayer is assessed on emoluments attributable to duties performed in the UK;

Case III – charges tax in respect of emoluments arising for any year of assessment in which the office holder or employee is resident in the UK but the emoluments escape tax under the two other Cases. The emoluments are assessed to tax to the extent that they are remitted to the UK.

Schedule F (s 20): this Schedule assesses tax on dividends and other distributions issued by a company resident in the UK.

The Schedules classify and tax income according to the source from which it is derived. Accordingly, if a source ceases to exist prior to the commencement of a year of assessment but the income derived from that source is paid or credited to the taxpayer during the year of assessment in question, the profit, subject to special provisions to the contrary, escapes tax. In *Bray v Best* (1989), a payment related to an employment that was no longer in existence at the time of the payment escaped income tax on the ground that in the year of receipt a taxable source did not exist. This Schedule E principle has been reversed for 1989–90 and following years by s 19(4A) of the TA 1988. Today, emoluments are assessable to income tax in the year of receipt, notwithstanding that these relate to services performed in earlier years.

The TA 1988 has created several sources of income within the Schedules, each with its special rules of computation, but one point which underpins the Schedules is that they collectively comprise one tax – income tax. Thus, income tax is a generic description of a tax levied under each of the Schedules. The effect is that income tax which is due to the Revenue under one Schedule (say Schedule A) may be used to reduce income tax which is overpaid under a different Schedule (say Schedule D Case I). In *London County Council v AG* (1901), the local authority received rents (net) from which income tax had been deducted under Schedule A. The local authority also received interest (net) from which income tax had been deducted. On paying interest on its consolidated stock, the local authority deducted tax under Schedule D Case III. It then reduced the tax for which it was liable to pay to the Revenue by deducting the tax that was paid or credited on its behalf under both Schedules A and D. The Revenue opposed this deduction. The House of Lords held in favour of the taxpayer.

Although the Schedules are inter-related, it seems that once a source of income is identified and taxable under one Schedule the same income cannot be assessed under a different Schedule. In *Fry v Salisbury House Estate Ltd* (1930), the company received rents from unfurnished offices in a building. (The assessment at this time was in respect of the *notional rent* namely the annual value of the property less a statutory allowance.) The notional rents, which were less than the actual profits, were assessable under Schedule A. The company also provided services for the offices such as heating and cleaning at an additional charge. These profits were assessable under Schedule D Case I. The Revenue purported to assess the company under Schedule D Case I in respect of the actual rents received as reduced by the notional rents. The House of Lords held in favour of the taxpayer. The assessment under Schedule A precluded the assessment under Schedule D.

The same principle applies to expenses which the taxpayer claims are deductible. Accordingly, where a taxpayer incurs expenses in respect of his Schedule E appointment which are not deductible from his Schedule E income, owing to the strict nature of this rule, the taxpayer is not entitled to deduct the expense from his Schedule D income, see *Mitchell and Edon v Ross* (1961), a doctor who was in private practice (Schedule D) also held a part time appointment as a consultant (Schedule E). His Schedule E expenses could not be deductible from his Schedule D income.

Although the Schedules are mutually exclusive, if a source of income falls within one Schedule with multiple Cases, the Revenue is entitled to select the Case which would yield the greatest amount of tax. In *Liverpool, London and Globe Insurance Co v Bennett* (1913), the taxpayer company was entitled to receive interest from its investments abroad but the interest was not remitted to the UK. Such profits of the business under Case I of Schedule D were taxable but under Case IV escaped tax if not remitted to the UK. The Revenue elected to assess the taxpayer under Case I. The House of Lords held that the Revenue was entitled to elect. It should be pointed out that, occasionally, an express provision may overrule this principle, for example, Schedule D Case VI may only be used in respect of profits or gains which do not fall under any other Case of Schedule D. Similarly, Schedule E Case III may not be used to tax emoluments within Cases I or II.

Question 2

Every man is entitled, if he can, to arrange his affairs so that the tax attaching under the appropriate Acts is less than it otherwise would be. If he succeeds in ordering them so as to secure that result, then, however unappreciative the Commissioners of Inland Revenue or his fellow taxpayers may be of his ingenuity, he cannot be compelled to pay an increased tax. [*Per* Lord Tomlin in *IRC v Duke of Westminster* (1936).]

Consider the accuracy of this statement.

Answer plan

In your answer, you should consider:

*   construction of documents in *IRC v Mallaby-Deeley* (1938);
*   Eveleigh LJ (dissenting) in *Floor v Davies* (1978);
*   *IRC v Plummer* (1980);
*   the 'emerging principle' in *Ramsay v IRC* (1981);
*   affirmation and further clarification of the 'emerging principle' in *Burmah Oil v IRC* (1982);
*   extension to 'linear transactions' in *Furniss v Dawson* (1984);
*   limitations in consolidated appeals in *Craven v White; IRC v Bowater; Baylis v Gregory* (1984);
*   re-enforcement of limits of the 'emerging principle' in *Shepherd v Lyntrees* (1989);
*   the scope of the limits in *Countess Fitzwilliam v IRC* (1990);
*   the extent of control in *Hatton v IRC* (1992).

Answer

The *Westminster* principle (so called) was concerned with the extent to which a taxpayer was entitled to adopt a scheme in order to avoid or mitigate his tax liability. The citizen is not liable to pay tax unless a taxing provision clearly imposes a fiscal liability on him. The issue in the *Westminster* case (*IRC v Duke of Westminster* (1936)), involved the extent by which a citizen may arrange his affairs in order to mitigate his liability to tax. The House of Lords decided in favour of the Duke. The approach of the courts was reflected in the principle laid down by Lord Tomlin to the effect that the court will not go behind the 'form' of a transaction in order to give effect to its 'substance'. But the *Westminster* principle did not lay down any test as to the methods of ordering one's affairs which would be conclusive for the purpose of avoiding tax.

It is clear that if the terms of the document or documents effecting the transaction are ambiguous, the court may look at all the circumstances in order to interpret the true nature of the transaction. In this context the court does not destroy the form in order to promote the substance but simply tries to discover the true nature of the transaction. Thus, in *IRC v Mallaby-Deeley* (1938), the Court of Appeal was entitled to decide that a capital obligation to pay a sum to another was incapable of being converted into an income obligation by the simple expedient of paying the relevant sum under a deed of covenant. Likewise, the status given by the parties to the transaction is inconclusive see *IRC v Land Securities Investment Trust* (1969), a property holding company purchased a number of freehold and leasehold interests in consideration of *rentcharges*. It was decided that the 'rentcharges' were partly capital payments.

The tax planner's hope of avoiding tax was based on the premise that the courts, in considering the 'form' of a transaction, will construe each step of an arrangement on its own merits. Accordingly, such taxpayers entered into tax avoidance schemes by introducing stages with the sole purpose of avoiding tax. The germ of rationalising the court's approach towards tax avoidance schemes was planted by the dissenting judgment of Eveleigh LJ in *Floor v Davis* (1978) at the Court of Appeal stage of the appeal. This case involved the *value shifting* provisions now included in ss 29–34 TCGA 1992. Briefly, these anti-avoidance provisions create a deemed disposal at market value for capital gains tax purposes if a person, with control of a company, exercises control so that value passes out of shares in his company and passes into other shares in a company. In this case the taxpayer (and two sons in law) wanted to sell their majority shareholding in an electronics company, A to an American company, D. To avoid a straightforward sale and liability to corporation tax, they formed a new company, B and agreed to sell their shares in A to B in return for preferred shares entitling them to one seventh of the surplus assets on a winding up. B then agreed to sell shares in A to the American company, D. Ordinary shares entitling the holders to six sevenths of the surplus assets were issued to a foreign resident company, C, formed by the taxpayers. B and C were then liquidated and the taxpayers became entitled to the surplus assets in both companies. The questions in issue were first, whether ss 29–34 were applicable and, secondly, whether the scheme adopted by the taxpayers was effective. The Court of Appeal and the House of Lords held that the value shifting provisions were operative. On the broader issue of the validity of the stages in the scheme, Eveleigh LJ was of the view that the scheme was of an artificial nature and ought not succeed.

The steps taken should not be viewed in isolation but in the context of a multiple stage transaction. This decision was followed by a tax avoidance scheme which succeeded before the House of Lords in *IRC v Plummer* (1979), the taxpayer entered into a transaction with a charity, the effect of which was that he received £2,480 from the charity in return for five annual payments of £500 to the charity. The taxpayer claimed to deduct the gross payments in computing his income for higher rate tax purposes. The court allowed the claim on the ground that the payments were annual payments. This decision has been reversed by s 125 of the TA 1988.

It was not until the House of Lords decision in *Ramsay v IRC* (1981) that the lead given by Eveleigh LJ was adopted. This principle revolutionised the courts' approach to tax avoidance schemes. The purpose of the scheme in *Ramsay* was to avoid tax by creating an allowable loss through a sale and leaseback transaction which was intended to reduce a gain made by the taxpayer. The House of Lords, *inter alia*, decided against the validity of the scheme. Lord Wilberforce gave the leading judgment and laid down the following propositions:

- *sham* transactions have no legal effect. A transaction is a *sham* if it professes to be one thing but is in fact something different;
- if a transaction is genuine, the court cannot go behind it to some underlying substance;
- but a step or stage inserted in a series of transactions intended as a whole is not to be construed in isolation but in its context. In other words, a *composite* transaction is construed in its context. A *composite* transaction is an accepted obligation to carry through a scheme in successive steps. This is the case where there is an expectation that the stages in the transaction will be carried through, and there is no likelihood in practice that it will not.

This case was followed shortly by another House of Lords decision, *Burmah Oil v IRC* (1982). In this case, the object of the scheme was to convert a disallowed loss into an allowable loss for capital gains tax purposes. The transactions were circular and artificial. The Law Lords found in favour of the Revenue and Lord Diplock seized the opportunity to reiterate the principles laid down in the earlier decision of the House. The new approach is in respect of *a pre-ordained series of transactions* or *a single composite transaction* (whether or not they include the achievement of a legitimate commercial end) *into which steps are inserted that have no commercial purpose apart from the avoidance of tax*. These steps will be ignored for tax purposes or will not be considered *in vacuo*. In other words, the inserted steps will not be treated for primary tax purposes as breaking the link between the first stage and the last, but otherwise, the inserted stage is treated as genuine and legally effective and as such may attract tax liabilities in its own right: see *Ingram v IRC* (1985), which involved an unsuccessful scheme to avoid stamp duty. The *Westminster* decision was reconcilable with *Ramsay* and *Burmah* on the ground that in *Westminster* the transaction was not composite, but a single step arrangement entered into by two independent persons with independent minds whereas, in *Ramsay* and *Burmah* the tax planning schemes involved companies controlled by the taxpayer.

In *Furniss v Dawson* (1984), the Law Lords were able to reflect on the 'new approach' laid down in *Ramsay* and *Burmah* and extend the principle even further to a 'linear' transaction. The arrangement in *Furniss* involved an intended tax deferment scheme consisting of a series of pre-arranged steps, some of which had no commercial purpose other than the deferment of tax. The court decided that tax was payable in accordance with the substance of the scheme as a whole even though the scheme was not circular.

A number of inferences were capable of being drawn from *Furniss v Dawson*. These were:

- the 'new' approach adopted in *Ramsay* and *Burmah* is restricted to composite transactions. In other words, the 'form' of a transaction may prevail in the context of a single step transaction;
- in a composite transaction each step may be considered independently provided that the same had a commercial purpose, irrespective of whether or not it achieves a commercial end;
- the boundaries surrounding the 'emerging' principle are required to be probed judicially;
- a 'composite' or pre-ordained transaction is a question of fact to be determined by the Commissioners;
- a pre-ordained series of transactions involves a scheme containing mandatory successive steps or an expectation that

such steps will follow provided that there is no likelihood that, in practice, the steps will not follow.

The limits of this new approach to tax avoidance schemes are illustrated by three cases heard by the House of Lords in a consolidated appeal. The cases were *Craven v White; IRC v Bowater Property Developments Ltd*; and *Baylis v Gregory* (1988). In these cases, the Crown argued that disposals of assets by the taxpayers to companies, followed by the disposals of the same assets by the recipient companies to the ultimate purchasers, should be regarded as direct disposals by the taxpayers to the ultimate purchasers. The Law Lords by a majority in *Craven* and unanimously in *Bowater* and *Baylis* decided against the Revenue. The meaning of a 'pre-ordained series of transactions' was considered at some length in the judgments although there was no complete agreement. Successive transactions may not be regarded as pre-ordained or a composite arrangement in order to attract the *Ramsay* rule, unless at the time the first stage was entered into, all the essential features of the remaining steps had been determined by persons who had the firm intention and ability to proceed. For example, a transfer from A to B with a further transfer to C will be treated as a transfer from A to C if, at the time of the transfer from A to B, it is a near certainty that the specific transfer from B to C will take place. Moreover, A is required to have control over the end result and there is no commercial purpose for the insertion of step B, other than the avoidance of tax. In all three of the above-mentioned cases, the sales to the ultimate purchasers were not determined at the time of the disposals to the companies. Those sales might not have taken place. It followed that the transactions were not pre-ordained.

Although the decision in *Craven v White* is viewed as a slight watering down of the 'emerging principle', it is clear that the 'new approach' was not intended to be undermined. The Law Lords in the consolidated appeals were intent in clarifying the *Ramsay* principle and accordingly reviewed all the previous cases. The decision of the House of Lords in *Craven, Bowater and Baylis* now stands as the leading authority in this field.

The limits of the 'new' approach were adopted by the High Court in *Shepherd v Lyntrees Ltd* (1989). The court allowed the taxpayer, a group of companies, to purchase a capital loss company in order to set off gains made by the taxpayer on the disposal of shares. In the House of Lords decision of *Countess Fitzwilliam v IRC* (1990), a capital transfer tax case, the court again considered the notion of a 'pre-ordained' series of transactions and on the facts decided that this requirement was not satisfied because the Commissioners found that the daughter, one of the beneficiaries under the scheme and a participant, had both an understanding and will of her own. The inference was that she could not be treated as a person over whom the originator of the scheme (mother) had control. There was also a real possibility that her mother might not have survived long enough to complete the scheme. In *Hatton v IRC* (1992), the High court decided that the taxpayer need not have control over the entire operation. The question was whether, on the findings of the commissioners, the essential elements identified in *Craven v White* were present in order to justify the court in treating two or more transactions as a single composite transaction.

In *R v HM Inspector of Taxes ex p Fulford-Dobson* (1987), the court decided that the Revenue were entitled to refuse to allow the taxpayer to use ESC D2 with the intention to avoid capital gains tax. In *IRC v Willoughby* (1997), the House of Lords decided that tax avoidance was a course of action designed to conflict with or defeat the evident intention of Parliament and not the adoption of an exception which Parliament had deliberately created. On the facts, when the transaction was entered into, tax avoidance was not in the mind of the taxpayer.

In *IRC v McGuckian* (1997), the House of Lords reviewed the *Ramsay* principle, and decided that the tax paying provisions were to be applied to the substance of the transaction, disregarding artificial steps inserted in a composite transaction with the purpose of avoiding tax. Once the artificial steps had been identified and disregarded, the language of the taxing Act was applied to the transaction. In this case, a transaction designed to assign the right to dividend was considered to be artificial and disregarded. The liability of the taxpayer fell within s 739 of the TA 1988.

Question 3

Norman and Mary have been living together for the last four years. They are considering whether to get married, and one consideration is the possible tax implications of marriage. Norman earns £25,000 a year and owns a house, subject to a mortgage to which Mary has been contributing. Mary earns £35,000 a year and owns investments and valuable jewellery. Both are aged 40.

Advise Norman and Mary as to the possible income tax, capital gains tax and inheritance tax implications which are relevant to their decision whether to marry or not.

Answer plan

Income tax:

- married couple's allowance;
- 'living together' – s 282 of the TA 1988;
- quantum of allowance available in the year of marriage;
- death of a spouse and allowances;
- separate assessment of income tax;
- apportionment of mortgage interest relief.

Capital gains tax:

- separate assessment to capital gains tax;
- losses;
- effect of inter-spousal disposals;
- private residence exemption and joint election.

Inheritance tax:

- whether a transfer of value between parties? – s 18 of the Inheritance Tax Act 1984 (IHTA);
- potentially exempt transfers – s 3(A) of the IHTA 1984;
- disposition for the maintenance of the family – s 11 of the IHTA 1984;
- liability of spouses to settle inheritance tax bills – s 199 of the IHTA 1984.

Answer

The question involves an examination of the income tax, capital gains tax and inheritance tax consequences of marriage as compared with the consequences of living together without going through a marriage ceremony. The policy of the independent taxation of married couples which was introduced for the year of assessment 1990–91 was designed to rectify the imbalance of the tax system against married couples. The effect has been a general amelioration of the position of married couples in respect of income tax, capital gains tax and inheritance tax.

Income tax

A husband living with his wife is entitled to a higher allowance compared to an unmarried couple. Each income tax payer is entitled to a personal allowance (£4,195 for the year of assessment 1998–99), but, in addition, the parties to a marriage, while they are 'living together', are entitled to a married couple's allowance (£1,900 for 1998–99). The allowance is given by way of income tax reduction. For 1998–99, the reduction is 15% (for 1999–2000 and subsequent years, the reduction is 10%). This additional allowance is claimable by the husband but may be transferred to his wife. Indeed, Norman and Mary (as a married couple) may consider an election to transfer the entire married couple's allowance to Mary in order to reduce her liability to higher rate tax. The expression, 'living together', as defined in the legislation, is expressed in negative terms and means more than living under the same roof. Thus, s 282 of the TA 1988 creates a presumption that a married couple is living together unless they are separated under a court order, or deed of separation or they are, in fact, separated in such circumstances that the separation is likely to be permanent. (This definition is also applied for capital gains tax purposes.)

In the year of marriage, in addition to a personal allowance the husband may claim one 12th of the married couple's allowance for each complete fiscal month in the year of assessment during which he is married. However, like married couples, each person will be separately assessed on his or her own income and is responsible for settling the tax with the Revenue.

Accordingly, Mary is liable to income tax on her earnings and the income from her investments and is required to settle her income tax with the Revenue. Similarly, Norman will be liable to income tax on his income. The main income tax detriment, as a single person, will be the loss of or non-availability of married couple's allowance.

If a wife dies, the surviving husband is entitled to claim married couple's allowance for the year of assessment in which she dies. If the husband dies, the married couple's allowance and other reliefs available to the deceased husband will be set against his income for the year of assessment up to his death. In addition, the surviving widow is entitled to widow's bereavement allowance in that year and the following year of assessment.

The mortgage interest which is payable on the house used as the borrower's only or main residence qualifies for income tax relief. Interest on a mortgage with a ceiling of £30,000 is the limit in respect of any residence. In relation to loans made after 31 July 1988, if qualifying interest is payable by more than one of the parties the relief is apportioned between each contributor up to his or her 'sharer's limit': see s 356(A) of the TA 1988. The 'sharer limit' is the amount arrived at by dividing the interest by the qualifying maximum number of persons through whom qualifying interest is payable (for example, if a loan of £30,000 was made to Norman and Mary, the sharer limit will be £15,000 each. In other words, each borrower will be entitled to relief on interest paid on a loan of up to £15,000). Whereas, if Norman and Mary were married and both contributed substantially to the repayments on a joint mortgage, both parties will share the mortgage relief equally. The parties may make a joint election to the effect that the tax relief be allocated between them in any way they choose. Thus, since Mary's taxable income may subject her to higher rate of tax, it would be prudent to allocate all the relief to Mary.

Capital gains tax

Allied to the income tax rules, a married woman living with her husband is separately liable to pay capital gains tax on her gains and is entitled to a separate allowance annually. If Mary (whether married or unmarried) makes a chargeable disposal of her jewellery at a gain, then, after deducting her relief for the year of assessment, she is liable to settle the tax bill with the Revenue. The losses made by a spouse may only be set off against that spouse's gains in the same or future years.

However, a married woman living with her husband who makes a disposal to her husband is not liable to capital gains tax. The disposal is treated as giving rise to no gain and no loss. The party acquiring the asset is treated as standing in the shoes of the other party to the marriage and will adopt the other's base cost and date of acquisition: see s 58 of the Capital Gains Tax Act 1992 (CGTA). On the other hand, unmarried couples are treated as separate individuals and disposals from one to the other may give rise to a chargeable gain or allowable loss as the case may be under general principles.

A married couple living together may only have one matrimonial home in order to enjoy the exemption under s 222 of the CGTA 1992. If there is more than one home, the parties are required to make a joint election declaring the exempt residence.

Inheritance tax

Transfers of value between spouses, whether living together or not, are exempt from inheritance tax to the extent that the value transferred is attributable to property which becomes comprised in the estate of the transferor's spouse, see s 18 of the IHTA 1984. Thus, a transfer by Mary to Norman at a time when they are married will be exempt, but if they are unmarried such disposition may give rise to chargeable transfer on death or may be a potentially exempt transfer, if made *inter vivos*.

If immediately before the transfer, the transferor was domiciled in the UK but his or her spouse was not, the exempt transfer is limited to £55,000: s 18(2) of the IHTA 1984.

A disposition by one party to a marriage in favour of the other party is not a transfer of value if it is made for the maintenance of the other, see s 11 of the IHTA 1984.

Each spouse is primarily liable to pay his or her inheritance tax due in respect of transfers of value made: see s 199 of the IHTA 1984.

Question 4

Explain the concepts of 'residence' and 'ordinary residence' as applied to individuals, trustees and personal representatives, partnerships and companies.

Answer plan

Your answer should include discussion of:

- s 336 of the TA 1988;
- s 334 of the TA 1988;
- Revenue practice;
- ss 110–11 and 151 of the FA 1989;
- s 112 of the TA 1988;
- s 66 of the FA 1988.

Answer

The UK tax jurisdiction extends to England, Wales, Scotland and Northern Ireland. It does not extend to the Isle of Man or Channel Islands. This jurisdiction is subject to an important principle of international law that no country will enforce the claims of another country for payment of tax.

UK tax law is effective to the extent that there is a nexus between the taxpayer and the UK. This nexus is established where:

(a) the source chargeable to tax is within the jurisdiction; or

(b) the taxpayer is so closely connected with the UK that this becomes the proper tax jurisdiction.

Residence of an individual

The expression 'reside' is not statutorily defined but is given its ordinary dictionary meaning by the courts as indicating 'to dwell permanently or for a considerable time'. This is a question of fact. The commissioners and the courts may have regard to all the circumstances, including the individual's conduct prior to and subsequent to the year of assessment.

Section 336 of the TA 1988 enacts that an individual present in the UK for a period of six months or more in any one year of assessment, for some temporary purpose and not with a view of establishing his residence here, be treated as resident in the UK. The Revenue has interpreted this period to mean 183 days, ignoring the days of arrival and departure. Periods of less than a day are computed in hours. In *IRC v Wilkie* (1952), the taxpayer spent 182 days and 20 hours in the UK excluding the days of arrival and departure. He was treated as not resident in the UK. For 1993-94 and subsequent years the question is determined without regard to any available accommodation (s 336(3)). In the exceptional circumstances of *Re Mackenzie* it would appear that involuntary presence in the UK may make an individual resident. In *Re Mackenzie* (1941), an individual came to the UK on a visit. She was detained as a person of unsound mind and died here, still detained, some 52 years later. The court decided that she was resident and ordinarily resident in the UK.

Section 334 of the TA 1988 provides that a Commonwealth citizen or citizen of Eire whose ordinary residence is in the UK (see later) and has left the UK for the purpose of occasional residence abroad, continues to be resident in the UK. 'Occasional residence' has not been statutorily defined but is generally taken to mean temporary residence abroad or short stays on holidays or business trips. In *Levene v IRC* (1928), the taxpayer was a retired businessman who had been resident and ordinary resident in the UK before he left to live abroad. From the date of his departure until five years later, he maintained no fixed place of abode anywhere but stayed in various hotels. During this time he spent between four and five months each year in the UK. His purpose being to obtain medical advice for himself and wife, to visit relations, to attend the graves of his parents and to take part in certain religious observances. It was decided that the taxpayer left the UK and lived abroad for the purpose of *occasional residence* and remained resident in the UK. In *Reed v Clark* (1985), the taxpayer, a pop star ordinarily resident in the UK, was advised that he may avoid income tax on substantial advance payments for copyright during the year 1978–79 if he resided outside the UK. He left the UK for California on 3 April 1978 and did not return until 2 May 1979. The court decided that he was not resident in the UK and his presence in California was more than for 'occasional residence'.

The Revenue adopt the practice of treating an individual, who has left the UK for permanent residence abroad, as continuing to be resident in the UK, if the taxpayer pays frequent and 'substantial' visits to this country. The view of the Revenue is that 91 days presence in the UK in a year of assessment is considered to be substantial. A regular visitor to the UK becomes resident after four years if his visits during those years average at least 91 days per year. Where a visitor indicates from the start that regular visits for substantial periods were to be made, he would be regarded as resident from the first year. In *IRC v Lysaght* (1928), the taxpayer, a director, sold his English residence and went to live permanently with his family in Ireland. He came to England every month for director's meetings and remained in the UK on business for about a week on each occasion, usually staying in hotels. The court decided that the taxpayer was resident and ordinarily resident in the UK.

However, it would be more difficult to establish that the visits of foreigners, who have never resided in the UK, are resident in the UK. If the purpose of visits to the UK is merely in the course of travel and not as part of the regular order of life, that individual will not be resident in the UK. In *Zorab v IRC* (1926), a retired member of the Indian Civil Service spent five months in the UK. The sole purpose of his visit being to visit his friends. The court decided that he was not resident in the UK in the relevant year.

Ordinary residence of individuals

The term 'ordinary residence' has not been statutorily defined. Ordinary residence as opposed to residence connotes some degree of continuity or a settled state of mind in one locality, for example, the UK, see *IRC v Lysaght* (1928). An individual may be resident but not ordinarily resident when he comes from abroad and stays here for more than six months in a year of assessment. In *R v Barnet LBC ex p Shah* (1983), five overseas students who entered the country at least three years earlier and obtained educational qualifications at their expense, applied to the local authority for a grant for a course of further education. Their applications were refused on the ground that they were not ordinarily resident in the area of the local authority. The court allowed their appeals and decided that they were ordinarily resident because they were habitually and normally resident here.

Residence of trustees and personal representatives

Following the decision of *Dawson v IRC* (1990), ss 110 and 111 of the FA 1989 were passed to reverse the decision. The position today is that from 1989–90 onwards, where one of the trustees of a settlement is non-UK resident and at least one is UK resident (a mixed trust) and the settlor (or where there is more than one, any of them is) resident or ordinarily resident or domiciled in the UK, then the non-resident trustee(s) is (are) treated as resident in the UK for income tax purposes. Similar rules determine the residence of personal representatives (s 111 of the TA 1988).

Residence of a partnership

Partnerships are treated as resident in the place where the control and management is situated. Section 12 of the TA 1988 enacts that where a trade or business is carried on by two or more persons in partnership, and the control and management of the trade or business is situated abroad, the trade or business shall be deemed to be carried on by persons resident outside the UK, notwithstanding that some of its members are resident in the UK and some of its operations are conducted within the UK.

Residence of corporations

For a company incorporated in the UK, the test of residence is determined by s 66 of the FA 1988, as the UK. In respect of companies not incorporated in the UK the pre-1988 test is still applicable namely, the place where its central control and management is located. Central management and control is located where board meetings are held (see *De Beers Consolidated Gold Mines v Howe* (1906)).

It is possible that the central management and control of a non UK incorporated association may be divided between several countries, so that no one country could be recognised as the only seat of control. In such a case, if a substantial degree of control is exercised in the UK, the company is resident here, notwithstanding that an equal or greater degree of control is exercised elsewhere, see *Unit Corporation v IRC* (1953).

Question 5

Outline the new system of 'self-assessment' for individuals, trustees and partnerships, indicating when these changes will take effect.

Answer plan

Good answers will make mention of:

- timing of self-assessment;
- filing of returns;
- amendments to returns;
- penalties;
- discoveries;
- time limits for assessment.

Answer

Sections 178–99 and Schedule 19 of the FA 1994 (as amended by the FA 1995) have established the framework for a new system of personal compliance and, together with the new rules on the taxation of the self-employed, represent one of the most fundamental changes to the administration of personal taxation in many years. The term, 'self-assessment', refers to the system whereby the annual tax returns filed by individuals and trustees should include a self-assessment of the taxpayer's liability for income tax and capital gains tax. Alternatively, the Revenue will compute the tax, provided that the returns are submitted earlier to enable its officers to make the necessary calculations in time. Payment deadlines are tightened and more stringent penalties relating to late returns and non-payment of tax have been introduced. In addition, the basis of income tax assessment for Schedule D is standardised on the current year basis as opposed to the preceding year basis.

This revolutionary system takes effect for the tax year 1996–97 and subsequent years, although certain transitional arrangements apply, particularly for partnerships. Businesses commencing after 5 April 1994, or deemed to commence on or after this date under s 113(1) of the TA 1988, are taxed on the new current year basis immediately.

The Revenue may issue a notice to an individual requiring him to make a return of such information as may reasonably be required for the purpose of establishing the amount on which he is chargeable to income or capital gains tax for the year of assessment (s 8 of the TMA 1970). The normal time limit for the submission of the return is 31 January in the year following the year of assessment to which it relates. However, if notice of the requirement to make a return is not given by the Revenue by 31 October in the year following the year of assessment, the time limit is extended to three months after the date on which notice is given (s 7 of the TMA 1970). The returns involving the year of assessment 1998–99 will be sent out in April 1999. Such returns will normally be required to be filed by 31 January 2000. Where an individual carries on a trade, profession or vocation in partnership, his return should include his share of income, loss or charge for the year of assessment. Similar provisions, including the same time limits, are introduced for returns made by trustees. Taxpayers who do not wish to compute their liability will be required to file earlier returns, the deadline is normally 30 September following the year of assessment. The Revenue need not give notice to deliver a return, and self-assessment will not be required in cases where the tax deducted under the PAYE system is equal to the full tax liability of the taxpayer, or the income is chargeable under Schedule F, or is other income from which income tax has been, or is treated as having been deducted, provided that the chargeable person is not liable for that year other than at the basic or lower rate.

Any partner may be required by notice to complete and deliver a return of the partnership profits together with accounts, statements, etc. The return must include information as to partnership reliefs, allowances, tax credits, tax at source, tax repayments and the names, residences and tax references of all persons who were partners during the period specified in the notice. In addition, the notice may require the person to include such other information as may reasonably be within his knowledge, such as information relating to the disposals and acquisitions of partnership property. The notice will specify the relevant period to be covered by the return which is normally the period of account of the partnership and the date by which the return should be delivered (the filing date): see s 12AA of the TMA 1970.

Moreover, each partnership return must include a statement showing each partner's share of income (and gains) and allocating the net profits or losses between the partners: see s 12AB of the TMA 1970.

For the purpose of making an assessment to income tax in respect of a trustee, settlor or beneficiary, an inspector may issue a return form to any number of trustees. The trustees may choose to make a self-assessment of the trust's income and gains, alternatively the Revenue may make an assessment on their behalf if they submit their return before 30 September following the end of the tax year.

A person who may be required to make and deliver a return will be statutorily required to keep all necessary records and to preserve them until the end of the 'relevant day'. The relevant day is normally:

(a) in the case of a person carrying on a trade (including any letting of property), profession or business alone or in partnership, or a company, the fifth anniversary of 31 January following the year of assessment or, for partnerships, the end of the period covered by the return; and

(b) in any other case, the first anniversary of 31 January following the year of assessment.

The penalty for a failure to make a return for income or capital gains tax is £100. For continuing failure, a further penalty of up to £60 per day may be imposed by the Commissioners. If the failure continues for more than six months beginning with the filing date, a further penalty of £100 is payable. If the failure continues after the anniversary of the filing date, and there would have been a liability to tax based on a proper return promptly submitted, a further penalty is chargeable on an amount not exceeding that liability. For 1996–97 and subsequent years a penalty carries interest calculated from the due date of payment. (The original sanctions for fraudulently or negligently delivering an incorrect return continue to apply: see s 95 of the TMA 1970). The maximum penalty for failing to keep records in relation to a year of assessment or accounting period is £3,000.

Where the Revenue have issued a notice requiring a person to deliver a return and the return is not delivered by the due date, the Inspector of Taxes may make an estimated assessment, that is, an assessment to the best of his information and belief. Tax is payable as if the determination were a self-assessment with no right of appeal. A determination is automatically superseded by any self-assessment, whether made by the taxpayer or the Revenue, based on information contained in a return. Such self-assessment must be made five years beginning with the filing date or, if later, within 12 months beginning with the date of the determination.

Within nine months beginning with the delivery of a return, the Revenue may by notice amend his self-assessment to correct obvious errors. At any time within 12 months beginning with the filing date the taxpayer may by notice amend his self-assessment. But no such amendment of a self-assessment may be made after the Revenue have given notice of its intention to enquire into his return.

An enquiry into a return may be initiated by the Revenue after notice has been given. The time limits are 12 months beginning with the filing date, provided that the return was filed on or before the filing date. Otherwise, the date of notice of enquiry is on or before the quarter day (31 January; 30 April; 31 July; 31 October) following the first anniversary of the day of delivery of the return. At the same time, the Revenue may by notice in writing require a person, within a specified time, to produce such documents and such accounts or particulars as the officer may reasonably require in order to check the accuracy or validity of a return. There is provision for a person to appeal within 30 days beginning with the date of notice.

For 1998–99 and subsequent years, if the Revenue 'discovers' that any profits have not been assessed which should have been assessed or any relief given is or has become excessive, the inspector may make an assessment of an amount which it is felt should be charged. But no such assessment will be made if the taxpayer acted honestly and the Revenue could reasonably have been expected to be aware of the deficiency when the inspector concluded his inquiries. In *Coy v Kime* (1987), a London taxi driver who worked five evenings each week, mainly serving the West End theatre goers, declared takings of £24 to £25 per night. The Revenue raised further assessments based on estimated income, taking into consideration the taxpayer's family living expenses and his petrol claims. The court upheld the assessments. An additional assessment is not precluded by an agreement between the taxpayer and an inspector settling the dispute in respect of an earlier assessment, if the information on which the agreement was based was misleading or incorrect, see *Gray v Matheson* (1993), the court decided that the Revenue had made a 'discovery' of further facts. Their decision to issue a further assessment could not be barred by an agreement between the parties, since the taxpayer had supplied inadequate information and omitted to make full disclosure of his affairs.

In general, an assessment must be made within six years of the end of the chargeable period to which it relates. Any objection to an assessment on the grounds that it was made out of time must be made by way of appeal against assessment. This rule is subject to the qualification that the standard time limit may be increased in the case of fraudulent or negligent conduct. In respect of claims for reliefs, the claim must be made within six years after the end of the chargeable period to which it relates.

Question 6

Outline the occasions when an Inspector of Taxes may make a discovery in respect of an underpayment of income tax and state, in brief, the consequences in civil law of such discoveries.

Answer plan

Answers should discuss:

- occasions for making a further assessment following discoveries;
- meaning of a 'discovery';
- Practice Statement SP 8/91;

- four types of default of major significance – fraud, negligence, failures and errors;
- extended time limits for assessments;
- interest payable on late tax;
- penalties.

Answer

An Inspector of Taxes who 'discovers' that:

- any profits which should have been assessed, have not been assessed;
- an assessment which had been made proves to be insufficient;
- any relief given is or has become excessive may make an assessment of an amount which it is felt ought to be charged, see s 29 of the TMA 1970 and s 191 of the FA 1994.

The interpretation of a 'discovery' appears to be settled and means 'to find out'. Indeed, a discovery may be made even where the taxpayer has made a full disclosure and the inspector was originally in error. In *Commercial Structures Ltd v Briggs* (1948), Schedule A assessments were found to be incorrect, although all the relevant information was in the possession of the inspector. Additional assessments were made to correct the error. This decision was affirmed by the House of Lords in *Cenlon Finance Co v Ellwood* (1962). However, in some cases, the Revenue may forego arrears of income tax due to official error, details are contained in ESC A19. Once an assessment or additional assessment is made, the inspector cannot make a new assessment on the same income for the same year even if he discovers a fresh point of law. This is determined objectively. The question is whether the evidence would lead a reasonable inspector to the conclusion that he has decided not to assess the taxpayer (see *Olin Energy Systems Ltd v Scorer* (1985)).

It appears that if the Revenue have reasonable grounds for believing that an assessment is inaccurate, it is entitled to make an additional assessment. In *Coy v Kime* (1987), a taxi driver, who worked five evenings a week, mainly serving the West End theatre-goers, declared £24 to £25 per night. The inspector raised further assessments based on estimated income, taking into account the taxpayer's family living expenses and fuel expenditure. The court upheld these assessments.

The Revenue's view is set out in a Statement of Practice (SP 8/91). Two main principles are:

(a) where a computation has been agreed by the inspector containing an issue which is both 'fundamental to the whole basis of the computation' and 'was clearly and immediately apparent', the Revenue will not go back and raise a discovery in respect of the same issue;

(b) the Revenue regard themselves as bound by the inspector's acceptance of a computation if the issue in the computation was based on full and accurate disclosure of all the relevant facts.

However, an amended assessment to capital gains tax issued by the Revenue by mistake and erroneously stating that the taxpayer's liability was nil, when the original assessment had been £3 m was not binding on the Revenue: see *Schuldenfrei v Hilton* (1998).

The statement concludes that, subject to the above, the inspector may make a discovery where:

• owing to fraudulent or negligent conduct, profits have not earlier been charged to income tax;

• the inspector has been misled or misinformed about the issue, see *Gray v Matheson* (1993), a publican's trading accounts were agreed by the inspector of taxes. On the basis of these figures, a different inspector began an investigation and raised further assessments on the taxpayer based on inaccurate figures in the accounts. The court held that the additional assessments were not barred by the agreement because the trading accounts were drawn up incorrectly;

• an error is made in a computation which had not been noticed at the date of the agreement and which can be corrected by making a discovery assessment.

However, it is questionable whether the Revenue is entitled to raise a discovery assessment, where the facts surrounding the circumstances giving rise to the issue have been disclosed, and the point has been raised by the inspector, or could have been within the contemplation of an 'ordinary, competent inspector'.

Under the 'self-assessment' regime which came into effect in 1996–97, the taxpayer is given the choice of computing his own tax liability if he wishes, or to leave it to the Revenue to calculate his liability to income tax. In the latter event, the Revenue will require an earlier submission of the return. More stringent penalties will be imposed relating to late and inaccurate returns. But under the new self-assessment regime, no further assessments will be made on the taxpayer provided that he acts honestly (that is, without fraud or negligent conduct) and the Revenue could reasonably have been expected to be aware of the deficiency when the inspector concluded his enquiries.

The Finance Act 1989 (FA) made several changes to the old notion of 'fraud, wilful default and neglect'. Today there are four kinds of default which are of major practical importance. They are fraudulent conduct, negligent conduct, failures and errors. There is no statutory definition of 'fraudulent and negligent conduct'. But the changes in terminology and concepts may be more significant in form than in practical effect. In particular, it appears that:

- anything which was 'wilful default' under the old law will almost certainly be fraudulent or negligent conduct under the post-1989 law;

- anything which was 'neglect' under the old law is most likely to remain negligent conduct under the post-1989 law;

- 'failure' to give notice, make a return etc, required by or under the TA 1988 may be relevant to the interest provisions of s 88 of the TMA 1970 and also to various penalty provisions. For practical purposes, such provisions are limited to failures without reasonable excuse to give the required notice, etc;

- an 'error' in any information, return etc, delivered to the Revenue may be relevant under s 88 of the TMA 1970 – default interest. There is no statutory definition of 'error' and there is no 'reasonable excuse' exception. The effect is that an 'error' still amounts to an error for these purposes even if the taxpayer had a reasonable excuse for it.

The consequences of default proceedings give rise to any one or more of three different kinds of options in civil law available to the Revenue. These are:

(a) extended time limits for assessments;

(b) interest under s 88 of the TMA 1970;

(c) penalties.

Time limits

Generally speaking, an assessment is required to be made within six years of the end of the chargeable period to which it relates.

The Finance Act 1989 made significant changes in the law. An assessment may be made on any person to make good loss of tax attributable to his fraudulent or negligent conduct up to 20 years after the end of the chargeable period to which the assessment relates (see s 36(1) of the TMA 1970 and s 149(1) of the FA 1989).

Interest

In certain circumstances where a default leads to late payment of tax, the taxpayer is liable to pay interest under s 88 of the TMA 1970. The kinds of default which attract interest are:

(a) failure to give notice, make returns etc;

(b) errors in information, returns etc, delivered to the Revenue.

In a Statement of Practice published by the Revenue (SP 6/89), the view of the Revenue is that interest will be payable on unpaid tax where a late or inadequate assessment is made and where the delay is 'substantial'. A 'substantial' delay in respect of filing a tax return is a date beyond the filing date of 30 days from the date of issue or, if later, by 31 October following the end of the tax year. The Board of Inland Revenue have a discretion in mitigating the interest charge.

Penalties

Most penalties may be 'determined' by an inspector, subject to an appeal to the commissioners. In other cases, the commissioners (or in cases of fraud, the High Court) impose a penalty on application from the inspector (s 100 of the TMA 1970; Schedule 19, para 31 of the FA 1994). Where a penalty is determined by an inspector it becomes due 30 days from the issue of the appropriate notice. It is treated as tax due and a debt payable by the taxpayer.

Penalties may be reduced from the maximum amounts according to the extent of co-operation by the taxpayer and other factors. In *Brodt v Wells Commissioners* (1987), the High Court reduced the award of penalties because the size of the award was out of line with other awards and the specific panel had not given reasons for their decisions.

The most important penalties arise in three kinds of cases:

(a) failure to notify the Revenue authorities of the taxpayer's chargeability to tax;

(b) where a return is not made or is made late;

(c) where a return is made but is incorrect.

Persons who are chargeable to tax but do not receive return forms are obliged to notify the Revenue of their chargeability within 12 months of the end of the year of assessment (s 7 of the TMA 1970, ss 196, 199 and Schedule 19 of the FA 1994). The time limit is reduced to six months under the self-assessment regime applicable from 1996–97. Omission to notify is a 'failure' and puts the individual at risk of penalties. The maximum penalty is equal to the tax chargeable.

Penalties are imposed for not making returns or for making them late and are also treated as 'failures'. The maximum penalty is £300 and if the failure continues after the imposition of a penalty, a further penalty of £60 is imposed for each day that the failure continues: s 93 of the TMA 1970.

Penalties for incorrect returns may be imposed in cases of fraud or negligence. The maximum penalty for fraud or negligence is equal to the tax on the amount by which the return is incorrect: s 95 of the TMA 1970; Schedule 17, para 27 of the FA 1994. If a person discovers that a return is incorrect and he fails to notify the Revenue authorities within a reasonable time, he is deemed to have submitted the return negligently: s 97 of the TMA 1970. Subject to this limitation, there is no penalty for an 'innocent' incorrect return.

From 1996–97, a person who may be required to submit a general return of income/gains must, on penalty of an amount of up to £3,000, keep appropriate records.

CHAPTER 2

INCOME FROM LAND

Introduction

The taxation of all income from UK real property, including furnished lettings, was amended, for income tax purposes, as from 6 April 1995 and, for corporation tax purposes, from 1 April 1998. The new rules introduce the concept of a 'Schedule A business'. In computing the profits most of the rules applicable to Schedule D Case I will also apply to Schedule A businesses.

Income tax under the new Schedule A rules will be charged on the *annual profits or gains* arising from any business which exploits rights over land in the UK in order to produce rents or other receipts. Moreover, to the extent that any transaction is entered into for exploiting, as a source of rent or other receipts of any estate, interest or rights in or over any land in the UK, that transaction shall be deemed to have been entered into in the course of a business. Thus, the casual letting which may lack the features of an adventure in the nature of a trade, will be chargeable to income tax under Schedule A.

Receipts, in relation to land, include:

- any payment for a licence to occupy or otherwise to use any land or in respect of exercising any other right over the land;
- rentcharges, ground annuals and any other annual payments reserved in respect of, or charged on or issuing out of, the land;
- rents from immobile caravans and permanently moored houseboats;
- sums payable or valuable consideration provided by a tenant or licensee for the use of furniture, unless they constitute receipts of a trade.

Excluded from the Schedule A charge are profits and gains:

- from a person's entitlement to receive yearly interest;

- charged to tax under Schedule D, for example, farming, market gardening, mines, quarries, etc;
- from letting tied premises, the rent from which is deemed to be a trading receipt.

Income tax under the new Schedule A is computed on the full amount of the profits or gains arising in the current tax year. Subject to any express rules to the contrary, the profits or gains, or the amount of any loss, are computed in accordance with Schedule D Case I rules, including the deduction principles.

Question 7

Alfred purchases a freehold investment property for £100,000 with the assistance of a mortgage. The interest repayments in respect of the loan amounts to £3,000 per annum during the current year of assessment. Alfred spends £800 on a new central heating boiler, £12,000 on installing an air conditioning system, £3,000 on redecorating the property, £1,000 in advertising for tenants and £500 on premiums for insuring the premises.

Alfred leases the property unfurnished to a firm of management consultants for a period of 21 years at a premium of £10,000 and a rent of £15,000 per annum.

Advise Alfred as to his tax liability.

Answer plan

Your answer should consider the following matters:

- the freehold property is a capital asset liable to capital gains tax;
- no capital allowance is available in respect of buildings and structures – FA 1994;
- Alfred's rental income is chargeable to tax under the remodelled Schedule A;
- part of the premium received may be assessable as rent;
- interest payments may be deductible under s 74 of the Income and Corporation Taxes Act 1988 (TA);

- expenditure on the central heating boiler may be deductible under s 74 of the TA 1988;

- expenditure on the air conditioning system is not deductible but capital allowance may be claimed;

- decorating, advertising and insurance premiums may be deductible.

Answer

The Finance Act 1995 (FA) introduced new provisions which recast the method of assessing profits under Schedule A with regard to individuals. The new provisions apply as from 6 April 1995.

In outline, s 39 of the FA 1995 inserts a new Schedule A, enacting that income tax is charged under Schedule A on the annual profits or gains arising from any business (within Schedule A), carried on for the exploitation of a source of rents or other receipts from land in the UK, including any transaction entered into for the exploitation of income from land. The effect under this Schedule is that the profits are computed by applying Schedule D Case I principles, although the income is not itself treated as earned income. Schedule A assesses not only rents but also other profits derived from land. The chargeable persons are 'the persons receiving or entitled to the income in respect of which the tax is directed by the Income Tax Acts to be charged' (s 21(1) of the TA 1988). Further, the tax is computed on the full amount of the profits or gains arising in the year of assessment (s 21(2) of the TA 1988).

The rent of £15,000 per annum is an annual profit chargeable to income tax under Schedule A. But part of the premium received is treated as rent and is assessable to income tax. A premium is a capital sum paid by the tenant to the landlord in connection with the grant of a lease. But for special statutory provisions to the contrary, the receipt of a premium would have been taxable as a capital profit. Section 34 of the TA 1988 enacts special 'deeming' provisions treating a portion of a premium, in limited circumstances, as income. The provision states that if a lease is granted for a period not exceeding 50 years and the consideration includes a premium, a proportion of that premium is treated as additional rent taxable under Schedule A. This proportion of notional rent is the surplus remaining after deducting 2% of the premium for each complete year of the lease other than the first. The effect of this discount of 2% is that the amount of the premium charged to income tax falls with the length of the lease. Thus, Alfred will be treated as receiving an additional rent of £6,000. This is computed thus:

Length of lease – 21 years	Premium	£10,000
Discount 2% x £10,000 x 20 years =		£ 4,000
Chargeable slice = £10,000 – £4,000 =		£ 6,000

The remainder of the premium (£4,000) is capital and liable, subject to exemptions and reliefs, to capital gains tax. This figure is lower than Alfred's annual exemption and if the position remains unchanged Alfred will be exempt from capital gains tax.

The acquisition of the freehold property by Alfred is a capital asset which is liable to capital gains tax on its disposal or part disposal (see s 42 of the Tax and Chargeable Gains Act 1992 (TCGA)). A part disposal is effected whenever 'on a disposal of an asset, any description of property derived from that asset remains undisposed of' (see s 42(1) of the TCGA 1992). In short, the creation of a right or interest in or over an asset involves a part disposal. In Alfred's case, the creation of a lease out of the freehold property involves a disposal of part of the asset. In order to compute the gain, the acquisition cost of the asset disposed of is required to be ascertained, as well as improvement expenditure, incidental costs of acquisition and disposal and taper relief. Any part of the premium which is chargeable to income tax under Schedule A is not charged to capital gains tax. Thus, £6,000 of the premium is discounted from the acquisition cost of the asset.

Section 42(2) of the TCGA 1992 creates a formula in order to compute the acquisition costs of the lease. The formula is $A/A + B$. Where A is equal to the consideration for the disposal, and B is equal to the market value of the asset remaining undisposed of. This formula is treated as a proportion of any expenditure which is wholly attributable to the asset from which the part disposal is effected. In Alfred's case it is necessary to value the undisposed freehold interest retained by him. No value is given on the facts presented and it would not be possible to compute Alfred's liability.

Moreover, s 117 of the FA 1994 provides that land, buildings and structures cannot be treated as plant and accordingly is incapable of attracting capital allowances.

Alfred's interest payments in respect of the mortgage are capable of attracting income tax relief under the new rules subject to Schedule A. The test today is whether the annual sum is payable wholly and exclusively for the Schedule A business. The leading case on this test is *Bentleys, Stokes and Lowless v Beeson* (1952). The approach of the courts is to ascertain whether the sole purpose of the expenditure is commercial. A non-commercial element may not destroy the commercial nature of expenditure if the non-commercial factor is purely incidental to the commercial purpose. In the absence of evidence to the contrary it would appear that the payments are deductible. We have been furnished with information that the asset purchased is an investment property. There appears to be no element of domestic or private or non-commercial purpose included in this expenditure and the entire interest payment is deductible from the Schedule A income.

The same principle is applicable in respect of the deductions of £1,000 for advertisement expenses and £500 concerning premiums on a policy insuring the premises. These are all allowable expenses.

Alfred spends £800 on installing a new central heating boiler on the premises. On the assumption that the expenditure is wholly and exclusively laid out for the purposes of the business (see above), the remaining question is whether the expenditure is of a revenue or capital nature. Two prohibitions are enacted in s 74(d) and (g) of the TA 1988. These are respectively:

> ... any sum expended for repairs of premises occupied ... for the purposes of the trade, etc, beyond the sum actually expended for this purpose ...

and 'any capital employed in improvements of premises occupied for the purposes of the trade ...'. The first part of s 74(d) permits a deduction by implication of the actual amount spent on normal repairs to business premises. The effect of s 74(g) is that expenditure will not be deductible if the work done is in substance an improvement of facilities on the premises. It is essentially a

question of degree whether money spent on an asset is
maintenance or improvement expenditure. A weighty (though not
conclusive) piece of evidence is commercial accounting principles.
Without such guidance the test propounded by the courts seems to
focus on whether the subject matter of the expenditure relates to
part of the entirety or the entirety itself, *per* Buckley LJ in *Lurcott v
Wakeley and Wheeler* (1911):

> Repair and renew are not words expressive of a clear contrast.
> Repair always involves renewal; renewal of a part; of a subordinate
> part ... Repair is restoration by renewal or replacement of
> subsidiary parts of a whole. Renewal, as distinguished from repair,
> is reconstruction of the entirety, meaning by the entirety not
> necessarily the whole but substantially the whole subject matter.

In *O'Grady v Bullcroft Main Colleries* (1932), replacement of an
obsolete chimney was capital. But in *Samuel Jones & Co v IRC* (1932),
the renewal of a chimney was treated as a revenue expenditure and
deductible. Another approach adopted by the courts is to ascertain
whether the trader acquired the asset in a state of disrepair. It is a
question of degree whether the cost of repair in such a case is
capital or revenue. If the asset is incapable of producing income in
its acquired state, the expense of renovating it is capital (see *Law
Shipping v IRC* (1924)). Conversely, if the asset is capable of
producing income, notwithstanding its state of disrepair, the
expenditure is deductible (see *Odeon Associated Theatres v Jones*
(1972)).

The replacement of the central heating boiler appears to be
merely maintenance rather than improvement expenditure. The
expenditure does not seem to add a new asset, that is, something
which was not in the premises in the first place. It would have been
different had Albert been replacing or changing the heating system
in the premises, perhaps from hot air to gas central heating. But it is
not the case that Albert is seeking to update his central heating
system. If this is the case the expenditure is of a revenue nature and
deductible from the gross annual profits.

The same principle applies to the redecorating expenditure of
£3,000.

In the light of what was said above in the context of the
distinction between maintenance and improvement expenditure, it

would appear that Alfred's expenditure on air conditioning equipment is capital. This expenditure creates an asset which did not exist on the premises in the first place. On this assumption, the expenditure is not deductible for income tax purposes. However, capital allowance may be claimable in respect of this expenditure amounting to £12,000.

An allowance is claimable by a trader in respect of capital expenditure incurred in the provision of *inter alia* machinery wholly and exclusively for the purposes of the trade, etc. 'Machinery' has been defined in the Oxford dictionary as meaning 'apparatus for applying mechanical power, having several parts each with a definite function'. Thus, assets with moving parts are treated as machinery. It would follow that air conditioners fall within this definition.

In addition, in order to qualify, the machinery must belong to the taxpayer and be used in the course of the trade. There appears to be no doubt that these conditions are satisfied. We have been told that Albert purchases the equipment and there is no evidence that he has transferred property in the machinery.

The allowance is available as a writing down allowance at the rate of 25% per annum of the qualifying expenditure on a reducing balance basis. In the case of individuals the allowance may be claimed in whole or in part. Thus, a maximum of £3,000 of capital allowance is claimable by Albert in respect of the expenditure on the air conditioner. The allowance is available from the end of the chargeable period in which the expenditure is incurred. The allowance is deductible from taxable profits in the relevant tax year.

Question 8

Mrs Hubble, a spinster living near the Sussex coast, owns two properties, 'The Leys' and 'White Cottage'. Mrs Hubble lives in the Leys and lets a furnished room to a student from the nearby University. The cost of electricity and heating is included in the rent. She receives a total of £4,000 from her tenant during the current year of assessment.

White Cottage is let during the holiday period which Mrs Hubble informs you lasts for five months in a calendar year. During the year of assessment Mrs Hubble informs you that White Cottage was actually let for a period of 102 days, although it was available for letting for a considerably longer period. Mrs Hubble's net income from her lettings of White Cottage during the year of assessment was £8,000.

Advise Mrs Hubble as to her liability to income tax in respect of her profits from both properties. She informs you that she is hoping to increase the rent payable in respect of the 'Leys'.

Answer plan

The Leys

Consider:
- liability to income tax under Schedule A;
- rent a room relief.

White Cottage

Discuss the following:
- Schedule A liability;
- furnished holiday letting;
- simplified tax return.

Answer

The Leys

Section 39 of the FA 1995 repeals and substitutes a new s 15 of the TA 1988 which is applicable to individuals, partnerships and trustees. The section enacts that with effect from 1995–96, income tax shall be assessed under Schedule A in respect of the *annual profits and gains* arising from a business carried on for the exploitation of any estate, interest or rights in or over any land in the UK. In short, the revenue receipts derived from land are treated as a Schedule A business.

'Receipts' in relation to land include:

(a) any payment in respect of any license to occupy or otherwise to use any land or in respect of the exercise of any other right over land;

(b) rentcharges, ground annuals and feu duties and any other annual payments reserved in respect of, or charged on or issuing out of the land (s 39(1) of the FA 1995).

Deductions are allowed in respect of trading expenses and capital allowances in much the same way as a trader is entitled to claim deductions.

Where any rent or other consideration is received for the use of furnished premises (including a caravan or houseboat) and is taxable under Schedule A , any additional sums received for the use of the furniture are also within Schedule A. Thus, Mrs Hubble's receipts of £4,000 from the student tenant for the benefit of the use of the room is primarily assessable under Schedule A, subject to statutory provisions to the contrary. From the gross rent Mrs Hubble is entitled to deduct expenses incurred in the provision of the facility. Alternatively, had Mrs Hubble provided services to her tenant, other than accommodation (such as meals, cleaning and laundering) the total amount of rents would have been required to be apportioned and the profit derived from the services would have been assessable under Schedule D Case I.

However, in pursuance of the government's objective to encourage owner occupiers who have a spare room in their home to let it out, a special relief was created by s 59 and Schedule 10 of the FA (No 2) 1992.

The relief applies to an individual receiving sums for the use of furnished accommodation in a 'qualified residence' or for ancillary services consisting of the provision of meals, cleaning, laundry etc, in respect of all of which the individual would otherwise be chargeable to income tax under Schedule D Case I and/or Schedule A. Subject to an election, and provided the gross sums received do not exceed the individual's limit (1998–99: £4,250) for the year, the profits (or losses) of the basis period for the year of assessment are treated as nil.

A 'qualifying residence' is a residence which is the individual's only or main residence at any time in the basis period for the year of assessment. A 'residence' means a building (or part) occupied or intended to be occupied as a separate residence, or a caravan or a house boat.

On the facts given, the 'Leys' appears to be a qualifying residence and Mrs Hubble's gross rent from the lodger is £4,000 for the year of assessment. It follows that this rent is exempt from income tax, provided that Mrs Hubble makes an election to this effect.

Mrs Hubble has requested advice concerning the effect of increasing the rent payable by her lodger. The relief limit for the year of assessment is capable of being increased by Treasury order. If Mrs Hubble's income from the lodger is greater than the relief limit Mrs Hubble may elect for the profits or gains of the basis period to be treated as equal to the excess. In other words the gross sum exceeding the relief limit for the year may be assessable to income tax. Alternatively, the individual may decide to pay tax in the normal way, that is, the gross receipts may be reduced by actual expenditure. A material factor in deciding on the latter option is the availability of losses in respect of other lettings. An election in respect of the first option mentioned above must be made in writing within one year of the end of the relevant tax year (or such longer time as the Board may allow). Such election remains in force until it is withdrawn.

White Cottage

Generally, from 1995–96 and later years, furnished lettings are taxable under the new Schedule A provisions as a business (see the outline above).

Sections 503–04 of the TA 1988 provide for income from furnished holiday lettings run on a commercial basis to be treated as trading income. The assessment to tax remains Schedule D Case VI but to all intents and purposes the profits are treated as trading. The effect of this arrangement is that:

(a) loss reliefs are available under ss 380–90;

(b) capital allowances are claimable for machinery and plant;

(c) the income is classified as earned income with the consequence that retirement relief and roll-over relief are available.

'Commercial letting' is defined as a letting with a view to the realisation of profits. This is a question of degree. Accommodation is let 'furnished' if the tenant is entitled to the use of the furniture. 'Holiday accommodation' is accommodation which:

(a) must be available for commercial letting to the public generally as holiday accommodation for at least 140 days in a 12 month period; and

(b) is so let at least 70 such days.

The accommodation must not normally be in the same occupation for more than 31 consecutive days at any time during a period of seven months.

In satisfying the 70 day test, averaging may be applied to letting periods of any or all of the accommodation let by the same person which would be holiday accommodation if it satisfied the 70 day test. A claim for averaging must be made within two years of the end of the year of assessment or accounting period to which it is to apply.

The circumstances regarding Mrs Hubble's profits from 'White Cottage' are such that she may or may not satisfy the tests within ss 503–04 of the TA 1988. Assuming that her lettings are treated as commercial (and there is no evidence to suggest otherwise), she has let the premises for 102 days. This certainly satisfies the 'actual lettings' test (of a minimum of 70 days). But the facts are rather vague concerning the period of availability of commercial lettings to the public. The availability is a minimum of 140 days. No difficulty arises if the requirement is satisfied. It should be added that the 'averaging' provision (outlined above) is not available to her for this is only possible where it is the 70 day principle which is not satisfied and, in any event, there are no other properties which may enter the equation.

The effect of not being within ss 503–04 of the TA 1988 is that Mrs Hubble's net profit of £8,000 is liable to income tax under Schedule A, as outlined above. Finally, since Mrs Hubble's total gross income from the exploitation of the properties may fall below £15,000, she is entitled to file a simplified return with the Revenue. She is required to state the gross property income, the total amount of allowable expenses and the net income or profit. There is still a need to keep accurate records.

CHAPTER 3

PROFITS FROM TRADES, PROFESSIONS AND VOCATIONS

Introduction

Schedule D Cases I and II assess the *annual profits or gains* arising from a trade, profession or vocation. A trade is partially defined as including 'every trade, manufacture, adventure or concern in the nature of a trade'. In special circumstances, the court will have regard to the 'badges' of trade and case law in order to determine whether a casual transaction amounts to an adventure in the nature of a trade. The expressions, 'profession' and 'vocation' have not been statutorily defined. Generally, the rules for computing the profits under Cases I and II are the same.

The expression, 'annual profits' has not been statutorily defined, but means the surplus of taxable receipts over deductible expenses. In practice, the trader submits to the Inspector of Taxes:

(a) a profit and loss account and balance sheet for the accounting period; and

(b) a computation showing the adjustments needed for tax purposes.

It is essential to distinguish a capital receipt from a revenue receipt. Capital receipts are excluded from the trading accounts and only revenue receipts of the trade, etc, are assessable to income tax. In *Van den Berghs v Clark* (1935), Lord Macmillan stated:

> The Income Tax Acts nowhere define income any more than they define capital ... What constitutes income they discreetly refrain from saying ... Consequently, it is to decided cases one must go in search of light.

There is no shortage of authorities on the distinction between capital and revenue receipts.

The gross trading receipts are reduced by deductible expenses in order to ascertain the *net trading profits*. To be deductible, an expense is required to be:

(a) of a revenue nature as opposed to a capital expense. The distinction between a revenue and capital expense is a mixed question of law and fact. In *British Insulated and Helsby's Cables Ltd v Atherton* (1926), Viscount Cave laid down a test, 'Where the expenditure is made, not only once and for all, but with a view to bringing into existence an asset or advantage for the enduring benefit of a trade ... such an expenditure is of a capital nature.' There are numerous cases which have considered and applied this test;

(b) incurred 'wholly and exclusively' for the purposes of the trade, etc, see s 74 of the Taxes Act 1988 (TA), and is not prohibited by any statutory provision.

The profits are required to be computed by using the 'earnings' basis, which gives a true reflection of the relevant transaction. It requires sums earned, but not yet received, to be credited against the expense incurred in respect of the transaction. With respect to periods of accounts beginning after 6 April 1999, profits are required to be computed on a basis which gives a 'true and fair view' (see ss 42 and 45 of the Finance Act 1998 (FA)). A receipt is 'earned' when the trader has fulfilled all the conditions imposed on him to require the debtor to pay the consideration. The High Court decided that interest on bank deposit accounts, accruing quantitively and paid into a suspense account in the bank's name, 'arose' on being credited to the depositer when the accounts were closed: *Girvan v Orange Personal Communications Services Ltd* (1998).

The other basis for computing the profits is the 'cash' basis. This method is frowned upon by the Revenue but has been accepted in practice in respect of some professions where undue fluctuations of profits are likely, for example, the profits of a barrister or an author. The cash basis simply involves the deduction of cash payments against cash receipts.

Barristers in early years of practice

Barristers may use the cash basis to calculate their profits for periods of accounts ending during their first seven years of practice: see s 43 of the FA 1998. This basis must be used consistently and must be changed to the statutory 'true and fair prices' basis after seven years. An earlier change over is permissible but, once made, is irrevocable.

At the end of an accounting period, a trader is required to value his unsold stock and work in progress. It is permissible to value certain items or groups of items at the lowest figure of 'cost', 'market value' or 'replacement price'. *Cost* means all expenditure incurred directly in the purchase or manufacture of the stock including transportation expenditure, if any, together with the relevant proportion of overhead expenditure of the business. *Market value* means the amount which it is estimated will be realised from the disposal of stock in the ordinary course of business. *Replacement price* means an estimate of the amount for which, in the ordinary course of the trade, the stock could be replaced or produced. For work in progress the costing methods that are acceptable are prime cost (wages, materials and expenses directly expended thereon), marginal cost (prime cost plus overheads). The figure for unsold stock or work in progress at the end of the accounting period, is treated as a notional receipt earned by the trader. At the start of the next accounting period the stock in hand (opening stock) or work in progress must be entered into the accounts as a notional expense for that year at the same figure.

With regard to new businesses commencing on or after 6 April 1994, and existing businesses taxable under Schedule D from 6 April 1997, the basis of assessing profits is on the current year. There are special rules for the first and the second years of assessment and the final year of business.

Question 9

Problems Ltd has entered into the following transactions in its last accounting period. Advise the company on the tax liabilities it will incur in the following transactions:

(a) a sum of £12,000 was spent on running conferences for the training of some of the independent retailers who sell the company's products. Of this total amount, £1,000 was expended on food, drink and social functions;

(b) £27,000 was paid to a competitor, Facile Ltd, as the consideration for an undertaking given by that company not to market certain specified products in South West England for a period of three years;

(c) £5,000 held as deposits for orders which had been placed by three customers two years ago, and which had since been held in a separate account, were paid into the company's bank account. The orders have never been completed and the company takes the view that the deposits have been forfeited by the customers. The goods in question have been sold to other buyers.

Answer plan

Your answer should make reference to:

- liability to corporation tax but computation of profits based on income tax principles;
- deductibility of expenses;
- entertainment expense disallowance;
- restrictive covenant, capital or revenue expense;
- change of ownership of deposits;
- date of receipt in the company's accounts.

Answer

Companies (and unincorporated associations but not partnerships) are assessable to corporation tax on their trading income as computed under the law and practice applicable to Schedule D Cases I or II (see s 9 of the TA 1988). Under Schedule D Case I, tax is charged on the profits or gains of the trade carried on wholly or partly in the UK (s 18 of the TA 1988). Generally, the Taxes Act lays down no affirmative rules as to what sums are to be treated as trading receipts and what expenses are deductible. It is a question of law as to which receipts and expenses should be included in the accounts. Accounts prepared in accordance with commercial accounting principles are treated as a starting point before being adjusted in accordance with tax law.

Part (a)

The expenditure of £12,000 on running conferences for the training of independent retailers who sell the company's products may be wholly or partly deductible. In order to qualify as a deductible expense, an item of expenditure is required to be of a revenue nature and permissible by statute. From the facts it would appear that the training conference has been organised as a means of marketing the company's products by training retailers who sell the company's products. This appears to be a revenue expense in that no asset has been acquired by Problems Ltd for the enduring benefit of its trade, *per* Viscount Cave in *British Insulated and Helsby's Cables v Atherton* (1926), who laid down a test to identify a capital expense. The expense by Problems Ltd may be of a continuing nature in that as new products are manufactured by the company further training conferences may be held.

Section 817 of the TA 1988 stipulates that no deduction shall be made unless expressly allowed by statute. Section 74(1)(a) and (b) of the TA 1988 enact the general rule, albeit in a negative form. The effect is that an expense is allowed if it is incurred *wholly and exclusively for the purposes of the trade*. In *Bentley, Stokes and Lowless v Beeson* (1952), Romer LJ explained this requirement by having regard to the purpose of the expenditure. If the sole or main purpose is directly connected with the business venture, the expense is deductible. This is the position even if the expense involved some incidental non-commercial purpose. But if the expenditure embraces two main purposes one commercial and the other a non-commercial purpose (dual purposes) the entire expense is strictly not deductible. Another approach is to consider whether the expense was incurred exclusively for the purpose of earning profits or made for other purposes after profits have been ascertained.

Applying this principle to the facts, Problems Ltd incurred the training conference expense solely for commercial purposes, that is, in order to train its retailers so that its products could be more efficiently marketed. In *British Sugar Manufacturers Ltd v Harris* (1937), payments were made by a company to two other companies under an agreement to pay them, for four years, a specified percentage of its net profits 'in consideration of their giving to the company the full benefit of their technical and financial knowledge and experience'. The payments were deductible. In *Wickwar v Berry* (1963), fees paid by a farmer for the attendance of his sons (employed as farm labourers) at an agricultural course at a college, were deductible. On analogy with these cases it would appear that the expense is deductible.

We have been informed that £1,000 of the sum expended was paid out on social functions. Section 74(1)(b) disallows expenses of a domestic or private nature. It would seem that despite the non-commercial nature of this expense, the purpose is inherent or incidental to the main commercial purpose and does not disentitle Problems Ltd from deducting this amount. This is a question of degree and presumably part of a package negotiated with the conference providers. In *Watkins v Ashford, Sparkes & Harward* (1985), the court allowed a firm of solicitors to deduct expenditure on providing food, drink and accommodation for the partners at the firm's annual weekend conference at a hotel. No distinction was to be made between the cost of accommodation and that of food and drink. The partners were providing a method of enabling them to continue their discussions over the weekend.

Alternatively, if the claim to deduct the expense on social functions is disallowed, the company may be entitled to apportion the remainder of the expense and claim a deduction in respect of such expenditure. Although apportionment is strictly not permitted under s 74(1)(a) and (b), in practice, the Revenue permits this process.

Part (b)

Problems Ltd pays £27,000 to a competitor, Facile Ltd, for an undertaking not to market specified products in south west England for three years. This is a payment for agreeing to enter into a restrictive covenant for commercial purposes. The question in issue is whether the payment is of a revenue or capital nature. Capital expenditure is not deductible in computing the profits of a trade. The test in order to identify capital expenditure was laid down in *British Insulated and Helsby's Cables v Atherton* (1926), *per* Viscount Cave:

> When an expenditure is made, not only once and for all, but with a view to bringing into existence an asset or advantage for the enduring benefit of a trade ... I think such expenditure is properly attributable not to revenue but to capital.

The approach adopted by the courts is to consider whether an asset has been acquired by the person expending the sum. No doubt, the amount of the payment as well as the length of the covenant are material factors to be taken into consideration. In *Associated Portland Cement Manufacture Company v Kerr* (1946), a company made lump sum payments to two directors in consideration of them entering into restrictive covenants. The court held that the payments were capital because the effect of the payments enhanced a capital asset namely, goodwill. The court considered that the effect of buying off two potential competitors by its very nature affected the value of the company's goodwill. On the other hand, in *Commissioners of Taxes v Nchanga Consolidated Mines* (1964), the respondents, a copper mining company, paid just under £1.5 m to another company to keep it out of production for 12 months. The court held that the payment was of a revenue nature for it was a cost incidental to the production of copper. The court considered the duration of the covenant to be a significant factor in its decision.

Applying these principles to the facts before us, the duration of the covenant is three years, the payment does not open a market in south west England. This market, it would seem, existed before the payment was made. But the payment simply gets rid of one competitor temporarily. Although it is a question of law whether a payment is of a capital or revenue nature, it would appear reasonably certain that the payment on these facts is of a revenue nature. It follows that if the payment is of a revenue nature it is deductible as it satisfies the test laid down in s 74.

Part (c)

There are two issues to be considered with respect to £5,000 of customer deposits which have been paid into the company's bank account. The first issue concerns ownership of the sum. The second issue concerns the date when such sums become taxable.

In *Morley v Tattersall* (1938), a firm of bloodstock auctioneers received sums from sales for which they were liable to account to the vendors, their clients. These sums were not in law trade receipts but were the clients' money. Substantial sums were never collected by the clients and remained in the firm's hands as 'unclaimed balances'. In due course when such sums were unlikely to be claimed, they were transferred to the credit of the individual partners. The court held that these sums were not trading receipts of the firm. The status of a receipt was determined at the time of the receipt and could not be subsequently changed. On the other hand, in *Jay's the Jewellers Ltd v IRC* (1947), a company of pawnbrokers had unclaimed balances representing the proceeds of sale of unredeemed pledges. Some of these balances became the property of the pawnbroker after a period of time by virtue of the Pawnbrokers' Act 1872, and these were held by the court to become trade receipts by virtue of the Act. Other receipts outside the Act were held to become trading receipts after six years under the Statute of Limitation 1939. A similar result was reached in *Elson v Prices Tailors Ltd* (1937). The defendants, tailors, took 'deposits' from customers who ordered clothes. When the clothes were uncollected the deposits were transferred to an 'Unclaimed Deposits Account' and would ordinarily be returned to dissatisfied customers. It was held that the payments were true deposits representing part payment of the purchase price and were trading receipts.

In view of the conflicting principles derived from these cases, it is not a simple matter to advise Problems Ltd. Five thousand pounds were received as 'deposits'. The question here is whether the receipts were true deposits in law. It should be added that the name placed by the taxpayer on the status of the receipt is inconclusive. Much would depend on the terms of the contract between the company and the customer. Assuming in favour of the company that the receipt is a true deposit, that is, a part payment of the price of the service by the customer, it would appear that *Elson*'s case above is indistinguishable. The complication that arose in *Morley* will thereby be avoided. It is interesting to note that the company has taken the view that the deposits by customers are forfeited after a period of two years. This assessment would depend on the contract between Problems Ltd and its customers.

The remaining issue concerns the date when the sum may be credited to the company's trading receipts. In *Elson*, the court decided that the year of initial payment was the year in which the sum may be treated as a trading receipt. This follows logically from the status of the payment. If the sum is to be treated initially as a part payment of the purchase price, it ought to be credited in the accounts of the year when the contract was made. Whereas, in *Jay's the Jewellers* the sum became a trading receipt in the year when the status of the receipt was changed. On the facts before us, if £5,000 deposits were trading receipts initially but were forfeited two years subsequently, the sum is treated as trading receipts in the year of deposit.

Question 10

Try as you will, the word 'trade' is one of those common English words which do not lend themselves readily to a definition but which all of us think we understand well enough. We can recognise a trade when we see it, and also an 'adventure in the nature of trade'. But we are hard pressed to define it ... short of a definition, the only thing to do is to look at the usual characteristics of a 'trade' and see how this transaction measures up to them.

Consider the usual characteristics of a trade by reference to decided cases.

Answer plan

Good answers must consider:

- distinguishing questions of fact from law – *Edwards v Bairstow and Harrison*;
- subject matter of realisation;
- period of ownership;
- frequency of similar transactions;
- supplementary work;
- profit motive;
- circumstances responsible for realisation;
- illegal trading;
- mutual trading.

Answer

Schedule D Case I assesses tax on the annual profits or gains arising from any trade carried on in the UK or elsewhere (see s 18 of the TA 1988). The expression 'trade' has been defined inclusively as 'every trade, manufacture, adventure or concern in the nature of trade' (s 832 of the TA 1988). Although a trade ordinarily involves the regular buying and selling of property, it is wrong to assume that an isolated or casual transaction may not be liable to income tax under Schedule D Case I. Such an activity may involve an 'adventure in the nature of a trade' or alternatively, an accretion to capital liable to capital gains tax. Which tax regime is applicable may still be significant in determining the status of an isolated profit. In cases of doubt, the Revenue may raise alternative assessments.

The initial question, whether a taxpayer is engaged in an adventure in the nature of a trade, is determined by the Inspector of Taxes. An appeal from his decision goes to the Commissioners, usually, the General Commissioners. The findings of the Commissioners are decisions of fact, but an appeal from their decision lies to the High Court by way of case stated on a point of law. It is only in rare cases that the court will overturn the Commissioners' decisions on appeal. This would be the case where the conclusions of the Commissioners cannot be supported by the facts. In this event, the only reasonable conclusion that could be drawn is that the Commissioners misdirected themselves on a point of law (see *Edwards v Bairstow & Harrison* (1956)).

The question whether the profits from an isolated transaction are liable to income tax or not may only be comprehensively examined by having regard to decided cases. In 1955, the Royal Commission on the Taxation of Profits and Income (Cmnd 9474) concluded that the term 'trade' is incapable of a satisfactory statutory definition but suggested six *indicia* of trading activities. These are the subject matter of realisation, the length of the period of ownership, the frequency of similar transactions, supplementary work, the profit motive and the circumstances that were responsible for the realisation. Very rarely is any one of these badges considered in isolation or conclusive as to the nature of the transaction. In many marginal cases, all six badges are required to be considered.

Subject matter of realisation

The courts take the view that some commodities are more likely to be acquired as the subject matter of a 'deal' rather than as an accretion to capital. If the subject matter of the purchase does not yield an income but is enjoyed for its aesthetic value or pride of possession, any profit from its resale may escape income tax, for example, the profit arising from the purchase and resale of a work of art may be treated as a capital transaction. But this is a question of degree and the commercial nature of the transaction may be gathered from the nature and quantity of the subject matter purchased. In *Rutledge v IRC* (1929), the taxpayer, while on a business trip to Berlin, bought 1 m rolls of toilet paper for £1,000. Within a short time of his return to England he sold the entire consignment to one person at a profit of £10,000. The court decided that the transaction was an adventure in the nature of a trade and liable to income tax. There was no other conceivable purpose for the purchase than that of reselling the rolls at a profit.

Similarly, the means adopted for the resale of the commodity may play a significant role in determining the status of the activity. The more elaborate the machinery for the disposal of the assets, the stronger the inference that the activity constitutes an adventure in the nature of a trade. In *Martin v Lowry* (1927), an agricultural machinery merchant purchased the government's entire surplus stock of aeroplane linen amounting to 44 m yards. He set up an organisation to dispose of the material to the public. He rented an office, engaged a manager and staff and advertised extensively. He eventually disposed of the material over a period of 12 months and realised a profit of just under £2 m. The court decided that having regard to the methods adopted for resale of the material, the number of operations into which the taxpayer entered and the time occupied by the resale, the taxpayer was liable to income tax under Schedule D Case I.

The length of the period of ownership

This test is based on the assumption that a quick turnover is the essence of a 'deal' (see *Rutledge v IRC,* above). But a long period of ownership is some evidence to indicate that the asset was bought as a capital transaction. The value of this *indicia* varies with facts of each case. In *Johnstone v Heath* (1970), the taxpayer was the manager of a building company. The company gave permission to the taxpayer to purchase its real property. The taxpayer was unable to arrange a loan to purchase the land personally but entered into a contract with a sub-buyer to purchase the land from the taxpayer at a higher price than the taxpayer was required to pay to the company. The court decided that the profit made by the taxpayer was liable to income tax. On the other hand, in *Harvey v Caulcott* (1952), a builder constructed two shops in 1927 and a house in 1939 for his foreman to reside. The shops were let until they were sold in 1946 and 1948 respectively. The taxpayer contended that the properties were realisations of investments and were not liable to income tax. The court held that the transactions were not liable to income tax owing to the long period of ownership. A marginal decision under this heading is *IRC v Reinhold* (1953), where the taxpayer bought and resold four homes within three years. He admitted that he had bought the houses for resale and that he had once before engaged in a property transaction. The court held that the transaction did not constitute a trade. The properties yielded income from rents. The intention to resell the properties some day at a profit was not *per se* decisive to attract income tax on the profits.

Frequency of similar transactions

A characteristic of a trade is the regular buying and selling of property, that is, stock. The point here is that repeated transactions of a similar kind offer strong evidence of the trading nature of the transactions. In *Pickford v Quirke* (1927), a syndicate was formed to buy and sell cotton mills. There were four such transactions. The court held that although one transaction by itself may not constitute a trade, several similar transactions may have this effect. Where a transaction is repeated the court may use the nature of the subsequent transaction(s) to determine the status of the original transaction. In *Leach v Pogson* (1962), the taxpayer carried out 30 similar transactions. In respect of each transaction he established a motoring school and each in turn to a company. The taxpayer conceded that he was liable to income tax in respect of all the transactions except the first. The court rejected this argument and held that he was liable to income tax.

Supplementary work

The alteration of a commodity by the taxpayer for the purpose of resale may indicate that his intention at he time of purchase was to resell the property at a profit, that is, to embark on a trading transaction. In *Cape Brandy Syndicate v IRC* (1921), three individuals in the wine trade formed a syndicate and acquired a quantity of Cape brandy. This was shipped to the UK, blended with French brandy, recasked and sold to purchasers over a period of 18 months. The court held that the profits were assessable to income tax.

But it has been conceded that some limit ought to be placed on this principle. By merely incurring expenditure on the property in order to enhance the value of the asset for the purpose of resale, does not necessarily constitute a trade. It is quite natural for any vendor to seek the best price for his property. In *Taylor v Good* (1974), a taxpayer unexpectedly bought a large country house for a bargain price at an auction. He subsequently applied for and obtained planning permission for its demolition and erection of 90 dwellings on the site. He then sold the land to a developer at a profit. The Revenue conceded that the property was not initially bought as a trading transaction but contended that the property had been subsequently appropriated to a trade. The court decided in favour of the taxpayer on the ground that at the time of the purchase the taxpayer did not intend to realise a profit from the asset. The status of the transaction was determined at the earlier time and not at the time of applying for planning permission. The application to obtain planning permission was a step merely to enhance the value of the property for sale.

Profit motive

The question whether a taxpayer is trading is determined objectively. An important feature of a trading transaction is an intention to make a profit or an intention to avoid making a loss (see *Overseas Containers (Finance) Ltd v Stoker* (1989) and *Ensign Tankers (leasing) Ltd v Stokes* (1992), in respect of tax avoidance schemes). If commercial methods are used by the taxpayer this will constitute strong evidence of a trading transaction. In *Wisdom v Chamberlain* (1969), the taxpayer, an actor had assets worth between

£150,000 and £200,000. Fearing that sterling may be devalued, his accountant suggested that investments in silver bullion would be a suitable hedge against devaluation. He bought £200,000 worth of silver. The silver was eventually sold at a profit of £48,000 within little more than a year. The taxpayer's argument that he was merely seeking to avoid a loss and that he was not seeking to make a profit was rejected. The court decided that the motive and object of the transaction was to make a profit.

A taxpayer's motive may be considered when his actions are equivocal. If the taxpayer's activities produce a profit the onus of proof will shift to the taxpayer to show that the profit made on the sale of an asset is not taxable under Schedule D Case I. This is not an easy burden to discharge. In *Iswera v Ceylon Commissioner of Taxation* (1965), the taxpayer wished to reside near the school where her daughters were attending and bought a site for the erection of a house. The taxpayer was forced by the vendor to acquire a larger plot of land than she needed and afterwards disposed of the surplus land to nine sub-buyers at a profit. The court held that the profit was liable to income tax.

Moreover, the activities of a body may be construed as trading even though it is required by statute to apply a profit for a particular purpose. In *Mersey Docks & Harbour Board v Lucas* (1883), the Board was established by an Act of Parliament which enacted that moneys received by it will be applied to sinking funds to extinguish certain debts. The court held that the Board was liable to income tax in respect of any surplus funds. In addition, many institutions exist for the purpose of providing services to the community with no dominant intention of making a profit for itself, for example, charitable activities. Such organisations will be engaged in trading activities if the business is arranged on a commercial basis. In *Re the Estate of the ICLR for England and Wales* (1888), under the memorandum of the Council, all property and income of the Council were applicable solely to the objects of publishing law reports, etc and no part could be paid as a dividend, bonus or otherwise to any member. The court held that the Council was carrying on a trade.

On the other hand, if the organisation is incapable of making a profit it is unlikely to constitute a trade. In *Religious Tract and Book*

Society of Scotland v Forbes (1896), the society was founded for the diffusion of religious literature. It sold books from a shop and depots in Edinburgh and Belfast. The society also promoted the services of 'colporteurs', that is, persons who sold bibles and acted as cottage missionaries. The society claimed to set off its losses suffered by its colportage activities against its trading profits derived from its bookshops. This could only be done if colportage was a trade. The court held that such activity was not trading. Likewise, in *Graham v Greene* (1925), the winnings of an habitual gambler, not being a bookmaker, were not assessable to income tax.

Circumstances responsible for realisation

There may be circumstances or explanations for the sale of property which may negative any notion that the transaction (purchase and sale) is a trading transaction, for example, an emergency or other circumstances requiring a quick sale. The burden of proof will be on the taxpayer and each case will be decided on its own facts. In *Cohan's Executors v IRC* (1924), the deceased was a partner in a firm of shipbrokers. Before his death he had entered into a shipbuilding contract. The contract was completed by his executors and the ship was sold. The executors were assessable (on behalf of the deceased) on the resultant profit. The court decided in favour of the executors on the ground that they did not continue the trade but were merely performing their duty of realising the deceased's assets to the best advantage. In *West v Phillips* (1958), the taxpayer built 2,500 houses. Some were for letting and some for resale. The letting business started to make losses and the taxpayer decided to sell the let houses. The court decided that the forced sale did not constitute a trade.

In *Simmons v IRC* (1980), a scheme contrived by a group of property investment companies was abandoned because of the unfavourable investment climate. The group decided not to proceed with the scheme and to sell off the properties. The court decided that the profit realised was not by way of a trade. The group's intention at the time of the acquisition of the assets was not consistent with trading.

Illegal trading

It may be added that the profits of an illegal trade are taxable. In *Lindsay and Others v IRC* (1932), the profits obtained from the illegal shipping of whisky to the USA during the prohibition period were held to be taxable. Likewise, the profits of prostitution were held to be trading income assessable under Schedule D Case I in *IRC v Aken* (1990).

Mutual trading

Where individuals join together with common objectives and mutually subscribe funds to a common pool for their joint benefit, they cannot be considered to be trading, for example, a golf club with finances solely received from members' subscriptions. This is because individuals cannot trade with themselves. Thus, any surplus contributions returned to the members, on general principles and subject to statutory provisions to the contrary, is tax free (see *New York Life Insurance Co v Styles* (1899)). However, s 491 of the TA 1988 now imposes a charge to tax on the return of surplus assets in circumstances when the original contributions were tax deductible.

If the association makes profits out of activities involving non-members, the profits of such activities are taxable (see *Carlisle and Silloth Golf Club v Smith* (1913)), fees paid by visitors for the use of club facilities were held to be trading receipts.

Question 11

Rembrandt, an art dealer, had a busy year in 1998.

Part (a)

A drawing by Constable which he had acquired as a legacy from his father in 1994 and which he had since kept in his home was sold privately to a friend for £18,000.

Part (b)

He transferred a painting by Turner which he had bought as stock in 1996 for £50,000 to his house to take the place of the drawing and credited the business with £50,000 for it. The market price of this painting was £100,000 in 1998.

Part (c)

A second Turner painting, acquired in 1990 for £70,000 was exchanged for a painting by Holbein owned by Vermeer, also an art dealer. Both dealers considered the market value of each of these two works in 1998 to be about £130,000. The Holbein was displayed by Rembrandt for sale at a price of £140,000.

Part (d)

A decision was taken to sell off in the Spring sale in 1998 12 paintings which together cost £60,000 at sale prices totalling £40,000. Rembrandt's policy is to mark up his selling prices to not less than 50% more than his cost price.

Advise Rembrandt how the above transactions should be dealt with in his accounts at the end of the year for tax purposes.

Answer plan

Your answer should deal with the following issues:

- non-commercial acquisition and disposal;
- *Sharkey v Wernher*, market value disposal proceeds;
- commercial transaction between two dealers;
- revaluation of stock remaining unsold;
- possible commercial disposal at an undervalue.

Answer

Part (a)

Rembrandt acquired a drawing as a gift from his father in 1994. This acquisition by Rembrandt seems to be outside the course of his trade. There is no evidence that the drawing has been appropriated by Rembrandt into his art dealing business. Indeed, the evidence indicates that the drawing has been acquired as a legacy for his own personal benefit. Rembrandt kept the drawing in his home for pride of possession. Eventually the drawing was sold privately to a friend for £18,000. Since this asset never entered Rembrandt's trading accounts, it appears that the asset attracts not income tax but capital gains tax.

Capital gains tax is charged on the chargeable gains accruing to a person (other than a company) on the disposal of an asset during a year of assessment (see s 1(1) of the Taxation of Chargeable Gains Act 1992 (TCGA)). A chargeable gain means a gain accruing on the disposal of an asset after 6 April 1982. Such gains are computed in accordance with the principles enacted in ss 15–52 of the TCGA. Briefly, the disposal proceeds, actual or notional, are reduced by certain types of expenditure (the capital cost of acquiring the asset, actual or notional, as well as the costs of improving the asset and incidental costs of acquiring and disposing of the asset) and indexation allowance. For disposals after 6 April 1998, taper relief is available. The gain or loss is the difference between the disposal proceeds and deductible expenditure.

Applying these principles to Rembrandt, it appears that the specific legacy of the drawing acquired in 1994 has no actual acquisition cost incurred by Rembrandt. Indeed, s 62 of the TCGA 1992 provides that on a person's death, the assets acquired by a legatee are deemed to be acquired on the date and for the value at which the personal representatives acquired the property. The personal representatives are deemed to acquire the assets of the deceased for a consideration equal to their market value at the date of death of the testator. There is no deemed disposal. Thus, Rembrandt is treated for capital gains tax purposes as having acquired the drawing at market value. We have not been told of the market value of the drawing at the time of Rembrandt's acquisition of the asset. The sale of the drawing by Rembrandt to his friend for £18,000 amounts to an actual disposal of the asset. Assuming that the asset is disposed of at its market value, the gain or loss is assessable or deductible for capital gains tax purposes, subject to reliefs.

A final point is that it is highly unlikely that the profit or loss resulting from this transaction may be brought into account for income tax purposes as an adventure in the nature of a trade. The acquisition by Rembrandt is not in respect of a deliberate act by him to make a profit but rather a fortuitous event whereby a valuable drawing has been acquired.

Part (b)

The transfer by Rembrandt to his house of a replacement painting, by Turner, costing the business £50,000 and crediting the business with £50,000 is unlikely to be accepted by the Revenue. The general rule is that a trader may dispose of his stock, in the ordinary course of his trade, at whatever value he considers appropriate. If the transaction is commercial, objectively considered, the consideration received will be included in his trading account.

But exceptionally, if the trader disposes of stock otherwise than in the course of the trade, the market value of the asset at the time of the disposal should be ascertained and included in his accounts as a notional receipt. The assumption that is made is, but for the non-commercial disposal, the trader would have disposed of the stock at a commercial value. In any event, the trader would have debited his accounts with the expense of acquiring the asset. This is known as the rule in *Sharkey v Wernher* (1956), Lady Wernher ran a stud farm as a business, the profits of which were admittedly chargeable to tax under Schedule D Case I. She also carried on a hobby activity of horse racing and training which was not liable to income tax. Five horses were transferred from the stud farm to the racing stables. The cost of breeding these horses was debited in the stud farm's accounts. The question in issue was what figure should be credited as a receipt in the accounts. The taxpayer contended that the costs of breeding should be included in the account as a notional receipt. The Revenue argued that the market value of the horses on the date of disposal from the stud farm was the correct figure. The court decided in favour of the Revenue. The market value was the appropriate figure to credit the account on the ground that this sum would normally have been received by the trader in due course of the trade. Whether a disposal is commercial or not is a question of law.

In this case, Rembrandt acquired the Turner painting in the ordinary course of his trade in 1996 for £50,000. This sum has been debited in his accounts for that year as a trading expense. The transfer of the painting to Rembrandt's house, to replace the Constable, is an appropriation of stock undoubtedly for a non-commercial purpose. The approach of the courts is based on the proposition that a trader cannot trade with himself and not that trader cannot make a profit out of himself. On analogy with *Sharkey v Wernher*, it appears that Rembrandt would be unable to resist the Revenue's argument that the market value of the asset on the date of disposal, namely £100,000, is required to be credited as a notional profit in the trader's account. The suggestion by Rembrandt that he credits his trading account with a notional receipt, equivalent to the cost price of the asset has been rejected by the House of Lords in *Sharkey v Wernher*.

Part (c)

The exchange by Rembrandt in 1998 with another art dealer of the Turner for the Holbein painting amounts to an exchange or barter of stock. There is no evidence to suggest that this transaction is outside the course of Rembrandt's trade. On this assumption, the Revenue's view is that an exchange of stock between traders amounts to a realisation of trading stock and the simultaneous acquisition of new stock. The effect is that any profit or loss arising from such an exchange has to be taken into account in computing the trading profits. The *Sharkey v Wernher* principle applies to the disposal of stock, that is, the market value of the stock disposed of is included in the accounts as a notional receipt. In addition, the same figure is included as a notional expense in accordance with the reverse *Sharkey v Wernher* rule (see *Jacgilden (Weston Hall) Ltd v Castle* (1969), on the latter point). The estimating of the market value at the time of the exchange will not matter a great deal as the ultimate total profits will remain unchanged. The only consequence of an overvaluation or undervaluation will be to increase the profits of one period and decrease the profits of another. When the stock subsequently acquired is finally disposed of, the profit or loss is computed by deducting the notional acquisition cost from the disposal proceeds.

Applying this principle to the events orchestrated by Rembrandt, the market value of the Turner is ascertained in 1998 and enters the trader's account as a notional receipt. The traders estimate this to be £130,000. This would produce a profit on the Turner painting of £60,000. Moreover, another item of stock, namely the Holbein, has been acquired at the market value of the recently disposed Turner, that is, £130,000. This amount is treated as a notional expense on the date of acquisition. The profit in respect of this item of stock is realised when the stock is finally disposed of in the course of the trade or notionally transferred.

The alternative view which does not have the support of the Revenue is to treat the stock that has been exchanged as continuing to exist in the form of the stock acquired as a result of the exchange. This approach has the merit of postponing the taxation of profits until the newly acquired stock is finally transferred. This view is opposed by the Revenue not only because tax may be postponed without authority, but also the approach fails to give a true picture of the trader's activities which concern two items of stock, not one.

Part (d)

Rembrandt has made a decision to hold a Spring sale in 1998 and to sell 12 paintings at a discount, resulting in a loss of £20,000. Rembrandt's sales policy is to mark up his selling price to not less than 50% of the cost price, on the basis that the minimum sales prices of the paintings would have amounted to £90,000. It is imperative to ascertain whether the decision to hold a Spring sale and the selling prices of the paintings was reached by applying commercial principles, without any element of bounty. On the assumption that that is the case, transfers at an undervalue in pursuance of a commercial strategy will be treated as disposals outside the *Sharkey v Wernher* rule. The actual profit or loss arising from the transactions will be included in the trader's accounts.

~--estion 12

> The Income Tax Acts contain no rules which lay down affirmatively what sums are to be taxed as receipts ... in the compilation of an account ... It has been for the courts to lay down the principles to be observed. [*Report of the Committee on the Taxation of Trading Profits*, 1951.]

Consider this statement in the light of decided cases.

Answer plan

In answering this type of question, you should consider the following matters:

- receipts arising outside the taxpayer's trade are not trading receipts;
- the distinction between 'fixed' and 'circulating' capital;
- receipts from the sale of trading assets are *prima facie* capital;
- receipts in return for the imposition of substantial restrictions on the trader's activities are *prima facie* capital;
- receipts in *lieu* of trading receipts are of a revenue nature;
- receipts of a recurrent nature are likely to be of a revenue nature.

Answer

Section 18 of the TA 1988 assesses income tax on the 'annual profits and gains' arising from a trade, etc. The expression, 'annual' has not been statutorily defined but has been regarded as referring to trading profits. Such profits are ascertained by including only trading receipts as reduced by deductible trading expenditure in the profit and loss account. The Tax Acts do not prescribe rules specifying the appropriate methods of ascertaining the annual profits for tax purposes. *Prima facie* the courts accept the net profits shown in the profit and loss account provided that this is prepared in accordance with ordinary principles of commercial accounting. Such profits are then adjusted in accordance with tax principles: see

Odeon Associated Theatres v Jones (1970) on the significance of principles of commercial accounting.

Although a taxpayer is carrying on a trade, a particular receipt may still be excluded in the computation of profits if the receipt derives from activities outside the scope of the taxpayer's trade or the receipt is of a capital nature.

A trader who receives profits in respect of activities outside the course of his trade is clearly not liable to tax under Schedule D Case I. Such receipts may be treated as profits of another trade, or the sum may be assessed under Schedule D Case VI, or the sum may be treated as a capital receipt liable to capital gains tax. In *Simpson v Reynolds* (1975), an insurance broking company lost a valuable client on a change of control of the client's company. The client voluntarily undertook to pay the taxpayer £1,000 per annum for five years in recognition of past services. The court held that the gift was not chargeable to income tax, for the circumstances clearly indicated that the unexpected receipt was not connected with future broking services to be performed by the taxpayer. The gift was made in recognition of past services. In contrast, in *CIR v Falkirk Ice Rink Ltd* (1975), the taxpayer company operated an ice rink on a commercial basis and provided curling facilities to members of the public on payment of admission charges. It also leased rooms at a commercial rent to a club whose members were admitted at preferential rates. The charge for curling did not cover the cost of providing the quality of ice surface required and the club made a donation of £1,500 to the company. The court held that the donation was a trading receipt of the company. The donation, despite being voluntary, was not entirely unexpected and the payment was made by the club to continue links with the company.

The question as to whether profits originating from foreign exchange transactions are taxable as the profits of a trade has often arisen before the courts. If a trader purchases foreign currency in order to assist him in the purchase of goods abroad, any profit made on the foreign currency deal will be treated as part of his trading profits. In *Imperial Tobacco Company v Kelly* (1943), the taxpayer company purchased dollars in order to finance its purchase of American tobacco. The dollars were purchased by the British government at a higher price than the company paid for them. The court held that the profit made by the company was taxable. On the other hand, if the foreign exchange transaction can be regarded as a temporary investment or speculative venture outside the trade, any profit made is not taxable as a trading profit. In *McKinlay v Jenkins Ltd* (1926), stone merchants purchased Italian lira in anticipation of having to purchase marble in Italy some six months ahead. The lira purchased appreciated, and as the currency was not required immediately, they sold the lira at a gain. The court held that the profit from the foreign exchange transaction was not liable to income tax for the company embarked upon an exchange speculation.

Capital profits are excluded from the computation of trading profits, but it is no easy task to distinguish capital receipts from revenue receipts. The economists' distinction between 'fixed' and 'circulating' capital has its limitations in tax law. It is not possible to draw an exact line of demarcation between these two notions. An asset forms part of the fixed capital if it is retained in the business with the object of producing profit. Whereas an asset is part of the circulating capital of a business if it is acquired in the ordinary course of the trade and is sold or is used in the manufacturing of what is sold, for example, raw materials. This test, while it is of some help, is inadequate as a means of classifying the profits of businesses into capital and revenue receipts. The distinction remains a matter of degree to be determined by the facts of each case.

Receipts from the sale of assets are prima facie *capital*

When a trader sells all or part of his assets the profit is liable to capital gains tax even though the sum paid is recurrent or is in the form of a lump sum. But if the terms of the sale contain a collateral bargain for the future supply of goods, the profits from the subsidiary agreement may be liable to income tax. In *Orchard Wine and Supply Co v Laynes* (1933), partners in a wine and spirit business sold a secret formula, a trademark and the goodwill relating to a specific type of whisky liqueur which it manufactured on terms that they were entitled to commission on the future sales of liqueur. The court held that the commissions were trading receipts.

Receipts in return for the imposition of substantial restrictions on the trader's activities are prima facie *capital*

The issue here is whether compensation received by a trader for refraining from using some profitable asset is a capital or revenue receipt. Such receipt will be treated as capital if the asset surrendered can be said to involve the basis of the recipient's profit making apparatus. In *Van Den Berghs v Clark* (1935), compensation was received by an English company for the termination of a 'pooling agreement' with a Dutch company. The pooling agreement concerned an understanding as to the way the companies would run their businesses to their mutual advantage. The court held that the compensation was capital. It is a question of degree whether the compensation relates to the profit making apparatus (or structure) of the trader. If compensation is received in respect of part of the assets of the trader and the trader continues to make profits from that part of the assets retained, the compensation may be treated as a trading receipt. In *Kelsall Parsons and Company v IRC* (1938), the taxpayers were manufacturing agents and sold goods on a commission basis. It received compensation in respect of the termination of one of its agency agreements which had only one more year to run. The court held that the compensation was liable to income tax. The acquisition and loss of an agency was a normal incident of the trade.

A receipt in respect of the imposition of a substantial restriction on the activities of a trader is capable of being a capital receipt. Thus, compensation for undertaking a restrictive covenant may be capital. Much depends on the length and extent of the restriction. In *Higgs v Olivier* (1951), following the production of the film, *Henry V*, an actor entered into a restrictive covenant with a film company whereby he agreed not to produce, direct or act in any film for 18 months in return for a payment of £15,000. The court held that the sum was a capital receipt.

But, if the compensation for the restriction is an integral part of the agreement for the supply of goods, the receipt is treated as a revenue sum. This would be the case where the sum receivable for the restrictive covenant is linked with an agreement for the supply of goods. In *Thompson v Magnesium Elektron Ltd* (1943), one of the terms of an agreement for the supply of chlorine was that the taxpayers, magnesium manufacturers, would not manufacture chlorine. The court held that the sums receivable for such undertaking were of a revenue nature.

Payments in lieu of trading receipts are revenue receipts

The point here is that income tax is chargeable in respect of compensation paid to a trader instead of a receipt that would have formed part of the taxpayer's trading profits. If the subject matter of the compensation relates to a trading transaction, then it must follow that the compensation is of the same status. In *John Mills Productions v Mathias* (1967), the taxpayer company was formed to exploit the services of an actor. The taxpayer company entered into an agreement with a film production company to engage the actor exclusively for seven years in connection with a minimum of 10 films. After only two films were made the agreement was terminated in consideration of payment of £50,000 to the taxpayer company. The court held that the sum was liable to income tax as a trading receipt. Likewise, in *Burmah Steamship Company v IRC* (1930), the court held that compensation paid by a ship repairer to the taxpayer for the delay in the late return of a ship was liable to income tax. In *Donald Fisher (Ealing) Ltd v Spencer* (1989), compensation received by the taxpayer, tenant, for increased rent payable as a result of the default of its agents was liable to income tax.

Receipts of a recurrent nature are likely to revenue receipts

A capital receipt will not become a revenue receipt merely because it is one of series of payments of the same kind. Similarly, a revenue receipt will still be treated as such even though it is a once and for all amount. However, where a receipt is neither clearly capital nor revenue, light may be thrown on the nature of the receipt by considering whether any payments of a similar kind have been, or are to be, made to the trader in question. In *Evans Medical Supplies v Moriarty* (1957), the taxpayer company agreed to supply the Burmese government with all necessary drawings, plans, technical data and 'know how' to manufacture medical supplies in consideration for an annual sum. The court held that the consideration was a capital receipt. The company had parted with an asset which was the source or one of the sources of its profits. On the other hand, in *Rolls Royce v Jeffrey* (1962), the taxpayer company embarked on a deliberate policy of licensing companies in other countries to manufacture its engines on terms which involved the payment of 'capital sums' (so called) and royalties. The court decided that the sums were of a revenue nature.

Question 13

Advise the following traders as to their basis periods in respect of which their profits are computed.

Part (a)

Thomas commenced business on 1 August 1997 and produced accounts for the 12 months to 31 July 1998 and annually thereafter.

Profits (as adjusted for tax purposes) are:

12 months to 31 July 1998	£14,000
12 months to 31 July 1999	£20,000
12 months to 31 July 2000	£26,000

Part (b)

Howard started business on 1 August 1997 and produced accounts to 5 April each year until the year 2001 when the accounting date was changed to 30 June.

The adjusted profits are:

7 months to 5 April 1998	£ 8,000
12 months to 5 April 1999	£18,000
12 months to 5 April 2000	£24,000
15 months to 30 June 2001	£37,500

Answer plan

You should consider:

- opening year of trading – s 61(1);
- second year of trading – s 61(2);
- overlap relief – s 63(A);
- third year of assessment – s 60;
- change of basis period – s 62;
- conditions necessary for change – s 62(A).

Answer

Part (a)

The new, streamline, standard, current basis of assessment of Schedule D profits takes effect from 6 April 1996, but as regards a new trade commencing after 5 April 1994 takes effect for 1994–95 and subsequent years.

Section 61(1) of the TA 1988 (introduced by s 201 of the FA 1994) enacts that where the year of assessment is the commencement year of trading or business, the computation of profits chargeable to income tax under Schedule D Cases I or II shall be made on the profits arising in the year, that is, from the date of commencement to the following 5 April. Thus, on the present facts the basis period in the first year of trading is:

1997–98   8 months to 5 April 1998   £9,333

In respect of the second year of assessment, s 61(2) enacts that where either:

(a) the first accounts are made up for a period of less than 12 months; or

(b) no accounts are made up to a date in the second year of assessment,

the basis period for the second year is the period of 12 months from the date of commencement of business, notwithstanding the rules in s 62 regarding a change of accounting date. If neither (a) nor (b) applies, the basis period for the second year is determined under s 60 (the current year).

Applying this principle to the facts, s 61(2) does not apply because the accounting date in 1998–99 is not less than 12 months after the date of commencement. The basis period is determined under s 60. The second year of trading results are:

1998–99   12 months (1 August 1997 to 31 July 1998) £14,000

Note that this principle remains the same as the old preceding year basis.

Overlap relief may be available to Thomas in respect of 'overlap profit'. This is the amount of profits which, by virtue of the basis period rules, is included in the computations for two successive years of assessment. This arises *inter alia* as a result of the opening year rules. An 'overlap period' in relation to an overlap profit is the number of days in the period for which the overlap profit arose. In Thomas' case (using months for simplicity) the overlap profit is £9,333 computed by reference to an overlap period of eight months.

Relief for an overlap profit is given, by way of a deduction in computing profits. The Revenue will accept a calculation of overlap relief by reference to time periods otherwise than to days, for example, using months or fractions of months, provided that the same method is used consistently.

The third year of assessment is dealt with in s 60 of the TA 1988, tax is charged normally on the full amount of the profits of the year of assessment. In the case of Thomas the results of his third and fourth years of assessment are:

1999–2000 12 months (1 August 1998 to 31 July 1999) £20,000

2000–01   12 months (1 August 1999 to 31 July 2000) £26,000

Part (b)

Section 62 of the TA 1988 was redrafted by s 202 of the FA 1994. The purpose is to prevent avoidance or deferral of tax liability through the manipulation of accounting dates. Unless the conditions in the new 62A are met, the basis period will continue to be 12 months ending on the old accounting date (by apportionment of profits shown by the accounts). Section 62(2) identifies the basis period for the year of assessment where there is both a change of accounting date and either:

(a) the conditions of s 62(A) are satisfied; or

(b) the year in which the change takes place is the second or third fiscal year of a new business.

Where the 'relevant period' is less than 12 months or the year concerned is the second fiscal year, the basis period is the period of 12 months ending with the new accounting date. If the relevant period is more than 12 months (and the year concerned is not the second fiscal year), the basis period is the full relevant period. In both cases there will be profits for an overlap period which is included in the profits assessed for two successive years. A 'relevant period' is defined as one beginning immediately following the end of the previous accounting period and ending on the new accounting date.

The conditions enacted in s 62(A) are, first, the accounting period to the new accounting date must not exceed 18 months. The second condition is that notice of the change of accounting date must be given to the Revenue by 31 January, following the year of assessment in which the accounting change is deemed to take place. The taxpayer may therefore retain his existing year end for tax purposes merely by failing to give notice. The third condition is that no accounting change which has been effective for tax purposes has been made in any of the preceding five years of assessment, apart from the opening years. The fourth condition is that if there has been a change in the preceding five years of assessment, it is possible to set out in the notice of the accounting change, the reasons for the change. If the Revenue is satisfied that the change is made for *bona fide* commercial reasons, or does not object to the change within 60 days of receiving the notice, the new accounting date may be adopted for tax purposes.

The year of change is the first year in which accounts are not made up to the old accounting date. This could be a year in which no accounting date is specified. Where neither of the conditions in (a) and (b) above is satisfied, the basis period for the year of change is the 12 months from the preceding accounting date.

In Howard's case, there is no accounting date in 2000–01. Accordingly, this is the year in which the accounting date is deemed to change to 30 June. As the relevant period is less than 12 months, the basis period is 12 months to 30 June 2000. The profit of the period 1 July 1999 to 5 April 2000 is included in the assessments for both 1999–2000 and 2000–01, giving rise to an overlap profit of £18,000.

Applying these propositions, the basis periods and assessable profits are:

1997–98	7 months to 5 April 1998	£ 8,000
1998–99	12 months to 5 April 1999	£18,000
1999–2000	12 months to 5 April 2000	£24,000
2000–01	12 months to 30 June 2001	£25,000
	$(9/12 \times £24,000 + 3 / 15 \times £37,500)$	
2001–02	12 months to 30 June 2001	£30,000
	$(12/15 \times £37,500)$	

Question 14

Part (a)

In what circumstances may a loss sustained by a trader give rise to a relief from income tax?

Part (b)

Fred commenced trading on 1 February 1998 and prepared accounts to 31 December. He made a trading loss of £33,000 in the 11 months to 31 December 1998 and profits of £12,000 and £10,000 in the years to 31 December 1999 and 2000 respectively. He has other income of £7,000 for 1997–98 and £6,000 for 1998–99.

Advise Fred on the options available for claiming loss relief.

Answer plan

To answer this question, you need to discuss:

- the varieties of loss reliefs outlined;
- loss computation with notes.

Answer

Part (a)

There are a variety of ways in which trading losses may be eligible for relief:

- by set off against other income in the same year of assessment (s 380(1)(a) and (b) of the TA 1988);
- by relief against capital gains (s 72 of the FA 1991).
- by carry forward against subsequent profits of the same trade (s 385 of the TA 1988);
- by carry back of losses sustained in early years of trading (s 381 of the TA 1988);
- by carry back of a terminal loss (s 388 of the TA 1988);
- on a transfer of a business to a company (s 86 of the TA 1988).

Immediate relief

Where a person sustains a loss in any trade, profession, employment or vocation carried on by him either solely or in partnership, he may make a claim to obtain relief from income tax against his general income: (a) of the year in which the loss was incurred; or (b) of the year preceding that in which the loss was sustained. The period available for making the claim is within 12 months after 31 January following the year of assessment, that is, 31 January in the year which is 22 months after the end of the tax year in which the loss arose. 'Losses' mean losses computed in the same way and in respect of the same basis period as profits are computed under Schedule D Case I or II. In *Butt v Haxby* (1983), the taxpayer claimed relief under s 380 in respect of part of a trading loss, even though his other income was sufficient to absorb the loss.

He then claimed relief under s 381 (see below) in respect of the remainder of the loss. The court decided that the splitting of the loss was not allowed. If he claimed relief under s 380, only the excess, if any, of the loss which remains unrelieved was available for relief under s 381.

A loss will not be available for relief unless it is shown that, in respect of the tax year in which the loss was sustained, the trade was carried on:

- on a commercial basis; and
- with a view to the realisation of profits.

Relief against capital gains

Subject to a claim for relief under s 380 of the TA 1988 being made by the taxpayer (see above), a further claim may be made in the same notice of claim for a trading loss to be relieved against the capital gains of the trader of the same year. If there is insufficient general income in the preceding year to absorb the loss, the taxpayer may claim to set the excess loss against chargeable gains of that year. In other words, capital gains may only be used to offset trading losses to the extent that the trading losses cannot be made good against the taxpayer's income for the year (see s 72 of the FA 1991).

The claim under s 72 is in respect of the 'relevant amount' which is so much of the trading loss as cannot be set off against the claimant's income for the year of claim and has not already been relieved for any other year. The claim is not deemed to be determined until the relevant amount for the year can no longer be varied whether by the Commissioners on appeal or on the order of any court. More specifically, the Revenue have indicated that the appropriate loss relief claim becomes final:

- 30 days after the Inspector gives his decision on it; or
- when, after an appeal, agreement is reached between the taxpayer and the Revenue; or
- when the Commissioners determine an appeal; or
- when the courts decide an appeal.

The 'relevant amount', as finally determined, is to be treated for the purposes of capital gains tax as an allowable loss accruing to the claimant in the year up to the 'maximum amount', that is, the amount on which the claimant would be chargeable to capital gains tax for the year, disregarding the capital gains tax annual exemption: see s 72(4) of the FA 1991.

Losses claimed under this provision are relieved in priority to allowable (capital) losses brought forward.

Carry forward of losses

Trading losses which have not wholly been relieved under any other provision may be carried forward and set off against trading income from the same trade in subsequent years (s 385 of the TA 1988). It must be stressed that the relief is only available if the same trade is carried on by the taxpayer. Accordingly, changes in the nature of the business would deprive the trader of relief under this provision. Relief is given against the trading profits of the first subsequent tax year and then against the next year indefinitely. The claim to relief is required to be made within five years from 31 January following the tax year in which the claim relates.

In calculating the loss to be carried forward, annual payments made wholly and exclusively for the purpose of the trade, etc (trading charges), which cannot be relieved because of the lack of profits, may be treated as a loss for s 385 purposes. A similar treatment exists in respect of unrelieved interest payments.

Relief for losses in early years

Where a trader, etc, sustains a loss:

- in the tax year in which it is first carried on by him; or
- in the next three tax years,

he may claim relief by setting the loss against his total income for the three tax years preceding that in which the loss was sustained. The profits of the earlier years are taken into account before the profits of the later years (see s 381 of the TA 1988).

This relief is restricted in two ways, namely, the trade must have been carried on throughout the period on a commercial basis and the claim for relief must be made in writing within two years after the tax year in which the loss is sustained.

Terminal loss relief

On a permanent discontinuance of any trade, etc, losses sustained in the 12 months before the date of discontinuance, so far as not otherwise relieved, may be carried back and set off against the profits of the trade charged to income tax in the year of cessation and three years preceding the date of discontinuance (see s 388 of the TA 1988). Relief is given as far as possible against later rather than earlier years.

Losses for this purpose include:

- unrelieved capital allowances accruing within the 12 month period;
- any annual payments charged under s 349 of the TA 1988;
- any unrelieved interest payments so long as they are incurred wholly and exclusively for the purposes of the trade, etc.

Transfer of a business to a company

Section 386 of the TA 1988 provides that where the business of a sole trader or a partnership is:

- transferred to a company; and
- the whole or main consideration for the transfer is the allotment of shares to the former trader,

he may set his unrelieved losses against income which he receives from the company for any year throughout which he owns the shares allotted to him and during which the company continues to trade. The effect is that the trade or partnership is treated as continuing for the purpose solely of loss relief.

The claimant will normally be able to set the losses against either dividends received from the shares or salary received as a director or employee of the company. The order of set off is earned before unearned income.

Part (b)

Computation of taxable profits (allowable losses) are as follows:

		£	£
1997–98 1 February to 5 April 1998	(£33,000) x 2/11		(6,000)
1998–99 1 February 1998 to 31 January 1999			
1 February to 31 December 1998		(33,000)	
Less loss allocated to 1997–98		6,000	
		(27,000)	
1 January to 31 January 1999 £12,000 x 1/12		1,000	(26,000)
1999–2000	(y/e 31/12/99)	12,000	
	(overlap relief – £1,000)		
2000–01	(y/e 31/12/00)	10,000	

Notes

Losses available for relief for 1997–98 and 1998–99 are £6,000 and £26,000 respectively. Immediate relief may be available to Fred. For 1997–98, the loss of £6,000 may be relieved against Fred's other income arising in that year under s 380(1)(a) of the TA 1988. Fred has £7,000 of other income in this year. This may be used to frank Fred's loss. Similarly, Fred's adjusted loss of £26,000 may be partially relieved under s 380(1)(a) against his other income of £6,000 in the tax year, leaving a balance of £20,000 unrelieved losses at the end of this year.

The remainder of the losses may be rolled forward under s 385 of the TA 1988 and set off against the first available profits of the same trade without time limit. Thus, £12,000 of the losses may be set against the trading profits for 1999–2000, leaving unrelieved losses of £8,000 to be carried forward. For 2000–01, the losses brought forward may be relieved under s 385.

Alternatively, instead of claiming immediate relief under s 380, Fred may roll over his losses and set these off against his trading profits under s 385.

CHAPTER 4

SCHEDULE D CASES III–VI

Introduction

The main provisions of Schedule D Case III charges tax in respect of 'any interest of money, whether yearly or otherwise, annuities and other annual payments'.

'Interest' has been defined as the payment by time for the use of money, *per* Rowlatt J in *Bennett v Ogston* (1930). It is sometimes a difficult question to distinguish 'interest' from 'capital', for example, payment of a sum above a reasonable commercial rate of interest.

An 'annuity' is an annual payment made for a period with a duration determined by reference to a human life or lives. Section 656 of the TA 1988 provides that a purchased annuity is treated as containing a 'capital element' which is not regarded as taxable income. The 'capital content' of an annuity is determined by reference to 'official actuarial tables' and varies with the age of the annuitant and life expectancy. The older the annuitant the higher the capital content.

An 'annual payment' has been defined by Viscount Simonds in *Whitworth Park Coal Ltd v IRC* (1961), as containing the following features:

- the payment must be construed *ejusdem generis*;
- the payment must possess the quality of recurrence;
- the payment must be made under a legal obligation;
- the payment must form income in the hands of the recipient;
- the payment must be 'pure income profit' in the hands of the recipient.

Most annual payments were taken out of the tax net by s 347A of the TA 1988, in that, subject to limited exceptions, annual payments are not treated as charges on income and accordingly the payer's income is computed without any deduction being made on account of the payment. Moreover, the payment is not treated for tax purposes as part of the income of the payee. A major exception to this rule is covenanted payments to charities.

Annuities and annual payments are subject to deduction of lower rate of tax at source. If the payer makes the payment out of taxed income, he is *entitled* to deduct the lower rate of tax before making the payment. Alternatively, if the payment is made out of capital or income not liable to income tax, the payer is *required* to deduct tax at the lower rate.

Most deposits made by individuals with saving institutions are subject to a special tax deduction scheme. From 6 April 1991, banks, building societies, etc, are required to deduct and account for the lower rate of tax. The tax deductible is repayable where appropriate.

Income tax relief for the payment of interest is given if it relates to one of the specified categories of loan. These categories of loans are:

- to purchase machinery and plant. An employee or individual members of a partnership may claim relief on interest paid on a loan used to purchase machinery or plant on which capital allowance is claimed (see s 359 of the TA 1988);
- in acquiring an interest in a close company (see s 360 of the TA 1988);
- in acquiring an interest in a co-operative (see s 361(2) of the TA 1988);
- in acquiring an interest in an employee-controlled company (see s 361(3) of the TA 1988);
- in acquiring an interest in a partnership. The individual is required to be a member of the partnership (see s 362 of the TA 1988);
- to pay inheritance tax (see s 364(2) of the TA 1988);
- to purchase a life annuity where the borrower is at least 65 years old (see s 365 of the TA 1988).

However, relief will not be granted in the following circumstances:

- where interest is paid on an overdraft or under credit card arrangements;
- where interest is paid at a rate greater than a reasonable commercial rate.

Mortgage interest

Interest paid on a loan to purchase a main residence ('home loan') may be eligible for income tax relief. It is not necessary that the property be charged as security for the loan. As from 6 April 1994, relief is restricted to lower and basic rate taxpayers. The rate of relief for 1998–99 is 10% of the interest element of the loan, up to a maximum of £30,000 of the principal sum borrowed.

Schedule D Cases IV and V

These Cases deal with tax on income derived from foreign sources. Such income is taxed when received by someone resident in the UK. Case IV taxes interest on foreign *securities*, such as debentures in foreign companies or foreign government securities. Case V taxes income from foreign *possessions* including dividends on foreign shares, rents received on foreign properties, profits of foreign businesses controlled abroad and foreign pensions.

Schedule D Case VI

Case VI is a residual source of assessing income tax. The charging provision provides that tax is charged on 'any *annual profits or gains* not falling under any other Case of Schedule D and not charged by virtue of Schedules A, E or F'. In addition, several sources of income are, by statute, specifically assessable under Case VI, for example, receipts from the sale of 'know how' if not taxed as trade receipts or as a capital sums (see s 531(4) of the TA 1988), transactions in securities (see ss 703–09 of the TA 1988).

Question 15

John and his wife, Julie have separated in June 1998. John left Julie and their daughter, Sarah. Julie is now seeking a divorce and financial settlement for herself and Sarah, aged 5. The parties are considering the following alternative forms of financial settlement which may be ordered by the court:

(a) John pays Julie the sum of £2,000 per annum for herself during their joint lives and £3,000 per annum for the maintenance of Sarah until she attains the age of 21 or marries before attaining that age;

(b) John transfers 2,000 shares which he owns in BP plc and a holiday cottage in France to Julie for her use, and four valuable antique paintings to Julie upon trust for Sarah, in full and final settlement of his liability to Julie and Sarah;

(c) John transfers his half share in the matrimonial home (jointly owned with Julie) to Julie for the benefit of herself and Sarah in full and final settlement of his liability to them both.

Advise John and Julie as to the income tax, capital gains tax and inheritance tax implications of the above proposals.

Answer plan

Your answer should include discussion of the following points:

- married couple's allowance in the year of separation claimable by John;
- additional personal allowance claimable by Julie;
- periodic maintenance payments removed from income tax system;
- relief claimable by John in respect of 'qualifying maintenance payments';
- maintenance payments under s 11of the Inheritance Tax Act 1984 (IHTA);
- disposal within s 58 of the Taxation and Chargeable Gains Act 1992 (TCGA);
- disposal within ss 17 and 18 of the TCGA 1992;
- dispositions within ss 10, 11 and 18 of the IHTA 1984;
- relief under ss 222–26 of the TCGA 1992.

Answer

Part (a)

In the year of separation (that is, the year of assessment 1998–99), John will be entitled to the married couple's allowance for that year, in addition to his personal allowance. For 1998–99, tax relief for the married couple's allowance is given at a reduced rate of 15%. The allowance is no longer given as a deduction from John's total income, but is given instead by means of a reduction in John's income tax liability (see s 256 of the TA 1988). An election may be made to transfer the married couple's allowance to Julie, or the parties may share the relief equally. Moreover, in addition to her personal allowance, Julie may claim additional personal relief in respect of Sarah in the year of assessment of 'separation' from John. The basis of this claim is that Sarah is a 'qualifying' child resident with her mother. For 1998–99, the relief is given by means of a reduction (15%) in the claimant's income tax liability. For 1999–2000 and subsequent years, the relief is reduced to 10%.

A 'qualifying' child is a child of the claimant who, in the tax year:

- is born or is under the age of 16, or if over this age is receiving full time instruction at any university, college, school or other educational establishment; and

- is a child of the claimant, or if not such a child, is a child under the age of 18 and is maintained for the whole or part of any year by the claimant at his or her expense (see ss 259(5) and 261A(4) of the TA 1988).

The periodic payments contemplated by John, namely £2,000 per annum to Julie and £3,000 per year for the benefit of Sarah are, since 1988, not treated as charges on income. Accordingly, tax is not deductible at source. Such payments do not form part of the taxable income of Julie or indeed Sarah. It may be noted that if this payment constitutes Sarah's only source of income, her personal allowance will be wasted. The same applies to Julie. The effect is that such payments are generally removed from the income tax system.[1]

Where John makes 'qualifying maintenance payments' he is entitled to obtain some relief equivalent to a percentage of the amount of the married couple's allowance (15% of £1,900 for 1998–99). A 'qualifying maintenance payment' is defined in s 347B of the TA 1988 as a periodic payment (other than instalments of capital) which:

- is made under a UK court order or written agreement; and
- is made by one party to a marriage either to or for the benefit of the other party, or to the other party for the maintenance by that party of a child of the family; and
- is due at a time when:
  o the two parties are not married and living together; and
  o the recipient of the payment has not remarried.

It should be noted that John satisfies the above requirements but payments made directly to Sarah do not qualify for relief.[2]

Since John's payments are of an annual nature there are no capital gains tax repercussions concerning these sums. Indeed, this remains the position even if John transfers a capital asset in *lieu* of some or part of his continuing obligation. The reason is that the recurrent obligation constitutes an annual debt payable by John. The discharge of this debt, in whole or in part, even in respect of a transfer of assets does not alter the nature of the obligation.

For inheritance tax purposes maintenance payments made payable to a party to the marriage and/or the children of the marriage, are not treated as transfers of value and therefore exempt from inheritance tax (see s 11 of the IHTA 1984).

Part (b)

The transfers of the capital assets will not have any income tax significance to John, unless he is a dealer in these assets and they formed part of his stock in trade. There is no evidence to suggest that he is such a trader and the remainder of this answer is based on such premise.

It is of material significance to be able to determine the exact date (and consequently the year) of transfer. Section 28 of the TCGA 1992 enacts that a disposal under a contract takes place on the date of the creation of the contract and not on the date of the transfer or conveyance, if different. During the year of separation and while the parties are still married to each other, the disposal of the shares and cottage by John and acquisition by Julie, is treated as giving rise to 'no gain and no loss' (see s 58 of the TCGA 1992). The reason is that the parties are still married to each other and they are living with each other, even for part of the year of assessment. The effect of this provision is that the allowable expenditure in respect of the assets (including indexation up to 1 April 1998 and taper relief thereafter) is treated as the disposal proceeds of the assets. Likewise, in Julie's hands, the assets are deemed to be acquired for a consideration equal to John allowable expenditure. When this provision operates, the acquisition by Julie takes place on the date when John acquired the asset.

Alternatively, if John's disposals of the assets to Julie take place after the year of separation, the transfers shall be treated as between 'connected persons'. The effect of such transfers, from the point of view of both John and Julie, is that the disposals are deemed to be for a consideration equal to the market value of the assets at the time of the disposals (see ss 17 and 18(2) of the TCGA 1992). Thus, in John's hands, the difference between the market value of the assets and the allowable expenditure (including indexation up to 1 April 1998 and taper relief thereafter) is treated as a gain liable to capital gains tax. He is allowed to set off his annual exemption from such gains. In Julie's hands, she is deemed to acquire the assets at their market value.

The expression, 'connected persons' is defined in s 286 of the TCGA 1992. Section 286(2) enacts that an individual is connected with his or her spouse as well as relatives. If John transfers the assets to Julie after the year of separation but before the divorce decree absolute, the transactions are undoubtedly between connected persons.

For the same reasons, the transfer of the antique paintings by John to Sarah, or upon trust for Sarah, is treated as a disposal between connected persons at market value. This is the position irrespective of when the transfer is made.

For inheritance tax purposes, the transfers by John to Julie of the capital assets on or before the divorce decree, are exempt under s 18 of the IHTA 1984 as transfers between spouses, provided that John is domiciled in the UK. There is no necessity for the parties to live together. The simple test is whether the transferor and transferee are married. This will be satisfied before the decree absolute. If the transfers to Julie and Sarah (or on behalf of Sarah) are made after the divorce decree, the dispositions are not transfers of value if they are made by one party to the marriage in favour of the other party, or for the benefit of a child of either party, by way of 'maintenance' (see s 11 of the IHTA 1984). The expression, 'maintenance' is an unfortunate term used by the draftsman. It connotes (without being defined) periodic income payments as used in the family law context. But transfers of capital may amount to maintenance of the other party to the marriage. It is submitted that the transfer of capital to another party to a marriage or child of the marriage by way of financial provision is within the notion of 'maintenance' under s 11. In any event, s 10 of the IHTA 1984 provides that dispositions are not transfers of value if they are not intended to confer gratuitous benefits on the transferee and either:

(a) they were made in transactions at arm's length between persons not connected with each other; or

(b) the transactions were such as might be expected to be made at arm's length between persons not connected with each other.

Although John and Julie are connected persons up to the time of the divorce decree, and Sarah, his daughter, is connected with John, it is possible to attract the exemption within s 10 of the IHTA 1984 if John is capable of satisfying two conditions:

(a) that the transfers were not intended to confer any gratuitous benefit on Julie and Sarah; and

(b) that the dispositions were effected in similar fashion to transfers between unconnected persons.

In other words, John is required to prove, in addition to his subjective intention, that the connection between himself and Julie and Sarah was not reflected in the terms of the transactions. The fact that the transfers are part of a financial package for the upkeep of the parties on separation may assist in determining this issue.

In connection with s 10 of the IHTA 1984, the Senior Registrar of the Family Division issued a statement on August 1975, to the effect that transfers of property pursuant to a court order in consequence of a divorce will, in general, be regarded as transactions at arm's length and not intended to confer any gratuitous benefit.

Part (c)

The transfer of John's share in the matrimonial home to Julie for the benefit of herself and Sarah has very few income tax implications, save for the application of MIRAS. To qualify for tax relief on the mortgage, the borrower is required to own an interest in the property and occupy it as a main residence. We are told that John owned a half share in the house before the separation, presumably the other half is owned by Julie. Assuming the mortgage is transferred in the name of Julie, the appropriate tax relief will be enjoyed by her. Julie will be entitled to claim mortgage interest relief on the loan with a ceiling of £30,000. The rate of relief is 10% of the interest element of the loan for 1998–99.

If the disposal of John's interest in the matrimonial home took place in the year of separation, s 58 of the TCGA 1992 exemption will be available to John. The disposal and acquisition will be between spouses who have been living together, albeit for only part of the year of assessment. John will be treated as having disposed of his interest and Julie will be treated as acquiring an interest at no gain and no loss (see above). It would be relevant to ascertain the proportion of John's share acquired by Sarah. Such portion, of course, is outside of s 58 of the TCGA 1992, but may be exempt from capital gains tax under ss 222–26 of the TCGA 1992 (private dwellinghouse exemption).

We are told that Julie remained in the house with Sarah but John left the house. It is important to know the length of time that John failed to occupy the house and whether he had acquired ownership of another house prior to the transfer to Julie. There is no evidence of such acquired ownership by John and we will assume that none was acquired by John. If his absence is less than three years, and the transfer is made after the year of separation, the private residence exemption is claimable by John (see s 223(1) of the TCGA 1992). If the period of non-occupation exceeds three years, a proportion of the gain in excess of the aggregate of the periods of occupation and three years will be taxable. But this provision is subject to ESC D6 which establishes that if John ceases to occupy the matrimonial home and disposes of it as part of a financial settlement to Julie, the home will be regarded as continuing to be the residence of John from the date of non-occupation to the date of transfer, provided that it had been Julie's main residence throughout the period of John's non-occupation. These conditions appear to be satisfied and John will no doubt be able to claim the relief.

For inheritance tax purposes the transfer of the capital may be exempt under s 18 of the IHTA 1992 if made before the date of the divorce decree. But relief may still be available under ss 11 and 10 of the IHTA 1984 (see above).

For 1999–2000 and subsequent years, the married couple's allowance is reduced to 10% in respect of a claimant who proves that in the tax year he is a married man whose wife is living with him.

Notes

1   In relation to maintenance payments under 'existing obligations' (as defined), the payer may claim as a deduction only so much of the payment as exceeds an amount equal to the married couple's allowance (£1,900 for 1998–99). The first £1,900 of such payments attract 15% of relief. The payment forms part of the income of the payee who is taxable on the sum under Schedule D Case III. The former spouse receiving such payments is entitled to an extra allowance of 15% of £1,900 for 1998–99.

2   If payments are made to Julie for the maintenance of Sarah in respect of an existing obligation made under a court order, such income is for tax purposes treated as the wife's and not Sarah's. Thus, Sarah's reliefs would be wasted (see *Stevens v Tirard* (1939)).

Question 16

On 1 December 1998, Matthew executed a deed with the trustees of the Gallery of Modern Art, a charity, in order to pay the charity the sum of £1,000 per annum for four years. The execution of this covenant entitles Matthew to attend the gallery free of charge for two years (visitors normally pay £5 per visit), and to attend the annual Christmas dinner in London.

Matthew is employed, earning £40,000 per annum. He wishes you to explain to him the tax effects of the deed and requires you to consider other ways of making charitable donations with tax advantages.

Advise Matthew.

Answer plan

Answers should discuss:

- covenanted donations to charities;
- annual payment;
- deduction of basic rate of tax;
- relief from higher rate of tax;
- recovery by charity of basic rate of tax;
- deposit covenants;
- gift aid ss 25 and 26 of the FA 1990;
- payroll giving s 202 of the TA 1988;
- capital gifts s 257 of the TCGA 1992 and s 23 of the IHTA 1984.

Answer

The deed is capable of being construed as an annual payment which is specifically excepted from the general rule by virtue of s 347A(2) of the TA 1988. In other words, s 347A excludes annual payments from the tax system, except those retained by s 347A(2), namely a 'covenanted payment to a charity'. This expression is defined in s 347A(7) as a covenanted payment, made otherwise than for consideration in money or money's worth, in favour of the charity, provided that the payments are made for a period exceeding three years and is not capable of earlier termination under a power exercisable without the consent of the charity. The reference to money or money's worth within the definition is not an indication that the payment is required to be voluntary but rather a stipulation that the covenant is not made in return for services which the charity is obliged to perform. Further, the four year covenant executed by Matthew, by definition, exceeds three years and, assuming that there is no power retained by Matthew to terminate the agreement prematurely, the covenant will satisfy the definition.

An 'annual payment' within Case III of Schedule D (see s 18(3) of the TA 1988) has been defined by Viscount Simonds in *Whitworth Park Coal Co v IRC* (1961), as a payment which satisfies the following conditions:

- the payment must be construed *ejusdem generis* with interest and annuities;
- the payment must possess the quality of recurrence;
- the payment must be made under a legal obligation;
- the payment must form income in the hands of the recipient;
- the payment must be 'pure income profit' in the hands of the recipient.

The obligation undertaken by Matthew representing a covenanted payment *prima facie* satisfies the first four conditions laid down by Viscount Simonds. The notion of 'pure income profit', known as the *Earl Howe* principle, was created by the courts in order to distinguish ordinary business receipts from annual payments. Attention is focused only on the payee, charity. Case III provisions give no relief for expenses, indeed, it is assumed that no expense will be incurred in earning Case III income. The annual payment must be a receipt of such a kind that the whole of it can be properly regarded as an addition to the total income of the recipient. At the same time, not all conditions and counter-stipulations will deprive a payment of the character of 'pure income profit', see the *obiter* pronouncement of Lord Evershed MR in *IRC v National Book League* (1957). The essential issue is whether or not the covenanted payments are made in consideration of benefits and facilities to the covenantor in the ordinary course of business. The obligations undertaken by the gallery are to provide free admission to Matthew for two years and to invite him to its annual dinner. These do not appear to be services provided in the form of a 'disguised' covenanted payment and satisfies the test of 'pure income profit'. In addition, s 59 of the FA 1989 provides that the consideration for the payment, namely, the right of admission, shall be disregarded if the charity exists for the sole or main purpose, *inter alia,* for the preservation of property for the public benefit. It is not possible to decide this issue on the facts presented. Moreover, the practice of the Revenue has been to ignore *de minimis* benefits which are worth less than 25% of payments.

On the assumption that the payments by Matthew are charges on income within s 347A(7) and outside the anti-avoidance provision in s 660(A), Matthew is entitled to deduct the basic rate of tax under s 348 of the TA 1988 before making the payment. Section 348 is applicable if the payment is made wholly out of income brought into charge to income tax.[1] In short, this section is applicable if the payment is made out of taxed income. In this event, Matthew may deduct the basic rate of tax and pay the net amount to the charity. The basic rate of tax for the year of assessment 1998–99 is 23%, Matthew may retain £230 and pay the balance of £770 to the gallery. The charity is not entitled to prevent the deduction by Matthew and the payment of the net amount shall be a discharge of the obligation to pay the full amount (see s 348(1)(c)). Matthew is entitled to deduct the payment (£1,000) from his income liable to income tax, but suffers income tax at the basic rate of tax on the amount of the payment. In other words, the covenanted payment will reduce his taxable income for higher rate purposes, but has no tax planning effect for basic rate purposes.

The charity receives the covenanted sum net of tax and the basic rate of tax deducted by Matthew is treated as income tax paid by the recipient charity (see s 348(1)(d)). The charity, of course, is exempt from income tax and is entitled to recover the tax deducted on its behalf. The charity therefore receives the full amount covenanted partly from the covenantor (£720) and partly from the Revenue (£230).

Other tax effective ways of making charitable donations are:

- deposit covenants;
- gift aid ss 25 and 26 of the FA 1990;
- payroll giving s 202 of the TA 1988;
- capital gifts s 257 of the TCGA 1992 and s 23 of the IHTA 1984.

Deposit covenants

These are deeds whereby the covenantor agrees to pay one quarter of a specified amount over a four year period. The full amount (less the basic rate of tax) is 'deposited' with the charity which releases or withdraws one quarter of the specified sum per annum for charitable purposes. The Revenue have expressly stated that they will not challenge the legality of such arrangements.

Gift aid

Section 25 of the FA 1990 introduced a specific relief, 'gift aid', in respect of single gifts in money to charities. The scheme entitles individuals (and companies) to make gifts called 'qualifying donations', which do not exceed the total income of the individual (or company) for the relevant year. Such sums are paid to the charity after deduction of tax at the basic rate, and the charity is entitled to recover from the Revenue the tax deducted. In order to constitute a qualifying donation, the gift to the charity is required to be made by a UK resident individual and the gift must:

• constitute a sum of money not less than £250; and
• be subject to no repayment condition; and
• not be a 'covenanted payment to charity; and
• not fall with the 'payroll deduction scheme' (see below); and
• not be conditional or associated with an arrangement involving the acquisition of property by the charity, otherwise than by way of gift, from the donor or person connected with him.

(Similar conditions are required to be satisfied by companies.)

Donors who are higher rate taxpayers, are entitled to deduct the gross sum paid to the charity from their taxable income (and companies are entitled to treat gross payments to charities as charges on income).

The major difference between a 'covenanted donation to a charity' and 'gift aid' is that the former involves a continuing obligation, whereas the latter assumes a single donation of a minimum sum of £250. There is no ceiling or upper limit for gift aid.

Payroll Deduction Scheme – s 202 of the TA 1988

On the assumption that a recognised scheme is run by his employer, Matthew is entitled to make tax effective donations to charities of his choice, up to a maximum of £1,200 during a year of assessment. Matthew authorises his employer to deduct the relevant sums from his salary, before calculating PAYE tax due, and pay over the sums to an agent approved by the Inland Revenue. The agent then pays the relevant sums to the appropriate charity. The donations by Matthew are treated as deductible expenses. Thus, full relief is enjoyed by the donors even in respect of basic rate tax payers.

Relief from capital gains tax and inheritance tax

A donation of a capital asset to a charity is treated as giving rise to 'no gain and no loss' for capital gains tax purposes: see s 257 of the TCGA 1992. Thus, the disposal proceeds are treated as equivalent to the allowable expenditure with the effect that no capital gains tax is payable. For inheritance tax purposes, gifts to charities are exempt transfers of value (see s 23 of the IHTA 1984).

Note

1   Section 349 of the TA 1988 applies where the payer has no income or insufficient income to cover the amount of the annual payment and when he is not subject to income tax. Under this section, the payer is required to deduct the basic rate of tax and pay this sum over to the Revenue. Unlike s 348, deduction is compulsory, that is, the amount deducted does not belong to the payer, but to the Revenue. The position of the recipient remains the same whether the deduction is made under either s 348 or s 349.

CHAPTER 5

SCHEDULE E

Introduction

This Schedule charges tax in respect of the emoluments derived from an *office* (for example, trusteeship, directorship) or *employment* after deducting expenses (see ss 131–207 of the Income and Corporation Taxes Act (TA) 1988). The Schedule is divided into three Cases, but Cases II and III only apply where a foreign element is involved.

In essence, there are five issues to be considered under Schedule E:

(a) whether the taxpayer holds an office or employment;

(b) whether a receipt is an emolument;

(c) whether the emolument is derived from the office or employment;

(d) whether the taxpayer is entitled to deduct any expense from the emoluments;

(e) the appropriate Case under this Schedule for charging the emoluments.

An *office* means 'a subsisting, permanent, substantive position, which has an existence independent of the person who fills it, and which is filled in succession by successive holders', *per* Rowlatt J in *Great Western Railway v Bater* (1920).

An *employment* signifies something in the nature of a 'post'. It refers to a person employed under a 'contract of service' as opposed to a 'contract for services'.

An *emolument* has been partially defined by s 131(1) of the TA 1988 as 'including salaries, fees wages, perquisites and profits whatsoever'. This vague definition has been elucidated by the courts over the years. The basic proposition is that emoluments for services comprise not only wages and salaries, but a variety of other receipts such as *benefits in kind*. The various criteria adopted by the courts in order to determine whether a benefit in kind is an emolument, subject to statutory provisions to the contrary, are as follows:

- whether the benefit is convertible into money or not? If the benefit is not convertible into money then, on general principles, the advantage is not an emolument (see *Tennant v Smith* (1892)). But if a payment is made *in lieu* of a non-convertible benefit, the sum is an emolument (see *Sanderson v Durbridge* (1955));

- whether the benefit is provided by the employer or not? Based on the analogy with wages and salaries, a benefit to which the employee is contractually entitled affords strong evidence that the advantage is an emolument (see *Moorhouse v Dooland* (1955); *Machon v McLoughlin* (1926); *Heaton v Bell* (1970)). On the other hand, where the employer provides a voluntary gift for exceptional services *ex post facto* or a gift in recognition of the personal qualities of the employee, the gift is not an emolument (see *Seymour v Reed* (1927); *Moore v Griffiths* (1972)). But the regularity of voluntary gifts may create such an expectation on the part of the employee so as to be treated as equivalent to a contractual right and therefore taxable (see *Laidler v Perry* (1966));

- if the benefit is provided by a third party, then the advantage is an emolument if the employment customarily attracts the benefit (see *Blakiston v Cooper* (1909); *Calvert v Wainwright* (1947)).

The valuation of the benefit is determined in one of two ways, namely:

- a discharge of the obligation of the employee – the expense incurred in getting rid of the obligation (see *Nicoll v Austin* (1935));

- a gift of property to the employee - the value of the benefit to the employee. This may amount to the second-hand value of the property (see *Wilkins v Rogerson* (1961)).

Directors and certain employees: The general rule discussed above in relation to benefits in kind are subject to special statutory provisions inserted in ss 153–68 of the TA 1988 and applicable to directors and employees earning at least £8,500 per annum. The general scheme of the provisions is that expense allowances and benefits in kind (with their own valuation rules) are charged to tax under Schedule E, leaving the taxpayer to claim a deduction for expenses 'wholly, exclusively and necessarily' incurred in the performance of the duties of the employment.

Emoluments derived from the office or employment:

On general principles, it is necessary to establish that the advantage or benefit is directly referable to the office or employment. A mere connection with the office, etc, will not satisfy this requirement. In other words, the office, etc, is required to be the *causa causans* of the benefit. A *causa sine qua non* in itself is insufficient (see *Hochstrasser v Mayes* (1960); *Jarrold v Boustead* (1964)). With regard to directors and employees earning £8,500 per annum, s 168(3) of the TA 1988 enacts a deeming provision as follows:

(a) all sums paid to an employee by his employer in respect of expenses; and

(b) all such provision as is mentioned in this chapter which is made for an employee, or for members of his family or household, by his employer,

are deemed to be paid to or made for him or them by reason of his employment ...

Deductible expenses

Section 198 of the TA 1988 enacts the general expenses rule. The principle is divided into two categories of expenses namely:

(a) qualifying travelling expenses (as defined);

(b) any other expenses incurred wholly, exclusively and necessarily in the performance of the duties of the office or employment.

Generally, the deductible expenditure is very strict. In order to qualify, the expenditure must be:

• first, *necessary* to the office, etc. This requires the taxpayer to show that it would have been impossible to perform the duties of the office, etc, without incurring the expenditure (see *Brown v Bullock* (1961)); and

- secondly, the expenditure was incurred *in the performance* of the duties, that is, the expenditure was incurred not before or after the performance of the duties, but while the duties were being performed (*Lomax v Newton* (1953); *Humbles v Brooks* (1962)).

The basis of assessment under Schedule E is the full amount of the emoluments received in the year of assessment (see s 202A of the TA 1988).

Question 17

On 5 January 1997, Douglas was appointed Managing Director of Moneybags plc for three years under a service contract. On the same date, Douglas received £20,000 from Moneybags plc as an inducement to leave his previous employment and join Moneybags plc. Between 5 January 1997 and July 1998, Douglas received £80,000 by way of salary and £10,000 by way of bonuses.

On 1 August 1998, Moneybags plc dismissed Douglas in circumstances which he alleged amounted to a breach of his service contract and he commenced an action for arrears of salary and damages for breach of contract. The action for arrears of salary was compromised by an agreement under which Moneybags plc agreed to pay Douglas £10,000 in respect of arrears of salary. This action was settled by an agreement under which Moneybags plc agreed to pay Douglas £10,000 in respect of arrears of salary, a lump sum payment of £150,000 in full and final settlement of all claims against Moneybags plc and a further payment of £15,000 in consideration of Douglas agreeing not to disclose the facts to anyone (except in so far as he is required by law to do so).

Advise Douglas whether these payments and benefits are liable to income tax. Do not deal with personal reliefs or otherwise attempt to compute Douglas's liability to income tax.

Answer plan

Your answer should incorporate discussion of the following:

- emoluments;

- advance remuneration;
- arrears of remuneration;
- restrictive covenant;
- golden handshake – s 148 of the TA 1988;
- date of liability to income tax – s 202A of the TA 1988.

Answer

Douglas is appointed a director of Moneybags plc and, as such, is treated as an *officeholder* liable to income tax under Schedule E in respect of emoluments derived from his office: s 19(1) of the TA 1988. An 'office' has been judicially defined as 'a subsisting, permanent, substantive position which has an existence independent of the person who fills it and which is filled in succession by successive holders', *per* Rowlatt J in *GWR v Bater* (1920). This definition was affirmed by the House of Lords in *Edwards v Clinch* (1981). A director is treated as an office holder.

The expression, 'emoluments' has been statutorily defined in part by s 131(1) of the TA 1988 as 'including salaries, fees, wages, perquisites and profits whatsoever'. It is clear that not all payments from employers fall within this definition. An emolument is a profit made by reference to the services rendered by virtue of the office. In short, an emolument is a reward for services past, present or future, provided by an employee or officeholder. On these facts, the issue that needs closer examination is whether the benefits received by Douglas are treated as emoluments which are derived from his office.

The taxpayers who received sums in lieu of notice and redundancy payments which together were within the amount exempted from redundancy payments were liable to income tax on the amount received in lieu of notice: see *Thorn EMI Electronics v Coldicott* (1997).

Wages and bonuses

Undoubtedly, the remuneration or salary of £80,000 received by Douglas is an emolument. The bonus payments of £10,000 are within the definition of an emolument as representing a contractual entitlement referable to the services of the officeholder (see *Radcliffe v Holt* (1927); *Weston v Hearn* (1943)).

Inducement payment of £20,000

On general principles and subject to statutory provisions to the contrary, a payment which is made to a Schedule E taxpayer as compensation for giving up a right or a benefit is not treated as an emolument because the sum is not connected with services performed or about to be performed, but is paid for not performing services. In *Jarrold v Boustead* (1964), a signing on fee was paid to an amateur rugby player in order to induce him to become a professional and play for the club. The court held that the sum was not taxable under Schedule E. Likewise, in *Pritchard v Arundale* (1972), a chartered accountant who was induced to join a company as a managing director, received shares in a company in order to compensate him for giving up his practice. He was not liable to income tax under Schedule E. The profit from the shares accrued to him not for future services but in order to compensate him for the loss of his professional status. Such payments may now be liable to Schedule E income tax under s 148 or s 313 of the TA 1988 (see below).

Alternatively, payments made by an employer in anticipation of future services are treated as advance remuneration and liable to income tax. In other words, where a sum is paid (including benefits in kind) in order to encourage a potential employee to join a company the profit is treated as an emolument. Whether the purpose of the payment is compensatory or anticipatory is a question of causation and degree and the terms used by the parties are not conclusive. In *Glantre Engineering v Goodhand* (1983), a lump sum payment made to a chartered accountant in order to induce him to join the company was treated as an emolument for future services. The position remains the same if the payment is made by a third party rather than the employer (see *Shilton v Wilmshurst* (1991)).

In respect of the inducement payment of £20,000, it would appear that, on the facts, the sum ought to be liable to income tax as an emolument. The sum presumably was paid under a legally binding contract – it was paid by the new employer of Douglas – there is no evidence that the purpose was to compensate Douglas for giving up rights under his previous employment (in any event, Douglas will bear the burden of proving such purpose). In the light of these facts, it would appear that the *Jarrold* and *Pritchard* cases are distinguishable from the present facts.

Compromise agreement

The compromise agreement concerns three payments, namely, £10,000 in respect of arrears of salary, £150,000 as a golden handshake and £15,000 for a 'gagging' undertaking.

In respect of the arrears of salary, this clearly amounts to an emolument. The sum is payable in respect of past services performed under a contract of service. The fact that the payment is made as a result of a settlement of contentious proceedings is irrelevant. The origin of the claim remains namely, the sum was payable under the contract of employment as part of Douglas' salary. The case *Du Cros v Ryall* (1935), could be distinguished from the present facts. In that case, the taxpayer, a general manager of a company claimed damages for wrongful dismissal. The company compromised the action by paying the taxpayer, 'agreed damages' by reference to the relevant years during which the taxpayer was deprived of his salary. The court decided that the payment was not assessable as an emolument because the sum was paid for not performing services. The agreed damages was compensation for the loss that the taxpayer suffered. In Douglas' case, the £10,000 represents salary for services which have been provided at a rate which had been agreed.

The lump sum payment of £150,000 to Douglas may be chargeable to income tax under s 148 of the TA 1988. Such payments which are made in connection with the termination of Douglas' employment are chargeable to income tax, provided that the sum would otherwise escape tax. Thus, compensation payments made on the termination of an employment or change of functions are now assessable under s 148: see *Hunter v Dewhurst* (1932) and *Tilley v Wales* (1942). The first £30,000 of such sum is exempt from income tax: see s 148(1) of the TA 1988. The remainder of the payment is assessable in the year of receipt: see s 148(3).

The sum of £15,000 which was received by Douglas in consideration for entering into a restrictive covenant. The sum would appear to be assessable under s 313 of the TA 1988 which provides as follows:

> Where (i) an individual who holds, has held, or is about to hold, an office or employment (ii) gives in connection with his holding that office or employment (iii) an undertaking (whether absolute or qualified, and whether legally valid or not) the tenor or effect of which is to restrict him as to his conduct or activities, any sum ... paid, in respect of the giving of the undertaking ... and (iv) would not, apart from this section, fall to be treated as an emolument ... shall be chargeable to tax under Schedule E.

Of the four pre-requisites highlighted above, only two of these require consideration in respect of Douglas's circumstances. These are conditions (iii) and (iv). It appears that condition (iii) is satisfied on the facts of this case, for the agreement has the effect of restricting Douglas as to statements which he may disclose. *Vaughan-Neil v IRC* (1979), is distinguishable. In this case, a practising barrister was paid £40,000 by Wimpy Ltd to give up his practice and join the company. The court decided that this sum was not subject to tax under s 313. The taxpayer's inability to practice at the Bar stemmed from the rules of the Bar Council and not from the relevant clause in the contract. In Douglas' case, it would appear that his inability to disclose the relevant facts stems clearly from the agreement made between him and Moneybags plc. The other requirement concerns condition (iv). Before 1950, such profit was not liable to income tax on the ground that the sum is paid not as a reward for services, but for not performing services (see *Beak v Robson* (1943)). The effect as far as Douglas is concerned is that £15,000 received for undertaking a restrictive covenant is taxable under Schedule E in the year in which it is received.

One final point concerning the year in which emoluments are assessed concerns s 202A of the TA 1988. This enacts that emoluments are taxable in the year when they are received. Detailed rules have been enacted to identify the date when payment is received. In Douglas' case, payment is made when the sum is credited in his account.

Note

Section 148 of the TA 1988 was rewritten by s 58 of the Finance Act 1998 (FA). The new s 148 introduces a key amendment, namely, cash payments and other benefits which are assessable to income tax under s 148 are taxed in the year of receipt, and not on the date of the termination of the employment.

Question 18

Edward is a trainee chef providing services under contract for a period of three years at the Western Hotel. He receives a salary of £6,000 per annum. He is required by the terms of his training contract to reside in accommodation provided by the hotel in order to be available to work late at the numerous special functions organised by the hotel. He pays no rent for the accommodation and the hotel pays the costs of lighting and heating which amounted to £200 in 1998–99. Edward is provided free meals at the hotel. At Christmas 1998 Edward was given £100 by the managing director of the company with his gratitude for Edward's loyal and outstanding service to the hotel within the last year. Edward is allowed to purchase wine from the hotel at the same price as the hotel paid for it, subject to a ceiling of £300, but he is expressly prohibited from selling wine which he purchased from the hotel. In 1998–99, Edward purchased wine from the hotel at a cost of £150. The hotel provides Edward with a uniform while he is on duty. The hotel also provided Edward with an interest free loan of £700 to purchase a car.

Advise Edward as to the income tax consequences of these facts but do not attempt to compute Edward's liability to income tax.[1]

Answer plan

Good answers will examine the following:

* emoluments;
* living accommodation;
* costs of occupying living accommodation;

- personal gifts;
- free meals;
- advantage of underpriced wine;
- uniform;
- interest free loan.

Answer

As a trainee chef employed by the Western Hotel, Edward is liable to income tax under Schedule E in respect of his emoluments including certain benefits in kind: s 19 of the TA 1988.

Since Edward earns less than £8,500 per annum, including chargeable benefits and before any deductions for necessary expenses of the employment, he is not assessable under the special statutory provisions enacted in ss 153–68 of the TA 1988. The effect is that Edward is taxable, if at all, on general principles of Schedule E liability.

The general rule is that an employee is taxable in respect of emoluments derived from his office or employment. In other words, on the assumption that a benefit is treated as an emolument, the benefit is taxable if it is directly causally connected with the office or employment. This requirement may be satisfied if the benefit is contractually provided by the employer. In *Moorehouse v Dooland* (1954), a professional cricketer who was contractually entitled to receive cash collections from spectators for meritorious performances was liable to income tax. This test is satisfied in respect of each of the benefits received by Edward save for the Christmas gift of £100. The payment of £100 was made as a mark of personal esteem for Edward's loyalty and outstanding service. On the other hand, if the payment was made to Edward as part of his remuneration package for services rendered, for example, a bonus or a regular payment on special occasions such as Christmas, the sum could be treated as an emolument on the ground that the regularity of the payment created an expectation of a windfall on the part of the employee. In *Laidler v Perry* (1966), the House of

Lords decided that the receipt by employees of £10 vouchers paid by their employers at Christmas was an assessable emolument (Note that, although the facts of this case are now governed by s 141 of the TA 1988, the general principle remains unchanged). However, it would appear on the evidence that Edward received this amount on account of his personal qualities and as such will not be taxable. In *Seymour v Reed* (1927), the proceeds of a benefit match donated to a professional cricketer was not assessable as an emolument because the proceeds awarded were in the nature of a personal gift to the sportsman. Likewise, in *Moore v Griffiths* (1972), a member of the victorious England World Cup football team was not liable to income tax when, he along with his other members of the squad, each received a bonus of £1,000 from the Football Association.

The main issue in this problem is whether the other benefits enjoyed by Edward are to be treated as emoluments. The term, 'emoluments', includes 'salaries, fees, wages perquisites and profits whatsoever' (s 131(1) of the TA 1988). Undoubtedly, Edward's salary of £6,000 is an emolument.

But emoluments may take the form of other money payments or benefits in kind. Subject to statutory provisions to the contrary, not all forms of benefits in kind are taxable. Only benefits in kind which are convertible into money are assessable. In *Tennant v Smith* (1892), a bank manager was required to live in a flat situated above a bank. He was stationed there in order to transact special banking business outside bank hours. He was not allowed to vacate the premises, except with the permission of the directors, and was not allowed to sublet the flat. The court held that he was a 'representative occupier' and not liable to income tax. Applying this principle to the facts, the right to purchase wine at a preferential rate from the hotel, subject to the prohibition concerning resales, seems to be a personal right given to Edward which cannot be converted into money. Accordingly, he will not be taxed on this benefit. The provision of a uniform for Edward would appear to be restricted to his Schedule E duties and as such would not be taxable since he would not be able convert it into money. In respect of the loan, since the capital is repayable the amount loaned is not a benefit. The interest saved by the nil rate is not convertible and thus is not taxable in Edward's hands. Likewise, the provision of free meals in the hotel appears to be a personal right exercisable by Edward.

The modern rule with regard to living accommodation has been codified in s 145 of the TA 1988.[2] The rule is that any living accommodation provided to an employee or members of his family or household by his employer, is treated as an emolument (to the extent that it is *not otherwise taxable*) equal to the value of the accommodation to him for the period, less any sum made good by the employee to those providing the accommodation. The value of the accommodation is the annual value ascertained under s 837 (which is equivalent to the gross rateable value or the amount paid by those providing the benefit, if greater). But for any exemptions this rule would clearly be applicable to Edward's circumstances. However, s 145(4) creates a number of exceptions to liability under s 145(1). Section 145(4)(a) and (b) provide s 145(1) is not applicable:

(a) where the provision of accommodation is necessary for the proper performance of his duties; or

(b) where the employment is such that it is *customary* for employees to be provided with accommodation for the better performance of their duties.

Section 145(4)(a) and (b) have been judicially considered in *Vertigan v Brady* (1988). The court decided that a nursery foreman who was provided with rent free accommodation by his employer was not exempt from liability under s 145(1). On the evidence, the court decided that the accommodation was not necessary for the proper performance of the taxpayer's duties. Necessity was to be judged objectively by having regard to the relationship between the proper performance of duties and the dwelling house and not to the necessity based on the personal exigencies of the taxpayer in being unable to find suitable accommodation. There was other accommodation within a five mile radius of the nursery. Further, the court decided that the accommodation was provided for the better performance of the duties but the taxpayer's employment was not one of the type in which it was customary for employers to provide living accommodation for employees. Whether a practice was *customary* within 145(4)(b), three factors were to be considered: (i) the statistical evidence; (ii) the length of the practice; and

(iii) whether the practice has achieved acceptance generally. Applying s 145(4) to Edward's circumstances, it would be extremely difficult to adduce evidence to satisfy the courts under s 145(4)(b). But Edward may find it generally easier to establish his 'representative occupation' under s 145(4)(a). Factors to bear in mind are that Edward is required under the terms of his training contract to reside in the accommodation provided by his employer, objectively the duties of his employment attract the need for the provision of accommodation.

On the assumption that Edward is a 'representative occupier' and thus exempt from income tax in respect of the living accommodation, he would likewise be exempt from liability in respect of the living costs of occupying the premises. Thus, the expenses of lighting and heating amounting to £200 would not be treated as an emolument.

Notes

1 This question illustrates some of the general principles of Schedule E liability to income tax because Edward earns less than £8,500 per annum, inclusive of the benefits in question. The answer would have been different if Edward was earning at least £8,500 per annum.

2 This provision is applicable irrespective of whether Edward is a P11D employee or not.

Question 19

Peter is appointed a director of Sales Ltd. In addition to his salary of £60,000 per annum Peter is provided with a package of benefits. He is permitted to have either the use of a car up to 2,000 cc in the price range of £20,000 or alternatively an increase in salary of £1,000 per annum. Peter has elected to have the car instead of the increased salary. In addition, Peter is provided with free petrol for both private and business use and the bills for servicing and repairing the car are settled by Sales Ltd directly with the garage. Peter is provided with car parking facilities at his place of work. He is given an expense allowance of £5,000 for entertaining business clients. Sales Ltd also provides Peter with a mobile telephone and settles the bill for both business and private calls. Sales Ltd paid the school fees of Peter's child which amounted to £6,000 during the year of assessment.

Advise Peter of the income tax consequences of the above circumstances.

Answer plan

When answering a question of this type, you should include discussion of the following points:

- Peter is a director and is assessable on benefits within ss 153–68 of the TA 1988;
- election to receive the car benefit;
- liability in respect of provision of car;
- liability in respect of petrol;
- exemption in respect of car parking facilities;
- liability in respect of expense allowance;
- provision of mobile phone;
- provision of scholarship for Peter's child.

Answer

Peter is a director of Sales Ltd and is treated for income tax purposes as an office holder. He is taxable under Schedule E in respect of his emoluments derived from his office (see s 19 of the TA 1988). The expression 'emoluments' includes all 'salaries, fees, wages perquisite and profits whatsoever'. This expression includes not only Peter's salary of £60,000 but also benefits in kind which are taxable on general principles or statutory provisions.

It would appear that Peter's circumstances will attract the special provisions enacted in ss 153–68 of the TA 1988. These provisions are applicable to directors and employees earning £8,500 or more (see s 167(1)). The term, 'director', is defined in s 168(8) and Peter clearly comes within this definition. However, s 167(5) excludes certain persons from the definition of a director. These are, *inter alia,* full time working directors who have no material interest in the company. A full time working director is defined in s 168(10) as a person who is required to devote substantially the whole of his time to the service of the company in a managerial or technical capacity. On the facts, it is not possible to determine whether Peter is a full time working director. Similarly, there is no indication as to whether Peter has a material interest in the company or not. This expression is defined in s 168(11) as meaning that a person, with or without his associates, is the beneficial owner of, or able directly or indirectly to control more than 5% of the ordinary share capital of the company or on the company's liquidation would be entitled to more than 5% of its assets. Assuming that Peter is a full time working director without a material interest in the company, he does not escape the provisions in ss 153–68, because he earns more than £8,500 per annum.

Peter has a choice of acquiring the use of the car or an increased salary of £1,000 per annum. Should he be taxed on the value of the benefit in kind *per se* or with regard to the value placed on the benefit by the employer? Prior to 1995–96, if an employee had been offered a benefit in kind in return for reduced remuneration he would have been taxable under the general charge under s 19 of the TA 1988 on the amount of salary forgone (see *Heaton v Bell* (1969)). The reason for this rule is that the benefit in kind may readily be converted into money by surrendering it and thus restoring his salary to its former level. Likewise, where the taxpayer has a choice of accepting the benefit in kind or an increased salary the benefit may be converted into cash. This rule was used as a means of avoiding Class 1A national insurance contributions on cars provided by employers by arranging that the benefit was chargeable under s 19 in accordance with the rule in *Heaton v Bell*. However, s 157A (introduced by the FA 1995 and applicable as from 1995–96) excludes the principle in *Heaton v Bell* where a car is made available to a director or employee earning £8,500 or more. The mere fact that an alternative to the car is offered will not make the benefit chargeable to tax as an emolument under s 19 of the TA 1988. Thus, Peter who opted to receive the car instead of increased salary will be taxed in respect of its provision under s 157 of the TA 1988.

The principle governing the taxation of cars available to P11D employees (including the expenses for servicing and repairing) for their business and private use, without a transfer of the property in it, is enacted in s 157 of the TA 1988. The cash equivalent of such availability is 35% of the list price of the car and additional accessories after deducting any capital contribution to the cost by the employee. Thus, if we assume that the list price of the car and accessories available to Peter is £20,000, Peter will be treated as receiving an emolument equivalent to £7,000. This figure is subject to further reductions. If Peter drives 18,000 or more business miles in the tax year, the cash equivalent is reduced by two thirds. If the business miles exceed 2,500, but is less than 18,000 in any one year, the cash equivalent is reduced by one third. A further reduction of one third will be applied in respect of cars four or more years old at the end of the tax year. Further, there are additional reductions for each day that the car is unavailable to the employee. The reduction is measured on a daily basis. No separate charge is made in respect of the expenses of servicing and repairing the car. We have not been provided with the detailed facts to fully advise Peter as to his liability to income tax in respect of this benefit. But the various hypotheses for measuring Peter's liability have been drawn.

Petrol supplied by an employer to a P11D employee for driving a taxable company car is taxed according to a scale of charges laid down in s 158 of the TA 1988. The cash equivalent is measured by reference to the cylinder capacity of the car. Where, for any part of the year, the car is unavailable, the scale figure is reduced proportionately. The benefit scale charge is nil where the employee is required (perhaps by contract) to use the fuel for business only or to make good to his employer the whole of the expense for the fuel used for the employee's private use. Thus, unless Peter reimburses his employer the full expense for the use of fuel for private purposes, he will be taxable in accordance with the scale charges.

Car parking facilities provided by Peter's employer at or near his place of work are not taxable in Peter's hands (see s 155(1A)).

All payments for expenses, including sums put at Peter's disposal and paid away by him, are assessable, see s 153 of the TA 1988. The cash equivalent of the benefit is the amount of the allowance. In this case, Peter will be treated as having received £5,000 as additional emoluments. But s 153 is without prejudice to deductible expenses claimable, in particular, under s 198. However, the purpose of providing the expense allowance, we are told, was to provide entertainment for business clients. Section 577(1)(b) of the TA 1988 prohibits the deduction of expenses of business entertainment from the taxpayer's emoluments. But s 577(3) provides that where the employer is not allowed a deduction for business entertainment expenditure paid directly or indirectly to a member of staff, and the amount is also taxable as an emolument of the employee, the employee is allowed an equivalent deduction from taxable emoluments. The effect of this provision is that Peter may be entitled to deduct the expense allowance under s 198 of the TA 1988. He is required to establish that the amount was wholly, exclusively and necessarily incurred in the performance of his duties. More evidence is required in order to determine whether the sum is deductible.

Peter's private use of a mobile phone provided by his employer may give rise to a standard benefit of £200. No charge arises if there is no private use by Peter or if he refunds the expense incurred by his employer in respect Peter's private use (see s 159A of the TA 1988).

Section 331 of the TA 1988 exempts the holder of a scholarship from liability to income tax. Peter's son will not be liable to income tax. However, s 165 of the TA 1988 provides that if a scholarship is provided to a member of the family of a P11D taxpayer by reason of his employment the payments are assessable as a benefit under the general rule in s 154 of the TA 1988. A scholarship is to be taken to have been provided by reason of a person's employment if provided, directly or indirectly, under arrangements entered into by, or by a person connected with, his employer. Thus, since Sales Ltd pays the school fees of Peter's child amounting to £6,000 the scholarship is to be treated as provided by Sales Ltd. However, limited relief is available if the scholarship is awarded out of a trust fund, or under a scheme, to a person receiving full time instruction at an educational establishment, where not more than 25% of the total amount of the payments made from that fund or under the scheme, are to children of employees. It is not possible from the facts available whether this is the case or not.

Question 20

> ... the provisions of [s 198 of the TA 1988] are notoriously rigid, narrow and restricted in their operation ... The words are indeed stringent and exacting; compliance with each and every one of them is obligatory if the benefit of [the section] is to be claimed successfully. They are, to my mind, deceptive words in the sense that when examined they are found to come to nearly nothing at all. [*Per* Vaisey J in *Lomax v Newton* (1953).]

Discuss.

Answer plan

A good answer will deal with the following matters:

- deductibility of general expenditure under s 198;
- deductibility of travelling expenditure under s 198;
- comparison with s 74;
- Royal Commission recommendations.

Answer

The reference to s 198 (or to be more precise, its predecessor) in the above statement concerns the deductibility of expenses under Schedule E. There are two categories of expenses enacted in s 198. The section states that the Schedule E taxpayer may deduct expenses if he is:

> ... obliged to incur and defray out of the emoluments ...:
>
> (a) qualifying travelling expenses (as defined); or
>
> (b) otherwise to expend money wholly, exclusively and necessarily in the performance of those duties.

Travelling expenses

There are two requirements to be satisfied in order to deduct the expense – the cost must be 'necessarily' incurred 'in the performance of the duties'. The test of necessity requires the taxpayer to demonstrate that the nature of the duties of the employment obliges the employee to incur the expense. This is determined objectively and not from the personal circumstances of the taxpayer. In addition, the travelling expense is required to be incurred during the course of the performance of the duties.

The courts have drawn a distinction between travelling expenses which are preparatory to the performance of the employee's duties and expenses incurred while performing the duties. Accordingly, the expense of travelling from the taxpayer's home to his office or employment is preliminary to the performance of the duties and is disallowed. In *Ricketts v Colquhoun* (1926), the taxpayer, a barrister practising in London also held the appointment of Recorder of Portsmouth. His claim to deduct his travelling expense from London to Portsmouth on occasions when he sat as Recorder was disallowed. The duties of a circuit judge may only be performed in court. Thus, the expense of travelling to court was preliminary to the performance of his duties. In *Pook v Owen* (1969), the taxpayer carried on a general medical practice at his residence. He also held a part time appointment as obstetrician and anaesthetist at a hospital 15 miles away. On occasions, he was on call and during these periods he had to be accessible by telephone. His responsibility for a patient began as soon as he received a telephone call. On receipt of a call, he gave instructions to the hospital staff and usually set off immediately by car to the hospital. His claim for the deduction of travelling expense was allowed for his duties commenced the moment he received a call from the hospital. In other words, there were two places where his duties were performed, in his consulting room at home and at the hospital. The journey between the two places was undertaken in the performance of his duties. This approach was applied in *Taylor v Provan* (1975). The taxpayer, a Canadian citizen living in Toronto, was an expert in negotiating mergers. He travelled to the UK to negotiate a brewery merger. The court allowed his travelling expenses on the ground that the taxpayer had two offices – in Canada and the UK – and the expense of travelling between these offices was deductible.

There is some authority to suggest that if the above tests are satisfied, the taxpayer has to go further and establish that he could not equally well have performed his duties by means of cheaper transport, otherwise his claim will be apportioned. In *Marsden v IRC* (1965), the taxpayer, a tax inspector was disallowed the expense of using his car to visit towns in the performance of his duties. There was no evidence that he could not have travelled by public transport.

General expenses

The general expenses rule under s 198 is satisfied if three conditions are complied with namely, the expense is *necessarily* incurred, in the *performance of the duties* (these two requirements are similar to the travelling expenses rule). The third requirement is that the expense is *wholly and exclusively* incurred. The test concerning the latter requirement is similar to the Schedule D expenses rule under s 74 of the TA 1988. The courts consider the purpose for which the expenditure was incurred. This is determined objectively. In *Bentleys, Stokes & Lowless v Beeson* (1952), Romer LJ declared that if there were more than one purpose for expending the money, such as a commercial and a non-commercial purpose, none of the expenditure is allowed. But if the sole purpose is commercial the expense is deductible even though an incidental non-commercial purpose is inherent in the expenditure. This rule was applied in *Mallalieu v Drummond* (1983), where a barrister was disallowed the expense of providing a special wardrobe of 'dowdy' clothes for her court appearances.

It is extremely difficult for a Schedule E taxpayer to satisfy all three of these requirements. The test effectively means that it must be virtually impossible to carry out the duties of the office, determined objectively, without incurring the expenditure. Expenditure prior to the performance of the duties is disallowed. Examples are employment agency fees (*Shortt v McIlgorm* (1945)); mess expenses of a Territorial army officer (*Lomax v Newton* (1953)); headmaster's course in order to improve background knowledge (*Humbles v Brooks* (1962)); articled clerk's examination fees (*Lupton v Potts* (1969)); cost of ordinary clothing (*Hillyer v Leeke* (1976)); bank manager's subscriptions to a West End club as a condition of appointment (*Brown v Bullock* (1961)); journalists' expenditure on newspapers and periodicals (*Fitzpatrick v CIR (No 2); Smith v Abbott* (1994)); cost of domestic assistance where wife employed (*Bowers v Harding* (1891)).

The Royal Commission, in its report of June 1955 (Cmnd 9474), compared the Schedule D rule for the deduction of expenses with Schedule E and concluded that 'the Schedule D rule for deductible expenses is satisfactory and we have no alteration to recommend', but the Schedule E rule was too narrow and created hardships in a number of employments. Apart from limited instances of inherent differences in the nature of the income involved, there was no reason to treat deductibility under Schedule E less generously than under Schedule D. Proposals for change were considered by the Commission. One suggestion is that a lump sum or percentage allowance to Schedule E income should be given as compensation, without proof of actual expenditure. This idea was abandoned since the Commission could not decide on the amount of the lump sum. Another suggestion concerned specific rules which identified certain types of expenditure which would be allowed, if bearing on the employment. For instance, figures could be fixed for expenditure on books and periodicals. But the Commission decided that such a proposal could not work, though it would recommend granting relief in some cases where the existing rules worked inequitably. The Royal Commission suggested rewording the Schedule E expenses rule on less restricted lines allowing the deduction of: 'all expenses reasonably incurred for the appropriate performance of the duties of the office or employment.'

It is hoped that some time in the near future that the Schedule E expenses rule will be modified.

Question 21

The broad general principle which should govern the assessment of damages ... is that the tribunal should award the injured party such a sum of money as will put him in the same position as he would have been if he had not sustained the injuries ... To ignore the tax element at the present day would be to act in a manner which is out of touch with reality. Nor can I regard the tax element as so remote that it should be disregarded in assessing damages. [*Per* Lord Jowitt in *British Transport Commission v Gourley* (1956).]

Discuss how far this proposition is adhered to by the courts in reducing awards of damages, in order to take account of the tax that would have been paid by the taxpayer had there not been a breach of a duty.

Answer plan

When answering this type of question, remember to consider:

- the pre-*Gourley* situation;
- the *BTC v Gourley* decision;
- pre-requisites for a *Gourley* reduction;
- criticisms of the *Gourley* principle;
- six approaches to *Gourley*.

Answer

Before the decision of the House of Lords in *BTC v Gourley* (1956), it was settled practice in England that in assessing damages as compensation for loss of income, the court did not concern itself with the plaintiff's liability to income tax (see *Billingham v Hughes* (1949)). For example, a party is appointed under a three year contract of employment for a remuneration of £50,000 per annum. After the second year he is wrongfully dismissed and brings an action for loss of salary of £50,000 for wrongful dismissal. Before the *Gourley* decision, the plaintiff would have been entitled to claim his loss of salary, subject to the contractual principles of quantifying the loss (in particular, the principle of mitigation of the loss). No account would have been taken of the income tax he would have paid had his contract ran the full course.

The significance of the *Gourley* decision lies in the reduction of the award of damages by the court to take into account the tax that would have been paid but for the breach. In *BTC v Gourley*, the plaintiff, a successful engineer and Schedule D taxpayer, was injured as a result of the defendant's negligence. His loss of actual and prospective earnings was assessed at £37,720 and under the existing practice at that time would have received this sum tax-free. The defendant argued that, if the plaintiff had not been injured, £31,025 would have been paid in tax on those earnings and the plaintiff would have been paid a net sum of only £6,695. The House of Lords by a majority of six to one held that the plaintiff was only entitled to the net sum.

The effect of this decision is that tax calculations, and at times complex mathematical sums, have become an essential part of many claims for damages. The most common claims are in contract for loss of profit for wrongful dismissal, and in tort for loss of earnings or impairment or destruction of earning capacity following personal injury and death.[1]

The *Gourley* rule may be expressed thus: in assessing damages, not in themselves subject to tax, but which would have been subject to tax but for the breach of duty, the court is required to reduce the award by a sum which is broadly equivalent to the estimated liability to tax which the taxpayer would have incurred had he received the lost income.

In substance, there are two conditions to be satisfied:

(a) the award of damages must represent compensation for loss of income which would have been subject to tax, had there not been a breach of liability;

(b) the award of damages is not assessable to tax, in whole or in part, in the plaintiff's hands.

In respect of the first condition, damages are taxable, like other sums, if the source of the compensation is taxable. Frequently, in income tax law, the issue concerning an award of damages is to ascertain whether the compensation represents loss of income or capital. In *London & Thames Haven Oil Wharves Ltd v Attwooll* (1967), the taxpayer company owned several jetties at an oil installation where tankers could berth for the purpose of the discharge of oil. A tanker was negligently navigated and struck a jetty causing serious damage to it. The taxpayers brought a claim in negligence claiming £83,000 for the physical damage to the jetty and £21,000 for loss of profit. The company received one lump sum payment by way of compensation and the Revenue claimed that £21,000 of the damages was taxable as a trading receipt in the hands of the company. The Court of Appeal held that the payment for consequential loss was liable to income tax as loss of profit. The compensation was to be treated for income tax purposes in the same way as that sum of money would have been treated if it had been received, instead of the compensation. The mode of payment of the compensation does not alter the status of the payment (see, also, *Pennine Raceway Ltd v Kirklees MBC* (1989)).

The second condition, as stated above, concerns the specific determination of the court or the application of a statutory rule. Before 1960, 'golden handshakes' and sums paid for wrongful dismissal were not liable to income tax (see *Henley v Murray* (1950)). However, s 148 of the TA 1988 now assesses such sums to income tax. Section 148(2) applies to any:

> ... payment (not otherwise chargeable to income tax) which is made, whether in pursuance of any legal obligation or not, either directly or indirectly in consideration or in consequence of, or otherwise in connection with, the termination of the holding of the office or employment or any change in its functions, including any payment in commutation of annual or periodic payments (whether chargeable or not) which would otherwise have been so made.

If the relevant sum is taxable under s 148, s 188(4) exempts from income tax the first £30,000 of such receipts. The difficulty posed by *Gourley* is whether an award which is wholly or partly within the confines of s 188(4) ought to be subject to a reduction in order to take into account the tax which would have been paid, but for the breach. Before we examine the various applications of *Gourley*, it would be appropriate to examine the arguments which criticise the *Gourley* rule.

(a) The *Gourley* claim for the reduction of the award, in appropriate cases, will be made by the defendant in the action brought by the plaintiff. If the claim succeeds, the plaintiff suffers a reduction in his claim for damages. The reduction is equivalent to notional tax which would have been paid, but for the breach of duty by the defendant. The effect, if the *Gourley* claim succeeds, is that the defendant pays less damages. This may be unfair in that the defendant 'profits' from the breach by paying a lesser amount in damages as opposed to a full payment of compensation to the plaintiff, in view of the breach of duty.

(b) As a corollary to the above-mentioned point, the Revenue is not a party to the action between the plaintiff and defendant. The notional tax which represents the amount of the reduction of the award is not paid to the Revenue but is retained by the defendant, beneficially. The decision of the court concerning the reduction of the award will not bind the Revenue which is entitled to maintain, in appropriate cases, that the sum received by the taxpayer is taxable, for example, an award of £40,000 which is taxable under s 148 of the TA 1988 after a *Gourley* reduction may be liable to tax in respect of the sum exceeding £30,000 (exempt under s 188(4)). The plaintiff may be forgiven for feeling aggrieved at being effectively taxed twice. Once, by the court and, secondly, by the Revenue.

(c) The *Gourley* reduction tends to be inaccurate because the court proceeds on the assumption that there will be no changes in tax laws, the rates of tax and reliefs.

(d) Except in rare cases, a plaintiff awarded a net sum is deprived of the opportunity of arranging his affairs to his advantage. In exceptional circumstances, the court may take into consideration tax avoidance schemes but this requires fairly substantial evidence (see *Beach v Reed Corrugated Cases* (1956)).

(e) Occasionally, the courts refuse to apply the *Gourley* principle, but this is usually done on an *ad hoc* basis owing to the inequity in adopting the *Gourley* solution. In *Bartlett v Barclays Bank Trust Company Ltd (No 2)* (1980), shares held upon trust were sold at a loss and, as a consequence, damages for breach of trust were awarded against the trustees. The court held that the tax liability of the beneficiaries could not be taken into account in assessing the loss, distinguishing *Gourley*. The trustees' obligation was to restore to the trust estate the assets of which he deprived the estate. This obligation is fundamentally different from that of the contractual or tortious wrongdoer. This approach was followed in *John and Others v James and Others* (1986). The plaintiffs were a songwriter and entertainer and others associated with him, the defendants were music publishers. The plaintiffs claimed that under a number of recording and publishing agreements, the defendants were in breach of a fiduciary duty in retaining certain sums, which the plaintiffs were entitled to recover. The defendants claimed that, in arriving at the amount of the damages, there should be deducted an amount representing tax which the plaintiffs would have been liable to pay had the sums been paid when they fell due. The Court of Appeal rejected this contention and decided that the course of justice would be better served if there was no reduction of the award.

Indeed, there are occasions when an award by the court is increased to take into account the plaintiff's potential liability to tax on the interest on the capital awarded, but in estimating this liability the taxpayer's private income is ignored. This amounts to the principle in *Gourley* operating in reverse (see *Taylor v O'Connor* (1971)).

(f) There is no consistency in the application of the *Gourley* reduction.

To date, there appears to be no less than six possible solutions to the *Gourley* dilemma. These will now be considered in turn.

First, to ignore *Gourley*. In the context of s 148 receipts, s 188(4) exempts the first £30,000 of such receipts. This exemption, created by Parliament, is fruitless unless respected by the courts. Admittedly, by the same token, this requirement satisfies the second condition for the application of the *Gourley* rule. Unless the exemption is given effect, it will not amount to a relief. It is not open to the courts to deny a relief or exemption granted to the taxpayer by Parliament. The supporters of this are Master Jacobs and Sellers LJ (dissenting in the Court of Appeal) in *Parsons v BNM* (1962).

Secondly, the payment is not apportioned. If the gross sum does not satisfy both conditions necessary for the application of the *Gourley* rule (see above), the award by the court is not reduced, for example, if the compensation payable under s 148 of the TA 1988 exceeds £30,000, the award may not be reduced because the *Gourley* principle has not been satisfied. Alternatively, if the gross sum is less than £30,000, s 188(4) applies to exempt this amount and the *Gourley* reduction operates. The Court of Appeal (by a majority), in *Parsons v BNM* (1964), adopted this approach.

Thirdly, this approach involves a variation of the second approach as stated above. It involves applying the *Gourley* reduction first in order to ascertain whether the sum is below or above £30,000. If the reduction leaves a figure of less than £30,000, then the *Gourley* reduction will stand. Alternatively, if the conditional reduction leaves a figure exceeding £30,000 then the *Gourley* reduction will be added back. This view has the support of the *obiter* pronouncement of the majority members of the Court of Appeal in *Parsons v BNM*.

Fourthly, this approach requires the court to apply the *Gourley* reduction first and then apportion the resulting amount into two portions. The first £30,000 and the balance. The latter amount will suffer tax in the normal way in the taxpayer's hands. This view was referred to in *Parsons* case but has not found favour with the courts.

Fifthly, this involves an initial apportionment of the sum into two parcels, the first £30,000 and the balance. The first £30,000 will suffer a *Gourley* reduction but the remainder of the sum will be excluded from the *Gourley* rule, for example, in respect of a compensation claim of £40,000, an initial apportionment is made in respect of £30,000 and the excess. The *Gourley* reduction is made in respect of the first £30,000 but the excess is awarded gross to the taxpayer. This solution was adopted in *Bold v Brough Nicholson & Hall Ltd* (1964).

Sixthly, the court will estimate the net amount which would have been received by the plaintiff after deduction of income tax and award a sum which, after the relief under s 188(4) will leave the taxpayer properly compensated for the loss. This approach involves two calculations at the most. First, the plaintiff's real net loss is calculated on ordinary *Gourley* principles. If the real net loss is less than £30,000, that is the end of the matter. But, if the real net loss exceeds £30,000, the amount payable must be increased so as to produce a sum which, after it has been subject to tax under ss 148 and 188(4), will leave a sum equivalent to the net loss. In *Shove v Downs Surgical plc* (1984), on a claim for wrongful dismissal the court ascertained the compensation which the plaintiff was entitled to (£60,729) and awarded him a sum which, after deduction of his potential liability to tax, left that amount in his hands (£83,477). The difficulty with this approach is that both conditions necessary for the application of *Gourley* are not satisfied. Part of the compensation award is subject to tax and ought to be outside the *Gourley* principle.

Note

1   In 1958, the Law Reform Committee was unable to agree on the soundness of the tax reduction principle and considered that it would be desirable to review the practical implications of the decision in the future.

CHAPTER 6

SCHEDULE F

Introduction

For the year of assessment 1998–99, an individual who receives a qualifying distribution from a company resident in the UK is liable to income tax under Schedule F. The individual is entitled to a tax credit equivalent to the 'lower rate' of income tax (for 1998–99, 20%) in addition to the net dividend. If the individual is not liable to higher rate of tax he will suffer no additional liability in respect of the dividend, and if his circumstances permit, he will be entitled to a repayment claim in respect of the credit. But if he is liable to a higher rate of tax he will be required to pay the difference between the higher rate of tax and the lower rate (for 1998–99, this amount is 20%).

1999–2000 – the new rates

Income chargeable under Schedule F and equivalent foreign income will no longer be charged at the lower rate of 20%, but at the Schedule F ordinary rate: see s 1(a)(2) and (3) of the Income and Corporation Taxes Act 1988 (TA) (introduced by s 31 of the Finance Act (No 2) 1997 (FA)). This rate is fixed at 10%. Where such income is chargeable at a rate in excess of the basic rate, it will be charged at the Schedule F upper rate, which is fixed at 32.5% for the year of assessment 1999–2000. These rates may be amended by Parliament. For example, a UK company pays dividends of £800 on 1 June 1998 and 1 June 1999 to an individual who is liable to income tax at a rate in excess of the basic rate of tax. His liability will be:

		1998–99		1999–2000
Dividend		£800		£800
Tax credit		£200	1/9	£88.89
		£1,000.00		£888.89
Tax charge – 40% =	£400		32.5% – £288.89	
Less tax credit –	£200		£88.89	
Tax payable	£200		£200,00	

Question 22

In 1997, Agnes set up a discretionary trust using shares in her own company worth £300,000. The four beneficiaries of the trust are her two nieces, Brenda and Clare, and her two children, Debby and Enid. Brenda is aged 26 and is earning over £40,000 a year. Clare is aged 24 and is unemployed. Debby is aged 20 and earns £10,000 a year. Enid is aged 14, with no income, and is still at school.

The gross income of the trust is approximately £40,000 a year.

Advise the trustees of the income tax consequences during the tax year 1998–99 on the following alternative proposals:

(a) not distributing the income to the beneficiaries; and
(b) distributing the income equally between the beneficiaries.

Answer plan

Part (a)

Consider:

- trustees' liability to income tax;
- rate of tax applicable to trust;
- non-deductibility of management expenses, except as permitted under under s 686(2AA)(b) of the TA 1988.

Part (b)

Discuss:

- 'grossing up' of income received by beneficiaries;
- additional tax payable by some beneficiaries;
- repayment claims by some beneficiaries;
- 'settlements' and s 660(B) of the TA 1988.

Answer

Part (a)

Trustees, unlike individuals, are not liable to the higher rate of income tax nor entitled to claim personal reliefs. Generally, the trustees are liable to income tax at the basic rate. However, with regard to discretionary (or accumulation) trusts, trustees are liable to income tax at a special rate, namely, 34% (for 1998–99). This is known as 'the rate applicable to the trust' or the larger rate: see s 686(1A) of the TA 1988. With regard to distributions from UK resident companies, the trustees receive dividends net of tax at the lower rate of 20% together with a tax credit matching that lower rate of tax. For the year of assessment 1998–99, they will have a further liability of 14% tax to pay on the grossed up value of the dividends. However, the treatment of tax credits will be changed radically from 1999–2000 and subsequent years. The amount of tax credit attaching to such distributions is reduced from 20% to 10%. As compensation for the reduction of the tax credit on distributions, the rate of tax on distributions received by discretionary and accumulation trusts is reduced from 34% to 25% (a new Schedule F trust rate): ss 32, 33 and 34 of the FA (No 2) 1997.

When trustees are liable to income tax they are assessed under the Schedule and Case appropriate to the source of income. With respect to this settlement, the trustees may be assessed under Schedule F. Any one or more of several trustees is assessable in respect of trust income.

The management expenses of trustees (such as trustees' remuneration) are paid out of taxed income. Accordingly, such expenses are not deductible from income for the purposes of basic or lower rate of tax: see *Aikin v McDonald* (1894). However, for the purpose of liability beyond the basic rate of tax (11% for 1998–99) the trustees are entitled to deduct such expenses, provided that they are 'properly chargeable to income': see s 686(2AA)(b) of the TA 1988. In *Carver v Duncan* (1985), the House of Lords decided that the payments of life assurance premiums out of the trust income were not deductible under s 686(2AA)(b). This section permits expenses which are properly chargeable to income under the general law. The life assurance premiums were designed to benefit the capital and ought to have been borne out of the capital fund.

Part (b)

Brenda

Brenda is a higher rate income tax payer as she earns over £40,000 per year. In the circumstances, she is treated as receiving from the trustees a 'net amount corresponding to a gross amount from which tax has been deducted at the rate applicable to the trust': see s 687(2)(a) of the TA 1988. In other words, in the tax year 1998–99, Brenda receives £10,000 from the trustees. This sum is treated as a grossed up equivalent of an amount from which tax at 34% has been deducted. The income tax is payable by the trustees, but Brenda is given a tax credit in respect of the tax: see s 687(2)(b) of the TA 1988.

This gross income is added to Brenda's other income and is taxed at the higher rate of 40% in her hands. Against this liability of 40%, Brenda is entitled to offset the tax already paid on this source of income, that is, she is liable to pay an additional amount of tax on the dividends at the rate of 6%.

Clare

Clare pays the basic rate of tax on her unemployment benefit in so far as this exceeds her personal allowances for the year of assessment. Like Brenda, she is treated as receiving the gross equivalent of £10,000 plus a tax credit of 34% in respect of tax paid on this dividend. Depending on Clare's financial circumstances, she may be able to reclaim the whole or part of the tax paid on her behalf.

Debby

Debby is similarly treated as receiving £10,000 with a tax credit of 34%. In view of the fact that Debby is a basic rate taxpayer, she will be taxed on the full sum with a credit of 34% in respect of the tax paid on her behalf. Again, depending on her financial circumstances, she may reclaim the additional tax of 11% paid by the trustees.

Enid

Enid is Agnes' unmarried, infant daughter. By virtue of s 660(B) of the TA 1988, income under a settlement which is paid to the infant, unmarried child of the settlor is treated as the income of the settlor for that year of assessment. For these purposes, a settlement is defined in s 660(G) as including any disposition, trust, covenant, agreement or arrangement and, in respect of transfers on children, the definition was further extended to include a transfer of assets: see s 670 of the TA 1988. A *bona fide* commercial transaction without any element of bounty does not constitute a settlement: see *IRC v Plummer* (1980). Undoubtedly, the discretionary trust created by Agnes in 1997 is a settlement for these purposes. The effect is that the income paid to Enid from the trust is treated, for tax purposes, as the income of Agnes.

Since Agnes is likely to be a higher rate income tax payer, she will be treated as receiving the gross equivalent of £10,000 plus a tax credit of 34%, and will face an additional liability to income tax of 6%. Agnes has the right to reclaim from Enid or the trustees any extra tax paid in respect of the amount of the income paid to Enid: see s 660(D) of the TA 1988.

In the future, the trustees are advised to accumulate the income that they would be tempted to pay to Enid, until she attains the age of majority.

SECTION II
VALUE ADDED TAX

CHAPTER 7

VALUE ADDED TAX

Introduction

VAT is an indirect tax on the supplies of goods and services including the importation of goods outside the EC. The tax is collected at each stage of production or distribution. The burden falls on the final consumer of the goods or services. However, all those involved in the chain of production between the manufacturer and the retailer are first charged VAT and then pass it on to the next person in the chain. Customs and Excise are responsible for the administration of the tax.

A VAT registered business is entitled to a refund or credit of most of the VAT incurred on expenditure which it uses in making taxable supplies, that is, supplies taxable at the standard rate (17.5% from 1 April 1991), the zero rate or the lower rate of 5% which is applicable to domestic and charity fuel and power supplies made on or after 1 September 1997. Sales are called outputs (goods and services 'out' of the business). VAT charged on sales is *output tax*. Purchases are called inputs (goods and services 'into' the business). VAT incurred on purchases is *input tax*. The difference between output tax and input tax is normally paid to Customs and Excise on a quarterly or monthly basis. Alternatively, where the input tax exceeds the output tax a rebate is claimable from the Customs and Excise.

Some supplies of goods and services are taxed at the standard, zero or lower rates. Some supplies are exempt. Some supplies fall outside the scope of VAT altogether. Although no VAT is charged on zero rated and exempt supplies, the difference between them is important. Zero rating gives the supplier an entitlement to input tax credit, exemption does not. Examples of zero rated supplies are: young children's clothing and footwear; exports of goods; sales of most types of food. Examples of exempt supplies are, buildings sold, leased or hired (excluding hotel charges and holiday lettings); services provided by doctors, dentists, opticians, etc; most services provided by financial institutions.

Registration of a business may be compulsory (depending on the value of the turnover of the business) or voluntary. The consequences of registration are:

(a) the business becomes a registered person entitled to charge VAT on sales and to reclaim VAT on inputs;

(b) a VAT number is allocated to the business. This VAT number is required to be quoted on all invoices and credit notes;

(c) appropriate quarterly tax return periods are allocated to the business. Quarters coinciding with the business accounting year are normally given;

(d) satisfactory tax invoices and credit notes are required to be prepared to provide evidence of VAT charged;

(e) adequate records are required to be kept of all taxable goods and services received or supplied, as well as exempt supplies made by the business.

Question 23

Tony set up and managed a restaurant, the profits from which have grown substantially in recent years. The business has a turnover of a sum exceeding £400,000. Tony is contemplating converting the business into an incorporated association with himself as a major shareholder and managing director.

Explain to Tony in outline:

(a) the principles on which he is currently taxed; and

(b) assuming that he carries out his objective, the basis on which the company and he himself will be taxed.

Answer plan

A well structured answer should incorporate discussion of:

- Schedule D Case I liability on the annual profits or gains from a trade;
- bases of computing profits;
- valuation of unsold stock at the end of accounting period;

- current year of assessment;
- disposals within ss 17 and 18 of the Taxation and Chargeable Gains Act 1992 (TCGA);
- relief under s 162 of the TCGA 1992;
- Schedule F liability to income tax;
- Schedule E liability to income tax;
- mainstream corporation tax (MCT);
- advance corporation tax (ACT).

Answer

As a sole trader, Tony is liable to income tax under Schedule D Case I in respect of the annual profits or gains from the trade. The expression, 'annual' has been interpreted by the courts to mean revenue profits. Revenue profits are the gross trading profits (Tony's turnover in his trade) as reduced by deductible trading expenditure, that is, revenue expenditure incurred for the purpose of the trade and which is not prohibited by statute. In short, capital profits are excluded from liability to income tax. However, in exceptional circumstances certain items of capital expenditure, such as plant and machinery, may attract capital allowance which may be used to reduce the amount of profits liable to income tax.

The profits of the trade are computed by applying principles of commercial accounting. The usual method of aggregating the profits is on the 'earnings' basis, that is, by including into the account sums which have been earned whether or not they have been received. A sum is not treated as having been earned until the trader has fulfilled all the conditions which entitle him to payment. Correspondingly, Tony is entitled to deduct sums which are outstanding even though these amounts have not been paid. The alternative to the 'earnings' basis is the 'cash' basis under which the profits are computed by reference to sums received and not by reference to sums earned. Correspondingly, deductions may only be made in respect of bills paid and not on bills due.

At the end of each accounting period unsold stock may not be ignored when determining the net profits of the trade. Unsold stock is brought in as a receipt at the end of each accounting period.

At the beginning of each following accounting period, the unsold stock is treated as an expense. In valuing his stock, Tony is entitled to choose either the cost price or its market value, moreover Tony is entitled to pick and choose which item to value at cost or market value (see *IRC v Cock, Russell & Co* (1949)).

Since Tony's trade had commenced before 6 April 1994, he would have been assessed to income tax on the preceding year of assessment basis. With the introduction of the current year of assessment in the Finance Act 1994, transitional arrangements have been introduced for continuing businesses. The transition year is 1996–97. For this year, the assessable profit is a 12 month average of the profits earned in the financial years 1995–96 and 1996–97. The remainder of the 12 month average not utilised escapes tax completely. Income tax is payable to the Revenue on 31 January in the year of assessment and 31 July following the year of assessment.

If Tony converts his trade into a company, this *prima facie* involves a disposal by Tony in his personal capacity and an acquisition by the company, *inter alia*, of the assets of the trade. But for capital gains tax reliefs, Tony will be liable to pay capital gains tax in respect of the disposal. If no consideration is received by the taxpayer in respect of the disposal, the value of the disposal will be at the market value of the assets, including goodwill, at the time of the disposal. This is because s 17 of the TCGA 1992 enacts that a gift is deemed to give rise to a disposal for a consideration equal to the market value of the asset. Similarly, if Tony sells the assets to the company controlled by him the disposal is treated as taking place between connected persons (see s 286(6) of the TCGA 1992). The effect of such a disposal, as enacted in s 18, is that in respect of both Tony and the company, the transaction is treated as made 'otherwise than by way of a bargain at arm's length', thus attracting the market value rule enacted in s 17.

Section 162 of the TCGA 1992 provides a form of 'roll over' relief to Tony on the transfer of a business as a going concern and, in particular, in respect of business assets, to a company. The relief takes the form of postponement rather than exemption from capital gains tax. The relevant conditions to be satisfied are:

- the transferor of the business must be a sole trader (or partnership);
- the transfer is to a body corporate;
- the transfer of the business must be as a going concern together with all the assets of the business;
- the transfer is required to be wholly or partly in exchange for shares issued by the company to Tony.

It seems clear that all the above conditions have been satisfied (or will be) by Tony, with the consequence that s 162 relief will be available to him.[1] The effect of the relief is that the gains made by Tony on the disposal of the business assets will be deducted from the value of the shares received, that is, the gains are deferred, or the base value of the shares is reduced by the amount of the gain, until the eventual disposal of the shares. The company is treated as acquiring the assets at their market value at the time of the disposal. If Tony receives consideration[2] for the transfer, the gain is apportioned by applying the fraction – A/B – where A is the cost of the shares and B is the total consideration received by the transferor.[3]

Ownership of the shares by Tony entitles him to dividends. These are treated as qualifying distributions and are liable to income tax in his hands under Schedule F on the gross sum, that is, the net dividend plus a tax credit. The tax credit is equivalent to 20% of the gross dividend. This credit is equal to the income tax charge at the lower rate. Section 207A of the TA 1988 provides that income under Schedule F which is liable to income tax and which does not exceed the higher rate threshold shall be charged at the lower rate of tax. Thus, if Tony's taxable income does not exceed the higher rate threshold, no further tax is payable in respect of dividends received from the company. But, if his taxable income exceeds the higher rate threshold, he will be liable to income tax on the dividend on the difference between the higher rate and the lower rate. Alternatively, if Tony is not a taxpayer because his reliefs exceed his income, he may make a repayment claim in respect of the tax paid on his behalf.

Tony's income, derived from his post as a managing director of the company, is liable to income tax under Schedule E as emoluments from an office. These payments include not only money sums but also the cash equivalent of benefits in kind. The majority of these emoluments will be subject to the PAYE system, requiring deduction of tax at source.

Companies pay corporation tax (mainstream corporation tax or 'MCT') on its profits whether distributed or not. Profits for these purposes include both income and capital profits. The rate of corporation tax currently stands at 33%, although small companies pay tax at the rate of 25% if their profits do not exceed £300,000 in an accounting period. Where the company's profits exceed £300,000 but not £1.5 m tapering relief is available. The effect is that the company pays tax at the rate of 35% on profits which exceed £300,000 but below £1.5 m. MCT is payable on the later of the two following dates:

- within nine months of the end of the accounting period; or
- within one month of the date of the making of an assessment.

When the company makes a qualifying distribution (such as payment of a dividend) it is obliged to deduct and pay ACT to the Revenue. The amount of ACT currently payable is 20% or one quarter (that is, 20/80) of the net dividend. For the purpose of collecting ACT, the calendar year is divided into quarters (31 March; 30 June; 30 September; and 31 December). The company is required to file a return for each quarter indicating the amount of dividends that have been paid in the latest quarter. ACT is required to be paid to the Revenue within 14 days of the end of each quarter. The amount of ACT paid on dividends may be set off against the company's liability to MCT. Thus, dividend payments do not increase the company's liability to MCT, it simply is an advance payment of corporation tax.

When the company makes a non-qualifying distribution, no ACT is deducted and likewise no income tax credit is enjoyed by the recipient.

Notes

1   It appears that s 162 relief is available if the company acquires the business as a going concern and then disposes of the business to another. The first mentioned company acquires the business assets, of course, at market value (see *Gordon v IRC* (1991)).

2   Consideration, for these purposes, do not include the liabilities of the company subsisting at the time of the conversion.

3   The Revenue seem to accept that in appropriate cases retirement relief may first be deducted from the gains so that the remainder of the gains may be held over under s 162.

Question 24

John Smith makes taxable supplies of goods amounting to £53,000 in his trading year ending 31 January 1999. He anticipates that his sales will increase dramatically in the second half of next year. He comes to you for advice on VAT.

Advise John Smith on each of the following matters:

(a) whether he is required to register and the consequences of registration;

(b the VAT treatment of goods imported from and exported to countries outside the UK.

Answer plan

The following plan should provide the basis for a good answer:

•   penalties for non-registration;
•   annual and future turnover limits;
•   voluntary registration;
•   registration requirements imposed on 'persons';
•   accounting and set off requirements;

- imposition of VAT on the importation of goods from a country outside the EC;
- date and value of imported goods;
- reliefs available for trader;
- exports of goods to countries outside the EC are zero rated;
- supply of goods from a country within the EC to a UK registered trader;
- supply of goods by a VAT registered UK trader to a similar trader within a country in the EC;
- supply of goods by VAT registered UK trader to unregistered customers within the EC;
- supply of goods by a VAT registered trader in an EC country to an unregistered customer in the UK.

Answer

Part (a)

John Smith is strongly advised to apply for immediate registration for VAT purposes in view of the severe penalties that may be imposed for failing to register. The obligation to register is imposed on John. The penalty is based on the net tax due for the penalty period (that is, output tax less input tax) and is the greater of:

- £50; and
- a percentage of the tax due from the date when the trader should have been registered to the date when proper notification is made. The percentage rate for this purpose depends on the length of the delay in notification. A delay of nine months or less – 5%, a delay of nine to 18 months – 10%, a delay of over 18 months – 15% (see s 67 of the Value Added Tax Act 1994 (VATA)).

This late registration penalty is not payable if the trader can satisfy the Customs and Excise or a VAT tribunal that there is a reasonable excuse for the failure.

John Smith is required to register for VAT if his taxable turnover (including zero rated supplies) at the end of any month during a 12 month period exceeds the annual turnover limit (£50,000 as from 1 April 1998). Where a trader becomes liable to register by virtue of this rule, he is required to notify the Customs within 30 days from the end of the calendar month for which the turnover limit was exceeded. However, registration can take effect from an earlier date if Customs and John Smith agree to this (Schedule 1, para 5 of the VATA 1994).

Alternatively, if John Smith has reasonable grounds for believing that his taxable turnover (including zero rated supplies) within the next 30 days will exceed the annual turnover limit, he is required to register for VAT purposes.

Traders who either make or intend to make taxable supplies that will not take them above the threshold for compulsory registration, may request voluntary registration (Schedule 1, para 9(a) of the VATA 1994). Customs have a discretionary power whether or not to grant registration. In order to minimise the number of small registered traders, Customs take the view that voluntary registration will normally be granted where there is a compelling business need. Factors that are taken into account are:

- the trader must clearly make taxable supplies in the course or furtherance of a business. Thus, hobbies or casual activities will not count;
- the taxable supplies must contribute substantially to his livelihood;
- denial of registration will result in the trader incurring substantial irrevocable input tax.

If John Smith makes only zero rated supplies, he can, if he wishes, apply to be exempted from registration, even though his taxable turnover exceeds the registration limits: see Schedule 1, para 14(1) of the VATA 1994. If John Smith can cope with the administrative consequences of VAT registration it is advisable not to seek exemption because he would lose his right to reclaim input tax on taxable supplies.

It is a fundamental rule of the VAT code that 'persons' are required to register for VAT purposes, and not businesses. For VAT purposes, 'persons' include individuals, partnerships, companies and unincorporated associations. On the facts of this question, it is not clear whether John Smith trades a sole proprietor or not and whether he conducts a variety of other taxable activities. A person's registration covers all his business activities, regardless of how numerous or varied they may be. Thus, a sole proprietor of a confectionery shop who is registered for VAT purposes will be required to account for VAT on his other business activities. It also follows that the income of all business activities carried on by a registered person must be aggregated in arriving at that person's taxable turnover for registration purposes.

The effect of VAT registration is that John Smith is required to keep a record of the supplies which he makes in the course of any business carried on by him and the tax due on them (output tax). He is also required to keep a record of the tax suffered on taxable supplies received by him (input tax). John Smith will then be entitled to set off his input tax from his output tax. If his output tax exceeds input tax, he will pay the difference to Customs. Alternatively, if his input tax exceeds the output tax he will be entitled to reclaim the excess from Customs. The trader is required to make periodic VAT returns, drawn up on a quarterly basis (although some traders are allowed to complete monthly or annual returns) and submit these to Customs by the end of the month following the period to which it relates with a remittance for any tax due for the period.

Part (b)

The general rule is that the importation of goods[1] to the UK from outside the EC is a chargeable event, and VAT is due on it as though it were Customs duty, regardless of whether the person importing the goods does so in the course of a business (see s 1(4) of the VATA 1994). If the goods imported fall into the zero rated category, there is no liability on their importation. The tax is payable at the same time as any Customs duty arising. Evidence of VAT paid on the importation must be obtained by a trader as evidence for input tax recovery. The VAT paid on imports may be recovered as input tax in accordance with normal rules.

The date of importation into the UK is deemed to arise when:

- the goods are removed from a place outside the EC and enter the territory of the EC;
- they either enter the UK directly or through a Member State; and
- the circumstances are such that, on entry to the UK, any liability to customs duty arises (or would arise if the goods were dutiable).

The value of imported goods for VAT purposes is generally the same as the value for duty purposes plus taxes, duties, commission, packaging, insurance and transport costs arising prior to or because of the importation of the goods and ending at a time up to the place of importation (s 21 of the VATA 1994).

There are three main types of relief from VAT on the importation of goods from outside the EC countries:

(a) suspension of the charge – the charge is merely suspended while the goods are in some kind of suspension regime (such as warehousing). The liability crystallises, and VAT becomes payable, as and when the goods are removed from the suspension regime for free circulation in the UK;

(b) temporary import reliefs – these involve goods temporarily brought to the UK and escape the liability to VAT altogether. If the goods remain in the UK beyond the permitted period, a UK liability then arises;

(c) absolute reliefs – these involve complete exemptions from liability to VAT, for example, certain personal property imported by persons entering to take up permanent residence, certain trade samples, etc.

The export of goods to a country outside the EC is zero rated: see s 30(6) of the VATA 1994. It is generally necessary for exports to be made directly to a customer for zero rating to apply. In order to justify this treatment, it is essential to produce evidence that the goods have been exported. Such evidence may take the form of the bill of lading or other documents which establish that the goods have been transported to a customer outside the EC.

The general rule applicable to goods supplied within the EC is that they are taxed in the Member State to which they are dispatched. This rule was adopted as from 1 January 1993. Before this date, the supply of goods to the UK from an EC Member State was treated in the same way as the importation of goods from outside the EC.

In substance, the procedure is where a UK registered VAT trader acquires goods from another trader in an EC country, he does not pay VAT on importation, but must now account for VAT in the Member State of arrival. Thus, he accounts for VAT on the goods through his own VAT return. Where a VAT registered trader in the UK dispatches goods to a registered trader in another EC Member State, the supply will normally be zero rated (see s 30(8) of the VATA 1994). No VAT will be paid as the goods cross the frontier. The customer will acquire the goods and will account for VAT on his own VAT return at the rate in force in the country of receipt.

Where a VAT registered UK trader supplies goods to customers in an EC country, but who are not registered for VAT, the supplier is required to charge VAT at the rate in force for the UK. The same applies to the dispatch of goods by an EC registered trader supplying goods to an unregistered UK trader.

Note

1   Services are generally treated as made in the UK if the supplier 'belongs' to the UK (see s 7(10) of the VATA 1994). The effect is that a registered trader or professional is required to charge VAT in the UK. Section 9 of the VATA 1994 enacts rules for deciding where the supplier 'belongs'. The supplier of services is treated as belonging to a country if:

   •   he has a business establishment in that country and no other business establishment elsewhere; or

   •   he has no such establishment but his usual place of residence is by reference to that country; or

- he has such establishments both in that country and elsewhere, then the country in which his establishment exists which is most directly concerned with the supply.

Question 25

Part (a)

Outline the significance of distinguishing 'goods' from 'services' for VAT purposes.

Part (b)

Percy Paul has been in the retail business for several years. Ninety-five per cent of his retail business supplies are subject to VAT at the standard or zero rate; 5% are exempt. Percy envisages that, assuming the law remains unchanged, the exempt element of his business supplies is likely to increase to 10% during the next decade or so. He has decided to expand his business by financing the construction of a new building complex. Design plans are currently being drawn up. The new building will contain the shop and office and he foresees that the surplus space could be let out to other businesses. Percy has had preliminary discussions with potential tenants interested in using the surplus space. These possible tenants include a legal practice, an insurance company and a well known charity.

Explain to Percy Paul how VAT will affect the proposed building, indicating the circumstances under which irrecoverable input tax might arise.

Part (c)

Frank Turner, a registered VAT trader, seeks your advice in respect of relief for bad debts.

Advise him.

Answer plan

The following approach is suggested:

Part (a)

Consider:

- place of supply;
- time of supply;
- due date and rate of tax;
- status of transaction;
- supplies of goods – Schedule 4 of the VATA 1994;
- supplies of services – Schedule 4 of the VATA 1994.

Part (b)

You should discuss:

- partially exempt supplies;
- construction services taxable at standard rate;
- grant of an interest or right over land is exempt from VAT, unless the trader elects to waive the exemption;
- effect of lease to charity exceeding 21 years.

Part (c)

You will need to consider:

- bad debt relief – see s 36 of the VATA 1994.

Answer

Part (a)

VAT is charged on supplies of goods and services. The significance of distinguishing the two concepts are:

- whether a supply is regarded as made in the UK or elsewhere;

- the time when the supply is regarded as taking place and thus when tax is due, even the amount of tax payable and the rate of tax.

The legislation specifies a number of supplies which are treated either as supplies of goods or services (see Schedule 4 to the VATA 1994). Any supply which is not specified as one or the other will have been made for consideration and is deemed to be a supply of services (see s 5 of the VATA 1994).

The nature of a transaction is required to be analysed in order to determine its true status. This is often a question of degree. If a transaction involves a transfer of more than one item it will be treated as a multiple supply, for example, a sale of a sports ground and the services of the groundsman are treated as a supply of the sports ground and a supply of services.

The following supplies amount to a supply of goods unless they are specifically excluded from such treatment:

- any transfer of the 'whole property in goods': Schedule 4, para 1(1) of the VATA 1994. The term 'whole property' indicates that all rights of ownership existing in the goods must be transferred without retaining any reversionary rights. This is a question of law. It is immaterial whether or not title to the goods has passed (see *Excell Consumer Industries Ltd v Customs and Excise* (1985));

- although the transfer of possession in goods is normally a supply of services, such transfer amounts to a supply of goods where possession is transferred under an agreement for the sale of goods or under an agreement which expressly stipulates that property in the goods will pass in the future, for example, a hire purchase agreement (Schedule 4, para 1(2) of the VATA 1994);

- the production of goods by applying a process or treatment to goods belonging to another, for example, the cutting and sewing of a suit from cloth supplied by the customer (Schedule 4, para 2 of the VATA 1994);

- the supply of any form of power, heat, refrigeration or ventilation (Schedule 4, para 3 of the VATA 1994);

- the granting, assignment or surrender of a 'major interest' in land (Schedule 4, para 4 of the VATA 1994). A major interest in land is the freehold or leasehold interest having a term greater than 21 years.

A 'supply of services' is any supply undertaken for a consideration, but which is not a supply of goods (s 5(2)(b) of the VATA 1994). The following specific activities amount to a supply of services:

- the transfer of an undivided share of the property in goods or the transfer of possession of goods (Schedule 4, para 1 of the VATA 1994), for example, the sale of a half share in goods or the hire, lease or loan of goods;

- in pursuance of directions of a person carrying on a business, goods held or used for the purposes of the business are put to any private use or are used, or made available to any person for use, for any purpose other than a purpose of the business, whether or not for a consideration (Schedule 4, para 5(4) of the VATA 1994).

Part (b)

Any VAT registered business concerned with land or buildings is likely to make substantial exempt supplies and this is likely to lead to problems. In principle, input tax directly attributable to goods and services wholly used or to be used in making taxable supplies is fully recoverable and input tax directly related to exempt supplies cannot be reclaimed. If the whole of a business's VAT supplies is exempt it cannot register for VAT. But under the partial exemption rules, exempt supplies may, if they fall below specified *de minimis* limits,[1] be treated as taxable supplies so that the taxpayer is fully taxable and able to recover all input tax. It is necessary to quantify the amount of Percy Paul's exempt supplies. The rules also govern the calculation of the amount of input tax which can be reclaimed where the limits are exceeded. The remainder of input tax that relates to both taxable and exempt supplies, such as overheads, is deductible in the proportion that taxable supplies bear to total supplies. The proportion is expressed as a percentage. Alternatively, a 'special method' may be agreed with Customs and Excise.

Percy Paul expects that exempt supplies will increase proportionately in the future. This, together with the possible letting may mean that input tax will cease to be within the *de minimis* provisions, especially as the Capital Goods Scheme will require the input tax recovery to be reviewed each year over a 10 year period (assuming the building costs over £250,000). In this event, irrecoverable input tax would arise where the proportion of the input tax attributable to exempt supplies is above the *de minimis* limit.

Since the building is being constructed for use by Percy Paul in his business, the construction services are generally taxable at the standard rate.

Following the construction, Schedule 9, Group 1 of the VATA 1994, enacts that the grant of any interest in or right over land or any licence to occupy land is exempt from VAT, but Percy Paul is entitled to make an 'election to waive the exemption'. The election has the effect of converting what would otherwise be an exempt supply into a taxable supply: Schedule 10, para 2 of the VATA 1994. It would be in Mr Paul's interest to exercise the option because all supplies of the land and building made thereafter by Percy Paul will be treated as taxable supplies, save to the extent that the supply of goods and services relate to a dwelling or a building used or intended to be used for charitable purposes. The consequence of the election to Mr Paul is that he will be entitled to set off the input tax on the purchase or refurbishment or reconstruction of a non-residential building against taxable supplies which he makes.

On the other hand, if the option to tax is exercised, Mr Paul is required to take into consideration the impact this may have on his tenants. Exempt or partially exempt tenants, such as insurance companies and charities, will be unable to recover VAT charged to them and may only be willing to have a lower rent if this includes VAT.

If the lease to the charity were for a period exceeding 21 years, this would be treated as a grant of a major interest and eligible for zero rating and Mr Paul would be regarded as 'the person constructing' the building.

Part (c)

Relief from VAT in respect of bad debts became available from 1989: see s 36 of the VATA 1994. Relief is available where:

- a person has supplied goods and services for a consideration in money and has accounted for and paid VAT on the supply; and
- the whole or part of the consideration for the supply has been written off in his accounts as a bad debt; and
- a period of six months (beginning with the date of supply) has elapsed and the supplier holds the necessary records.

When the above conditions are met, the supplier may recover from Customs the VAT originally accounted for on the supply. If, however, the debtor subsequently repays the trader in whole or in part in respect of the bad debt, the VAT element within such repayments must be repaid to Customs.

The claim must be made within three years and six months from the later of the date of supply or the date when the consideration for it became payable.

A person who claims bad debt relief in respect of a supply made to a taxable person must notify the customer of this in writing within seven days of making the claim.

Note

1 The *de minimis* amount of exempt input tax is £625 per month on average or £7,500 per annum, provided that this exempt input tax is no more 50% of all input tax.

SECTION III
CAPITAL GAINS TAX

CHAPTER 8

CAPITAL GAINS TAX: GENERAL INTRODUCTION

Capital gains tax is charged on the *chargeable gain* accruing to a *person* (other than a company) on the *disposal* of an *asset* during a year of assessment.

A chargeable gain means a gain accruing on the disposal of an asset on or after 6 April 1982. The underlying notion is that gains accruing to a taxpayer before 6 April 1982 are exempt from capital gains tax. A *chargeable gain* (or allowable loss) is the difference between the disposal proceeds (actual and notional) as reduced by the aggregate of the cost of acquisition of the asset (including incidental costs of acquisition and disposal), the cost of improvement which is reflected in the asset at the time of disposal and indexation allowance up to 5 April 1998. For disposals after 5 April 1998 by individuals, trustees and personal representatives (PRs), indexation relief has been replaced by a taper relief which reduces the amount of the chargeable gains the longer the asset is held after that date, with a greater reduction for business assets: see s 2(A) of the Taxation of Chargeable Gains Tax Act 1992 (TCGA) (introduced by s 121 of the Finance Act 1998 (FA)). There is generally no tax advantage in holding an asset longer than 10 years, since the taper relief does not increase after this point. Taper relief is based on the size of the gain and the length of time an asset has been held. The relief ignores the amount of the initial investment. In assessing the chargeable gain eligible for taper relief on a disposal after 5 April 1998, the cost taken is the indexed cost up to 1 April 1998.

To attract taper relief, the asset either has to be a business asset owned for at least one complete year after 5 April 1998 or a non-business asset owned for at least three complete years after 5 April 1998 (these are the 'qualifying holding periods'). Gains realised by disposal of business assets qualify for a higher percentage of relief (with a maximum of 75% relief). Whereas the equivalent maximum relief with respect to non-business assets is 40%.

Companies generally continue to be subject to indexation allowance, although there are exceptions for companies which are settlors of trusts and also certain non-resident companies.

A *chargeable person* is a person 'resident' or 'ordinarily resident' in the UK. A partnership is not a separate legal person in English law. Each partner is liable to tax on his share of the gains realised by the partnership. Trustees and personal representatives are chargeable on the gains realised (actual or deemed) in the course of the administration of the trust or estate respectively. A company is not liable to capital gains tax as such but to corporation tax on the income profit and gains accruing on the disposal of assets.

An *asset* is defined in the widest possible manner in s 21 of the TCGA 1992. 'All forms of property' are assets including 'property created and property owned without being acquired'. This wide definition includes rights under a contract of a kind which is not assignable nor marketable, such as an employer's right to the personal services of an employee (see *O'Brien v Benson's Hosiery* (1979)). But a *spes* or hope of acquiring an interest is not a property right and, therefore, not an asset for capital gains tax purposes (see *Davenport v Chilver* (1983)).

The expression, *disposal*, has not been defined in the legislation. The Revenue take the view that a disposal is made 'whenever the ownership of an asset changes or the owner divests himself of rights and interest over the asset, for example, by sale, exchange or gift'. A disposal includes a part disposal of an asset. A part disposal is made whenever an interest in or right over an asset is created or where property derived from an asset remains undisposed (see s 21 of the TCGA 1992). The receipt by the owner of a capital sum derived from an asset amounts to a disposal even though no asset is acquired by the person making the payment (see s 22 of the TCGA 1992). Further, the destruction or loss of an asset is treated as a disposal (see s 24 of the TCGA 1992). The appropriation of a capital asset to trading stock is a disposal at market value if a chargeable gain or loss would thereby accrue. However, a trader assessable to income tax under Schedule D Case I may elect to bring in the asset at market value, less the gain or plus the loss, in computing the profits of his trade (see s 161 of the TCGA 1992).

The satisfaction of a debt is a disposal. However, no chargeable gain arises where the *original creditor* disposes of the debt. But there may be a chargeable gain when an assignee receives satisfaction of the debt or otherwise disposes of it (see ss 251 and 252 of the TCGA 1992). A disposal between a husband and wife living together gives rise to no gain and no loss. The spouse acquiring the asset is treated as acquiring the asset for its base value in the hands of the disponer. This rule does not apply if the asset is trading stock or the disposal is by way of a *donatio mortis causa*.

A gift or any other disposal, not by way of a bargain made at arm's length, is treated as a disposal and acquisition for a consideration equal to the market value of the asset (see s 17 of the TCGA 1992). Transactions made between connected persons are treated as made otherwise than at arm's length (s 18(2) of the TCGA 1992).

On the death of an individual, the assets of which he is competent to dispose:

(a) are deemed to be acquired by his personal representatives (PRs) for a consideration equal to their market value at the time of the death; but

(b) are not deemed to be disposed of by the deceased (see s 62(1) of the TCGA 1992).

If the PRs dispose of the assets to a person other than the *legatee* this may produce a gain (or loss) on general principles. But, if the PRs dispose of the asset to the legatee (or the assets are disposed of on intestacy), the legatee (next of kin) is treated as if the acquisition by the PRs had been his acquisition, without a chargeable disposal (see s 62(4) of the TCGA 1992).

There are special rules applicable to settlements made *inter vivos* or on death.

Question 26

What one is looking for is an entity which can be sensibly described as being a dwellinghouse though split up into different buildings performing different functions ... The question is one of degree, and as in all such cases the circumstances must be looked at as a whole. [*Per* Vinelott J in *Williams v Merrylees* (1987).]

Explain this statement and discuss how far the courts have clarified the meaning of a dwellinghouse for the purposes of the dwellinghouse exemption under ss 222–26 of the TCGA 1992.

Answer plan

A suggested plan is as follows:

- question of fact – *Edwards v Bairstow and Harrison* (1956);
- *Batey v Wakefield* (1981);
- *Markey v Sanders* (1987);
- *Williams v Merrylees* (1987);
- *Lewis v Rook* (1992);
- *Honour v Norris* (1992);
- *Makins v Elson* (1977);
- *Moore v Thompson* (1986);
- *Varty v Lynes* (1976).

Answer

Vinelott J, in *Williams v Merrylees* (1987), considered that the expression, 'dwellinghouse', included in the private dwellinghouse exemption within s 222 of the TCGA 1992, is a question of fact. This assessment of the status of the concept is disputed in a subsequent decision. But assuming that Vinelott J is correct, this would mean that the decisions of the Commissioners on questions of primary facts are final. An appeal lies to the High Court on points of law by way of case stated. The Commissioners' decisions based on findings of fact may amount to questions of law and are capable of being upset on appeal if those findings were such that no reasonable tribunal, properly instructed, could have come to the conclusion arrived at by the Commissioners. In other words, inferences drawn from facts are conclusions of law and, if the facts are not reflected in the conclusions drawn, the High Court has no option but to assume that there has been some misconception of the law. This principle is known as the rule in *Edwards v Bairstow and Harrison* (1956) which pervades not only tax law, but law generally. Thus, applying Vinelott J's approach to the question, what is a dwellinghouse? It would appear that the question, whether a structure within the grounds of a dwellinghouse is itself part of the dwellinghouse, is determined initially by the Inspector of Taxes but the taxpayer has a right of appeal to the Commissioners on a point of law or fact. A further right of appeal to the High Court exists but only on points of law. An initial issue for the High Court to ascertain is whether there was any evidence to support the decision of the Commissioners. Even if the judge would have come to a conclusion which is different from the Commissioners, the appeal would not be allowed if there is sufficient evidence to support the Commissioners' decision that the structure is or is not a dwellinghouse. With this limitation in mind, the question that arises is whether s 222 relief extends to multiple buildings within the same grounds owned by one person.

Section 222 relief from capital gains tax is available in respect of a gain made on the disposal by an individual of the whole or part of a dwellinghouse (or an interest in a dwellinghouse) which is his only or main residence. The relief extends to a garden or grounds of the dwellinghouse up to half a hectare or such larger area as is required for the reasonable enjoyment of the house as a residence. Generally, the relief is calculated by reference to periods of occupation as a main dwellinghouse.

The Revenue's view is that buildings which form part of the dwellinghouse are eligible for relief. Included in this classification are garages and fuel stores. Likewise, buildings which are ancillary to the gardens and grounds (such as greenhouses and sheds) qualify for relief if they fall within the permitted area. Whether other buildings (such as staff and aged relatives' accommodation) fall within the definition of 'dwellinghouse' is, as far as case law is concerned, surrounded by uncertainty.

The starting point for any discussion concerning the question of whether the existence of two or more units could be treated as part of a single dwellinghouse is *Batey v Wakefield* (1981). In this case, the taxpayer built a dwellinghouse for himself in 1.1 acres of land. He subsequently built a chalet bungalow with its own access on the land for occupation by a caretaker employee. The bungalow was physically separate from the main house and was separately rated, although the caretaker lived in the accommodation rent free and free from rates. The bungalow was sold together with 0.15 acres of land. The taxpayer contended that the bungalow formed part of the main house in a way similar to a wing added to a house to accommodate his servants. The Court of Appeal decided that the taxpayer was entitled to claim the relief under what is now s 222. A dwellinghouse may extend to several buildings not physically joined together. The fact that the bungalow was physically separate from the main building was irrelevant and the fact that the structure comprised separate accommodation or a self-contained flat was inconclusive in determining whether such accommodation was part of the dwellinghouse. It is necessary to identify the dwellinghouse which is the taxpayer's residence. That dwellinghouse may or may not be comprised in one physical building. If the dwellinghouse consists of a number of different buildings which are part and parcel of the whole, each part appurtenant to and occupied for the purposes of the main dwellinghouse, then each structure is to be considered as part of the dwellinghouse. The bungalow was built and occupied to provide services and caretaking facilities for the benefit of the main house. In effect, the bungalow was occupied by the taxpayer through his employee. The latter was employed for the purpose of permitting the taxpayer's reasonable enjoyment of his own residence.

In *Markey v Sanders* (1987), the taxpayer owned a country estate with a main house and several outbuildings. Some time later, she had built a three bedroom bungalow which had its own quarter acre garden. This was occupied rent free by her gardener and housekeeper. This structure was not separately rated. On the sale of the entire estate, including the bungalow, the question arose whether the taxpayer was eligible for the private residence exemption. The Commissioners decided in favour of the taxpayer, but the High Court reversed this decision because the only reasonable conclusion from the facts was that the bungalow was not part of the taxpayer's residence. The court propounded the 'entity' test, which is whether the group of buildings, looked on as a whole, could be fairly regarded as a single dwellinghouse used as the taxpayer's main residence. In order to satisfy this test, two conditions must be fulfilled. The first condition is that the occupation of the building in question must increase the taxpayer's enjoyment of the main house. The second condition is that the bungalow must be 'very closely adjacent' to the main building. On the facts of this case, the first of these conditions was satisfied, but the second condition (which is a flexible test) did not entitle the commissioners to apply it absolutely regardless of the facts. The only conclusion that could be drawn from the decision of the Commissioners is that they did not consider the second requirement, as stated above, or that they applied a different and incorrect test.

However, in *Williams v Merrylees*, the court doubted the emphasis given to proximity in *Markey v Sanders*. This case concerned a gardener's cottage situated 200 metres from the main house. The latter was set in four acres of land. The cottage was not disposed of until four years after the disposal of the main house. Nevertheless, the Commissioners found that part of the gain corresponding to the taxpayer's period of ownership of the main house was exempt. The court refused to interfere with that decision. The buildings were a single dwellinghouse. The test is whether there is an entity which can sensibly be described as being a dwellinghouse, although split up into different buildings performing different functions. This was a question of fact and degree. The closeness or otherwise of the buildings was a very important factor, but it was not right to isolate a single factor as essential before the Commissioners could conclude that separate buildings were a dwellinghouse. Regard must be had to layout and other characteristics of the property as a whole.

In *Lewis v Rook* (1992), a taxpayer purchased a large house, 10 acres of land and two cottages. Some time later she sold one of the cottages which was situated some 190 yards from her house and had been occupied by her gardener. The Revenue issued an assessment on the gain and she appealed claiming relief under what is now s 222. The Commissioners allowed her appeal but the Court of Appeal reversed this decision. The true test was whether the cottage was within the *curtilage* of, and *appurtenant* to, the main property so as to be part of the entity, that is, whether the cottage constituted part of the dwellinghouse occupied by the taxpayer as her main residence. This was not a question of fact, but of law. On the facts of this case, the cottage was some way from the main building and separated by a large garden.

In *Honour v Norris* (1992), it was held that one of four flats in different buildings in various locations in a London square, all occupied by the taxpayer and his family, could not be regarded as part of a single dwellinghouse as a matter of 'common sense'.

In the light of the above discussion, the current position is quite unsatisfactory concerning the status of multiple buildings within the same grounds. The imprecision of the word, 'curtilage' as a significant factor in resolving this issue must open the 'floodgates' to litigation. The Revenue's assessment of the position, as stated in the *Tax Bulletin* of August 1994,[1] is to draw a distinction between the curtilage of the main house and the curtilage of an estate as a whole. The fact that an entire estate may be contained within a single boundary does not mean that buildings on the estate should be regarded as being within the curtilage of the building.

In order to obtain the relief, the garden or grounds of the dwellinghouse (up to the permitted area) are required to be sold with the dwelling. Thus, the appropriation and disposal of part of a garden was liable to capital gains tax as a separate disposal, following the disposal of the house and part of the garden in *Varty v Lynes* (1976). In the *Tax Bulletin* in August 1994, the Revenue confirm that where a dwellinghouse and garden are sold together, but after the taxpayer had ceased to occupy the property they would not seek to charge the sale of the garden. Moreover, in *Makins v Elson* (1977), a dwellinghouse has been held to include a caravan raised up on bricks and connected to water and electricity supplies. On the other hand, in *Moore v Thompson* (1986), a caravan which was not connected to the services and used by the taxpayer while renovating his farmhouse was not included as a dwellinghouse.

Note

1   From the *Tax Bulletin*, August 1994:

Whether one building is part and parcel of another will depend primarily on whether there is a close geographical relationship between them. Furthermore, because the test is to identify an integral whole, a wall or fence separating two buildings will normally be sufficient to establish that they are not within the same curtilage. Similarly, a public road or stretch of tidal water will set a limit to the curtilage of the building. Buildings which are within the curtilage of a main house will normally pass automatically on a conveyance of that house without having to be specifically mentioned. There is a distinction between the curtilage of a main house and the curtilage of an estate as a whole. The fact that the whole estate may be contained within a single boundary does not mean that the buildings on the estate should be regarded as within the curtilage of the main house.

Question 27

On her father's death in April 1998, Helen (then aged 25) inherited two engravings worth £5,500 as a set, an antique necklace worth £15,000 and a tiara worth £20,000 (an heirloom which was subject to a term that it could not be disposed of by Helen but was to be retained and inherited by her eldest child).

For Christmas 1998, Helen gave one of the engravings to her brother and retained the other.

In March 1998, the necklace was stolen. It was then worth £19,000, but was uninsured.

In February 1998, Helen spent £1,000 having the tiara cleaned and reset. In March 1998, this item was stolen, but was insured. Its market value was £30,000, but was insured for only £25,000.

On her father's death, his life interest in a trust set up by Helen's grandfather passed to Helen. The property in the trust will pass to Helen absolutely when she is 30.

Advise Helen as to what charges to capital gains tax may arise on these facts.

Answer plan

A good answer should deal with the following issues:
* valuation and non disposal rule concerning death;
* uplift in legatee's base cost;
* gifts and disposals otherwise than at arm's length;
* disposals to connected persons;
* s 262 – relief on a disposal (including part disposal) of an asset not exceeding £6,000;

- s 24 – disposal on the occasion of the entire loss of an asset;
- deductibility of expenditure in computing net capital gains;
- notional disposal under s 22 when capital sum derived from asset;
- s 72 – deemed disposal but no charge on the death of a life tenant when the settlement continues;
- s 71 – deemed disposal where a person becomes absolutely entitled to settled property.

Answer

Capital gains tax is charged on the gains accruing to a chargeable person on the making of a chargeable disposal of a chargeable asset. The gain is taxed on a current year basis on the difference between the disposal proceeds (actual or notional) and allowable expenditure. Such expenditure includes the cost of acquisition (actual or deemed) improvement expenditure, indexation allowances up to 5 April 1998 and taper relief measured from 6 April 1998 and the incidental costs of acquisition and disposal.

The tax is payable on 1 December following the year of assessment.

For capital gains tax purposes, death is treated as an occasion giving rise to an uplift in the capital gains tax base at market value on the date of death. There is no liability to capital gains tax. Section 62(1) of the TCGA 1992 declares that on a person's death, the assets of which he was competent to dispose are deemed to be acquired by his personal representatives for a consideration equal to their market value at the date of death, but are not deemed to be disposed by the deceased. Thus, the personal representatives get an uplift in the capital gains base at market value. The expression, 'competent to dispose', is defined in s 62(10) and is generally regarded as the deceased's free estate. Section 62(4) enacts that when the personal representatives dispose of the asset to a legatee, the latter is treated as acquiring the asset on the date and for the value at which the personal representatives acquired the property. Accordingly, the legatee's acquisition relates back to the personal representatives and their base costs are acquired by the legatee. A legatee is defined in s 64(3) as including persons acquiring property under a testamentary disposition or on intestacy. Applying this principle to the facts, when Helen's father died in April 1998, the assets which Helen acquired are deemed to have notional acquisition costs equivalent to their market value on the date of death of Helen's father. These assets are the engravings valued at £5,500, the necklace valued at £15,000 and the tiara valued at £20,000. We have not been given the value of the trust assets at the time of the death of Helen's father.

The engravings

The donation of one of the engravings to her brother constitutes a disposal of the asset 'otherwise than by way of a bargain at arm's length', that is, the deemed disposal proceeds are treated as the market value at the time of the transfer (see s 17(1) of the TCGA 1992). In any event, the transfer of the engraving is to a 'connected person' as defined in s 286(2) of the TCGA 1992, and s 18(2) of the TCGA declares that a disposal to a connected person is treated as a transaction 'otherwise than at arm's length'. It is necessary to quantify the value of the asset transferred.

The gift of one of the set of engravings to Helen's brother constitutes a disposal of part of an asset for capital gains tax purposes. For this purpose, it is necessary to value the part retained by Helen. Indeed, it is necessary to value both engravings as a set prior to the disposal. In the absence of such values, it is necessary to make two assumptions as to the value of the set at the time of disposal. First, the value of the set did not exceed £6,000. Secondly, the value of the set exceeded £6,000. In each of these circumstances, it is taken for granted that the articles are identical. If they are not, then the market value of the asset remaining undisposed of will be crucial.

On the assumption that the market value of the set does not exceed £6,000, the disposal of the engraving to Helen's brother will be exempt from tax under s 262 of the TCGA 1992 as a disposal of tangible moveable property with a consideration not exceeding £6,000. Although one item of the set is transferred it is still necessary to aggregate the value of the remaining asset with the notional disposal proceeds, in order to ascertain whether s 262 of the relief is available or not (see s 262(5)(a) of the TCGA 1992).

On the other hand, if the market value of the set (that is, the aggregate of the notional consideration for the disposal and the market value of the remaining item) exceeds £6,000, s 262(5)(b) enacts a principle designed to reduce the tax limitation in proportion to the interest retained. Section 262(5)(b) provides that, where the sum of the consideration for the disposal and the market value of the undisposed of remainder of the set exceeds £6,000, the part of any chargeable gain that is excluded shall be so much of the gain as exceeds five thirds of the difference between the aggregate sum and £6,000, multiplied by the fraction equal to the consideration for the disposal divided by the aggregate sum. Thus, if the sum of the consideration for the disposal and the market value of the undisposed of remainder does not exceed £6,000 the limit of the consideration liable to capital gains tax is calculated by applying the following formula: $((A + B) - £6,000) \times A/A + B \times 5/3$, where A is the consideration received (actually or notionally) for the part disposal and B is the market value of the part retained by the disponer.

Finally, there are special rules enacted in s 262(5)(c) with the object of restricting loss relief where the aggregate amount of the consideration for the disposal and the market value of the undisposed asset is less than £6,000.

The necklace

As outlined above, the new acquisition cost of the necklace is its market value at the time of the death of Helen's father. Section 24(1) of the TCGA 1992 enacts that the occasion of the entire loss, destruction, dissipation or extinction of an asset shall constitute a disposal, irrespective of whether or not a capital sum is received by way of compensation or otherwise. The purpose of the deemed disposal under this provision is to enable a loss claim to be established by the taxpayer. Although the provision does not expressly refer to the date of the disposal, it is accepted that this occurs on the date of destruction. Accordingly, since the asset at this time is valueless the allowable expenditure (but not including indexation allowance: see s 53(2)(A), such allowance cannot create or increase a capital loss) will be treated as giving rise to a capital loss.

Losses must be relieved primarily against gains of the taxpayer in the same year. Any surplus losses may be carried forward and set against the taxpayer's first available gain in future years, without time limit. There are no provisions entitling a taxpayer to carry back losses and set them against gains of previous years, save for net losses created by an individual in the year of death. Moreover, capital losses cannot be set against the taxpayer's income for tax purposes. The consequence of this loss made by Helen under s 24 is that, apart from setting it off against any gains made in the current year, she is required to carry it forward and set it against future gains.

The tiara

The tiara was acquired on the death of Helen's father at a market value (and, thus, notional acquisition cost) of £30,000. Admittedly, the asset was subject to a restraint on disposal but this seems to be irrelevant to the circumstances because it has been stolen.

The expenditure of £1,000 on cleaning and resetting the tiara may not be wholly allowable. It would be sensible to apportion the expenditure and ascertain the amount spent on each purpose. Allowable expenditure is defined in s 38 of the TCGA 1992. Expenditure is required to be incurred 'wholly and exclusively' in the acquisition of the asset, including the incidental costs of acquisition and disposal and indexation allowance. Moreover, expenditure incurred for the purpose of enhancing the value of the asset which is reflected in the state or nature of the asset at the time of the disposal will be allowed. Enhancement expenditure relates to capital as opposed to recurring or revenue expenditure. By reference to income tax principles, it would appear that expenditure incurred in putting an asset in a marketable state such as cleaning, is a revenue expense. In other words, the cleaning expenditure does not create a new asset but is simply expenditure in order to maintain the asset. This portion of the expenditure of £1,000 may be disallowed by the Revenue. On the other hand, expenditure incurred in resetting the tiara may be allowed in computing the net gains for capital gains tax purposes.

Such expenditure has the effect of fundamentally altering the state or appearance of the asset and is reflected in the nature of the asset at the time of disposal.

The loss of the asset, as explained above, is itself considered to be a disposal (see s 24 of the TCGA 1992). Where the taxpayer receives compensation or insurance moneys for an asset which is totally lost or destroyed, there appears to be a further disposal under s 22 of the TCGA as it is a capital sum derived from the asset, namely, the insurance contract. This is the position even though no asset is acquired by the person paying the capital sum. In this respect, s 22(3) defines a capital sum as any money or money's worth which is not excluded from the consideration taken into account in the computation of the gain. Specifically, Helen would appear to have made a disposal under s 22(1)(a) and (b), which states:

(a) capital sums received by way of compensation for ... the loss, destruction or dissipation of assets ...;

(b) capital sums received under a policy of insurance of the risk of ... loss of assets ...

Although there is an apparent conflict in wording between s 24(1) and s 22(1), the view of the Revenue is that once an asset is lost or destroyed there can be no further disposal of it. Accordingly, where compensation is paid for the loss of an asset, the compensation is treated as the consideration on that disposal. Alternatively, it is arguable that when both sections overlap there are two disposals, first, when the asset is lost and, secondly, when compensation is received. The loss of the asset valued at £30,000 gives rise to a disposal and the receipt of the insurance proceeds of £25,000 gives rise to another disposal. On this basis, Helen would be treated as making a loss of £5,000, the difference between the insurance proceeds and the market value of the asset.

The trust

On the death of Helen's father the settlement continues with Helen becoming entitled to an interest under the trust until she attains the age of 30. The effect of this scenario is that there is a deemed disposal and reacquisition of the assets by the trustees at their market value at the time of the father's death. Capital gains tax is not chargeable and the trustees gain a tax free uplift (see s 72 of the TCGA).

However, s 71 of the TCGA 1992 provides that a deemed disposal of the assets occur whenever a person becomes absolutely entitled to the settled property as against the trustees. This will happen when Helen attains the age of 30. At this age, Helen will become the absolute equitable owner and the property will become unsettled within the meaning of s 60 of the TCGA 1992. The assets will be deemed to be disposed by the trustees at their market value. Further, any unused allowable losses accruing to the trustees in respect of that property will be surrendered to Helen to the extent that the same cannot be set off against the chargeable gains accruing to the trustees of the settlement.

Question 28

On 1 May 1998, Sam settles 50,000 shares in Electronics Ltd upon trust for Andy for life, then for Betty (Sam's daughter) for life, then for such of Betty's children as the trustees should (within the perpetuity period) by deed appoint and subject thereto, upon trust for Colin contingently upon attaining the age of 25 with gifts over. The trustees were given the power in the trust instrument to release the above-mentioned power of appointment.

All the parties are resident and domiciled in the UK and the shares have risen steadily in value.

Advise the trustees as to what charges (if any) to capital gains tax arise in the following sets of circumstances which take place in chronological order:

(a) Andy dies shortly after the creation of the settlement;

(b) the trustees sell 5,000 shares which they used in the administration of the trust;

(c) Betty releases her life interest;

(d) the trustees appoint 1,000 shares absolutely to Betty's 22 year old son, David, and then release their power of appointment;

(e) the original trustees retire from the trust and new trustees are appointed in their stead. The trust property becomes vested in these trustees;

(f) Colin attains the age of 25 but the remaining shares continue to be held in the names of the trustees;

(g) the following year, the trustees sold 2,000 of those shares at Colin's request.

Answer plan

To answer a question such as this effectively, you should consider the following points:

- definition of settled property;
- chargeable disposal on the creation of a settlement;
- connected persons and the effect;
- termination of a life interest in possession by virtue of death but with the continuation of the settlement;
- actual disposals by trustees;
- deemed disposal by trustees whenever a person becomes absolutely entitled to settled property – s 71 of the TCGA 1992;
- status of trustees – s 69 of the TCGA 1992.

Answer

The concept of a 'settlement' is not defined in the capital gains tax legislation. But 'settled property' has been defined in s 68 of the TCGA 1992 as 'any property held in trust other than property to which s 60 applies'. Section 60 enacts that:

- assets held for another by a nominee or bare trustee are treated as if they are vested in the person for whom the assets are held, that is, the beneficiary; or
- property is held upon trust for persons who would be absolutely entitled as against the trustees but for being an infant or other person under disability; or
- the fund is held for two or more persons who are or would be jointly (concurrently but not in succession) and absolutely entitled.

It follows that the definition of unsettled property in s 60 is used as a means of classifying settled property, and settled property is ascertained by reference to trust property not being unsettled. There are a number of difficulties inherent in this definition but such issues do not arise in this problem. It is clear that Sam's trust settlement in 1998 satisfies the definition of settled property. The property (50,000 shares in Electronics Ltd) is held upon trust and none of the beneficiaries is initially entitled to the property absolutely. The effect of the creation of the trust in settled property is that this, in itself, amounts to a disposal of assets by the settlor (see s 70 of the TCGA 1992). The position remains the same whether the settlement is revocable or irrevocable and notwithstanding that the transferor has some interest as a trustee or beneficiary under the settlement.

The value of the transfer by the settlor, Sam, is determined by reference to the 'connected persons' definition within s 286(3) of the TCGA 1992. Under this provision the trustees are connected with the settlor and individuals who are connected with the settlor. Thus, Sam and the trustees are connected. The effect of this determination is that a disposal between connected persons is treated as giving rise to a 'transaction otherwise than by way of a bargain made at arm's length' (see s 18(2)). Such transactions are deemed to give rise to disposals and acquisitions at market value (see s 17(1) of the TCGA 1992). The value of the shares disposed by Sam and the value of the shares acquired by the trustees are treated as the same. Sam's circumstances are taken into consideration in determining the amount of tax payable by him. As far as the trustees are concerned, they acquire the assets for a notional price, equivalent to the market value of the shares on the date of the creation of the settlement. During the continuation of the settlement, the trustees are subject to actual and deemed disposals of trust assets.

Part (a)

Since 1971, Parliament introduced the policy of not making death an occasion for a charge to capital gains tax. Andy, who enjoyed a life interest, dies shortly after the creation of the settlement but the settlement continues within the definition of s 68. In such an event, no charge to capital gains tax arises but a deemed disposal and reacquisition by the trustees at the market value of the assets corresponding to the deceased's interest takes place. A 'life interest' is inclusively defined in s 72(3) and includes a right to the income of settled property (as well as further exclusions and inclusions). As far as the quantum of the disposal is concerned, the policy of the Act is to treat an amount of capital corresponding to the proportionate amount of income as disposed and reacquired by the trustees. Since Andy was entitled to a life interest in the entire assets of the trust, the full capital of the trust is deemed to be disposed and reacquired by the trustees at market value but without a charge to tax, that is, a tax free uplift in the capital gains base is acquired by the trustees.

Part (b)

The sale of 5,000 shares by the trustees in order to facilitate the administration of the trust, amounts to an actual disposal by the trustees. The ordinary general principles concerning such disposals operate. Subject to exemptions and reliefs, the trustees are liable to tax for 1998–99 at the rate of 34%. If Sam is a higher rate income tax payer, it is imperative that he and his spouse are excluded from any benefit under the settlement, whether directly or indirectly: see s 77 of the Capital Gains Tax Act 1992 (CGTA). If Sam and/or his spouse is or may become entitled to a benefit under the settlement, the trustees will become liable to capital gains tax at the settlor's higher rate of income tax, that is, 40%. On the facts, it would appear that s 77 of the CGTA 1992 has been avoided.

The trustees may also be entitled to claim their annual allowances which is one half 'the exempt amount for the year': see Schedule 1 to the TCGA (for 1998–99, this amount is £3,400).

Part (c)

The release by Betty of her life interest in the trust assets amounts to a termination of a life interest in possession but the property remains settled. For capital gains tax purposes, no charge arises and no uplift in the capital gains base accrues. Had this event occurred by virtue of Betty's death the position would have been the same as existed for Andy.

We have not been told of the circumstances concerning the release by Betty. In general, no chargeable gain arises in the hands of a beneficiary where she disposes of an interest under a settlement, provided that she or someone before her did not acquire their interest for consideration in money or money's worth (see s 76 of the TCGA 1992). The proviso just mentioned does not apply to consideration consisting of another interest under the settlement. The exemption does not apply where, at the time of disposal, the trustees are neither resident nor ordinarily resident in the UK (see s 85(1) of the TCGA 1992). From the facts it would appear that none of these limitations apply when Betty releases her life interest.

The release of the trustees' power of appointment does not involve a disposal of a life interest in possession. The objects of a discretionary trust or power of appointment do not have an interest in the trust property but merely a *spes*, or hope, of acquiring an interest (see *Gartside v IRC* (1968)). This is not a chargeable event because the objects of the power (Betty's children) did not have an interest in the trust property before the trustees released their power of appointment.

Part (d)

The appointment of 1,000 shares absolutely to Betty's 22 year old son, David, attracts the exit charge in the hands of the trustees. Section 71(1) provides for a deemed disposal of the chargeable assets in the fund, whenever a person becomes absolutely entitled to any portion of the settled property. The assets of the fund are treated as being sold by the trustees for their market value on the date of appointment and immediately reacquired for the same value. To the extent that David becomes entitled to the property, the assets are treated as becoming unsettled.

Part (e)

The retirement and appointment of new trustees resulting in the transfer of the trust property in the hands of the new trustees does not amount to a chargeable event. Section 69 of the TCGA 1992 provides that the trustees of a settlement shall be treated as being a single and continuing body of persons distinct from the persons who may from time to time be trustees. Thus, the identity of the trustees is immaterial. The trusteeship as a whole is considered to be the same throughout the subsistence of the trust.

Part (f)

When Colin attains the age of 25, the trust property becomes unsettled because the beneficiary becomes absolutely entitled to the trust property as against the trustees. The effect is that a chargeable disposal is effected by the trustees. The assets of the trust to which Colin becomes entitled are deemed to be disposed of by the trustee and immediately reacquired by them as bare trustees. The consideration for the disposal is the market value of the assets on this occasion (see s 71 of the TCGA 1992). Since the event does not occur on the death of the life tenant, there is a charge imposed on the trustees.

Where a person becomes absolutely entitled to settled property as against the trustee, any unused allowable losses accruing to the trustee in respect of that property are carried forward to the person becoming absolutely. The procedure is that the trustees are required to set off such losses against gains accruing to them and any surplus is then surrendered to the person becoming absolutely entitled (see s 71(2) of the TCGA 1992).

Capital gains tax in respect of gains accruing to trustees may be charged on and in the name of one or more trustees (see s 65 of the TCGA 1992). With effect from 1996–97, a capital gains tax assessment may be made on any one or more of the 'relevant trustees' (s 65(1) TCGA 1992, as substituted by s 114(1) of the FA 1995). Trustees in the tax year in which the chargeable gains accrued and any subsequent trustees are 'relevant trustees'.

If the capital gains tax assessed on any trustee is not paid within six months from the time it becomes payable and the asset (or the proceeds), in respect of which the gains accrued, is transferred by the trustees to a person who is absolutely entitled, that person may instead be assessed (in the name of the trustees) at any time within two years from the time the tax became payable (see s 69(4) of the TCGA 1992).

Part (g)

The trustees, as bare trustees, sell 2,000 of the unsettled shares at Colin's request. In these circumstances, assets held on a bare trust for Colin are treated as if they are vested in Colin (see s 60(1) of the TCGA 1992). Accordingly, Colin's personal circumstances are taken into consideration in determining the amount of tax that is payable in respect of the disposal.

Note

A 'bare trustee' is a person who holds property for someone who is (or would be but for being an infant or mentally subnormal) absolutely entitled as against the trustee. In other words, the beneficiary(ies) has (have) the exclusive right, subject to any outstanding charge, lien, etc, for the payment of taxes and the like, to direct the trustees in the manner in which they may deal with the asset (s 60(2) of the TCGA 1992).

CHAPTER 9

EXEMPTIONS AND RELIEFS

Exemptions and reliefs

There are a number of exemptions and reliefs enacted. The main ones are mentioned below:

(1) annual exemption (s 3 of the Taxation and Chargeable Gains Act 1992 (TCGA)): an individual is not liable to capital gains tax if his net gains for the year of assessment does not exceed 'the exempt amount' (£6,800 for 1998–99);

(2) private dwelling house (ss 222–26 of the TCGA 1992): a taxpayer is entitled to total exemption from capital gains tax on a gain accruing to him on a disposal of a private dwelling house together with grounds of up to 0.5 hectare (or larger grounds as the Commissioners may determine). The taxpayer is required to establish that the dwelling has been his only or main residence throughout the period of ownership (ignoring the last three years). If the house has been his main residence for only part of the period of ownership, a proportion of the gain is exempt. Where a husband and wife are living together, there can only be one dwelling house subject to this relief;

(3) chattels sold for £6,000 (s 262 of the TCGA 1992): a gain on the disposal of tangible moveable property is exempt if the consideration for the disposal does not exceed £6,000. If the asset is sold for more than £6,000, the chargeable gain is five thirds of the difference between the value of the consideration and £6,000;

(4) wasting assets (s 45 of the TCGA 1992): the gains accruing on the disposal of tangible moveable assets, which have a predictable useful life not exceeding 50 years (wasting assets), are exempt from capital gains tax. The exemption does not apply if the asset has been used for the purpose of a trade and qualified for capital allowances;

(5) roll-over relief (ss 152–59 of the TCGA 1992): where a trader disposes of assets of the business ('old assets') for a gain and utilises the proceeds of sale to acquire new business assets

('new assets'), and the 'old' and 'new' assets are within the listed classes (s 155), the trader may elect to postpone his liability to capital gains tax. The gain accruing to the trader is deducted from the acquisition cost of the new asset. The postponement is until such time as the new assets are disposed of without being replaced or the discontinuance of the trade;

(6) retirement relief (s 163, 164 and Schedule 6): this relief is available to individuals who have reached retirement age (55 or over) and have made a disposal of a business, or shares in a family trading company in which he was a full time working director. The relief is also available to individuals who are compelled to retire below the age of 50 for reasons of ill health. The maximum amount of relief is £625,000 (that is, £250,000 + 50% of gains between £1 m – £250,000).

Following the introduction of taper relief for assets held long term, retirement relief is to be phased out over a period of five years, commencing with the year of assessment 1999–2000. The relief will be evenly reduced for each year within the five year period – see s 140 of the Finance Act 1998 (FA);

(7) transfer of a business to a company (s 162): a special form of 'hold-over' relief is available to a taxpayer when he transfers a business as a going concern to a company in exchange for shares in the company. The gain accruing on the disposal of the business is not chargeable until the shares are disposed of, and the acquisition value of the shares is reduced by the amount of the gain;

(8) deferred relief for reinvestment: where a gain in respect of shares issued to an individual and certain trustees after 5 April 1998 is reinvested in an enterprise investment scheme (EIS) shares, the gain may be set against the acqusition cost of those shares – s 150(A) of the TCGA 1992, as amended by s 74 of the FA 1998;

(9) gifts of business assets: capital gains tax liability may be postponed (or held over) on a disposal of certain business assets otherwise than at arm's length until the transferee subsequently makes a chargeable disposal. The relief must be claimed within six years of the end of the relevant year by both the transferor and transferee. Where the transferees are

trustees of a settlement, the claim for relief should be made by the transferor alone – s 165 of the TCGA 1992;

(10) miscellaneous exemptions. Section 51(1) of the TCGA 1992 enacts that winnings from betting, lotteries or games with prizes are not liable to capital gains tax.

Similarly, compensation or damage for any wrong or injury suffered by an individual in a personal or professional capacity are not liable to capital gains tax (see s 51(2) of the TCGA 1992).

The rights of an insurer under an insurance policy do not constitute a chargeable asset. Similarly, there is no charge to capital gains tax on the disposal of an interest in or rights under a policy of life assurance or deferred annuity. However, there is a disposal where the disponer is not the original beneficial owner and acquired the rights or interest for a consideration in money or money's worth (see s 210 of the TCGA 1992).

Motor cars and other road vehicles constructed or adapted for the carriage of passengers and of a type commonly used as private vehicles are not chargeable assets (see s 263 of the TCGA).

Likewise, decorations awarded for valour or gallant conduct, acquired otherwise than for money or money's worth are not chargeable assets (s 268 of the TCGA).

Question 29

Part (a)

Charles loaned Derek £6,000 repayable in six months time. Despite Charles' repeated requests for repayment of the loan Derek failed to repay the sum borrowed. Finally, Derek offered Charles a painting worth £3,000 and half of whatever he may receive under the will of his father, Fred. Charles reluctantly agreed to accept this offer and Derek transferred the painting to Charles. Charles was able to sell the painting for £6,300. Fred died shortly afterwards leaving Derek a legacy of £10,000. Derek fulfilled his promise and on receipt of the legacy paid Charles £5,000.

Part (b)

Charles gave a valuable brooch to his wife as a birthday gift. The market value of the brooch was £9,000. The item of jewellery was inherited by Charles on the death of his mother.

Consider the capital gains tax implications of the above facts.

Answer plan

A good answer will discuss the following:

- definition of a debt;
- s 251(1) – exemption in respect of debts;
- s 251(3) – property acquired by a creditor in satisfaction of a debt;
- s 262 – exemption in respect tangible moveable property transferred for a consideration not exceeding £6,000;
- s 22 – disposal in respect of a capital sum derived from an asset;
- s 62(4) – uplift in the legatee's capital gains base;
- s 58 – no gain and no loss disposal by a husband living with his wife;
- 'living together' definition;
- alternatively, the connected persons' rule.

Answer

Part (a)

The loan by Charles amounts to a debt repayable in six months time. A debt is a chargeable asset. The broad definition of an asset[1] inserted in s 21 specifically includes a debt (see s 21(1)(a) of the TCGA 1992). But the expression, 'debt' has not been defined by statute. It is generally taken to mean a sum payable in respect of a liquidated money demand. A mere contingent liability which may never ripen into a present debt, is not a 'debt' (see *Marson v Marriage* (1980)). The debt is required to be of an ascertainable amount payable at an ascertainable time (see *Marren v Ingles*

(1980)). On the facts presented, the loan creates a 'debt' in that the amount repayable is liquidated and the date of repayment is specific.

The general rule is that on the creation of a loan, whether in sterling or in some other currency, no chargeable gain accrues to the original creditor or his personal representative or legatee on the disposal of the debt, except in the case of a 'debt on security'[2] (see s 251(1)). A disposal of a debt includes the satisfaction of a debt or part of it (see s 251(2)). Thus, had Derek repaid the full amount of the debt, this would have been treated as a disposal for capital gains tax purposes but no liability to tax would have been incurred. The reason for this rule is to exclude a claim for loss relief in the event of the debt never being repaid.

However, s 251(3) enacts that where property is acquired by a creditor in satisfaction of his debt or part of it, then from the point of view of both the creditor and debtor, the property is acquired or disposed at its market value on the date of acquisition or disposal. On the facts, Derek disposes of a painting worth £3,000 to Charles in partial satisfaction of the debt. The remaining part of the consideration in satisfaction of the debt is the 'chose in action', that is, the right to claim 50% of whatever Derek may acquire under Fred's will. Derek will be treated as having disposed of the asset namely, the painting at its market value and after deducting his allowable expenditure and other deductions, his gain will be ascertainable. But, since the asset is tangible moveable property and the value of the consideration is less than £6,000, the gain will be exempt under s 262 of the TCGA 1992.

Likewise, Charles will be deemed to have acquired the painting at its market value of £3,000 in partial satisfaction of the debt, but no chargeable gain shall accrue to Charles in respect of the disposal of the debt. The base cost of the asset in the hands of Charles is its market value at the time of acquisition, that is, £3,000. The chose in action has a minimal acquisition cost, for although the entitlement of Derek to property under Fred's will is capable of being valued it is unlikely to be worth a large amount. The disposal of the painting for £6,300 is subject to relief under s 262(3) of the TCGA 1992. The chargeable gain is five thirds of the difference between the amount of the consideration (£6,300) and £6,000, that is, £500 and since this amount is within Charles' annual exempt limit, no liability to capital gains tax will accrue. By way of completeness, if the painting was received in full satisfaction of the debt, the base cost of the painting would have been the full amount of the debt released by Charles, namely £6,000.

The other asset received by Charles in satisfaction of the debt is the chose in action, that is, the right to half of the benefits receivable by Derek under Fred's will. The broad definition of assets in s 21 refers to 'all forms of property'. This definition includes choses in action. The base cost of the asset, as indicated above, may be negligible. When Charles receives £5,000 from Derek in final settlement of the debt, Charles will be treated as having made a disposal of the chose in action under s 22 of the TCGA 1992. In other words, a disposal of the assets by their owner is deemed to be made where any capital sum is derived from assets, notwithstanding that no asset is acquired by the person paying the capital sum. In particular, s 22(1)(c) refers to 'capital sums received in return for the surrender of rights, or for refraining from exercising rights'. This category includes payments received in return for releasing another person from a contract of employment (see *O'Brien v Benson's Hosiery Ltd* (1979)). The test under s 22 is subject to some inconsistency in judicial application. In *Davis v Powell* (1977) and *Drummond v Austin Brown* (1983), the courts focused on the expression, 'derived from' in the section. In these cases, the courts decided that the capital sum is required to be directly and causally connected with the asset disposed. If the asset is treated as a *causa sine qua non* of the compensation or capital sum, the sum is not taxable. On the other hand, in *Davenport v Chilver* (1983), the court decided that, on construction, s 22(1)(a)–(d) of the TCGA 1992 did not require the capital sum received to be causally connected with the asset. The court determined that the examples in paras (a)–(d) are specific occasions of sums which are treated as being 'derived from' the asset without requiring the Revenue to show a direct causal connection. On the facts posed in the problem, it appears tolerably clear that the legacy of £5,000 paid to Charles is directly linked with the chose created in his favour and is a disposal within s 22. Thus, Charles will be liable to capital gains tax on the difference between £5,000 and the value of the chose including indexation allowance and/or taper relief.

Part (b)

A legatee[3] who acquires property from a deceased is deemed to acquire the asset on the date and for the value at which the personal representative acquired the property. This is the market value of the asset on the date of death. There is no charge to capital gains tax, instead the legatee acquires a market value uplift in the capital gains base (see s 62(4) of the TCGA 1992).

Thus, when Charles inherited the brooch after the death of his mother, he is deemed to have acquired the asset on the date of his mother's death and at the market value at that time.

When a married man makes a disposal of assets to his wife during a year of assessment while they are living together, he is treated as having disposed of the asset at a value that gives rise to no gain and no loss (see s 58 of the TCGA). In other words, the disposal proceeds deemed to have been received by the husband (either spouse) is equivalent to his allowable expenditure, including indexation allowance and/or taper relief. In no circumstances, therefore, will the disponer spouse be capable of making a gain or allowable loss in respect of such transaction. Charles' transfer to his wife has the effect of surrendering his allowable expenditure to the receiving spouse, provided that they are living together. In addition, the recipient spouse obtains the date of acquisition of the disponer spouse, namely the date of death of Charles' mother.

Section 288(2) of the TCGA 1992 adopts the income tax definition of 'living together'. For income tax purposes, the definition of 'living together' is enacted in s 282 of the TA 1988. This is expressed in terms of a deeming provision. The parties to a marriage shall be deemed to be living together unless they are separated under a court order or deed of separation or are in fact separated in circumstances which are likely to be permanent. (In practice, a voluntary separation of 12 months is treated as likely to be permanent.) In addition, s 288(2) of the TCGA 1992 extends the meaning of not living together. The same consequences will ensue as if the parties had in fact separated in circumstances indicating that the separation is likely to be permanent if:

- one of the parties to a marriage is resident in the UK and the other is not resident for a year of assessment; or

- both are resident in the UK for a year of assessment but one is absent throughout and the other is not.

On the facts given there is no evidence that Charles is not living with his wife. The disposal is as described above.

In the alternative, if Charles and his spouse are not living together, the transfer by Charles will be treated as a disposal to a connected person as defined in s 286(2) of the TCGA 1992. The effect of a disposal between connected persons is declared in s 18 of the TCGA 1992, namely, that the disposal of the asset is deemed to be 'otherwise than by way of a bargain made at arm's length'. Section 17 declares that such disposals take place for a notional consideration equivalent to the market value of the asset at the time of the disposal.

Notes

1   The expression 'assets' is defined in the widest form in s 21 of the TCGA 1992. 'All forms of property' are assets, whether situated in the UK or not. This wide definition covers rights under a contract of a kind which are not assignable nor marketable such as an employer's right to the personal services of an employee (see *O'Brien v Benson's Hosiery* (1979)). However, a *spes* (or hope of acquiring a benefit) is not an asset, for it is not a form of property recognised in English law (see *Davenport v Chilver* (1983)).

2   A 'debt on security' has a limited and technical meaning. The expression 'security' is defined in s 132(3) of the TCGA 1992 as 'including any loan stock or similar security whether of the government of the UK or elsewhere, or of any company, and whether secured or unsecured'. It is not a synonym for a secured debt. The debt on security must be marketable, embodied in a contract and preferably in a document. It must be either loan stock or of a similar status. A debt on security is an asset and on disposal, by the original creditor or not, will attract a chargeable gain.

3   A 'legatee' is defined in s 64(2) of the TCGA 1992 as including 'any person taking under a testamentary disposition or on intestacy or partial intestacy ...'.

Question 30

David owns two houses and their contents which are situated in London and Surrey. The London house, which was acquired in 1974, has a four acre garden and is occupied by David, his wife and twin daughters. For a while David let part of the house to students. The cottage in Surrey, acquired in 1984, is occupied mainly at weekends and during holidays.

In May 1998, David sold one acre of the garden of his London home to a neighbour. In June 1998, he sold the house and a further two acres of land to another purchaser. The contents of the house were put in store but, in the course of removing the furniture, the removal contractors lost an impressionist painting worth £54,000 and damaged an Elizabethan table worth £12,000. In August 1998, David received insurance moneys of £54,000 in respect of the painting and £4,000 in respect of the Elizabethan table; the latter sum he used to repair the table. In July 1998, he sold the remaining acre of his garden to a developer.

In June 1997, David received a quotation from a firm of heating engineers for the installation of gas central heating in the Surrey cottage. He considered this to be exorbitant and decided to install the heating system on his own. He successfully completed the installation in July 1997, after purchasing the equipment and setting up the system, using his own expertise. In September 1998, David sold the cottage with its garden to a developer at its market value of £90,000, together with the right to receive one quarter of the amount of any increase in that market value which would result from the purchaser succeeding in obtaining planning permission to develop the property. In November 1998, the purchaser of the Surrey cottage obtained planning permission and since this permission increased the market value of the property, paid David an additional £20,000 in December 1998.

Advise David in respect of the charges that arise in respect of capital gains tax.

Answer plan

Answers should refer to the following points:

- s 222 – relief;
- election under s 222(5);
- 'permitted' area of grounds;
- sale of one acre of garden prior to sale of dwelling;
- s 223(4) – gains attributable to letting as residential accommodation;
- allowable expenditure attributable to the disposal of one acre of garden following disposal of dwelling – s 42;
- entire loss of painting – s 24;
- capital sum derived from asset – s 22;
- damage to table, disposal within s 22; election – s 23;
- allowable expenditure – s 38(1)(b); *Oram v Johnson*;
- time of disposal – s 28;
- deferred consideration – s 48.

Answer

David owns two houses or assets, one in London and the other in Surrey. Both assets have been disposed of by David at a gain. The question in issue is whether David is liable to capital gains tax in whole or in part in respect of the gains accruing on the disposal of the assets and the contents of the houses.

Relief from capital gains tax may be available to David in respect of the disposal of one of the dwellinghouses. Sections 222 and 223 of the TCGA 1992 create an exemption in respect of the gain made on the disposal of the whole or part of an interest in a dwellinghouse which is his only or main residence. Since David from time to time occupied both the London and Surrey houses, both are eligible for relief. At the same time, only one residence may qualify for relief at any given moment in time. The primary question is which of these residences is subject to the relief. David is entitled to make an election by giving notice to the Inspector within two years from the beginning of the period of ownership of the second home and may be varied by a further notice to the Inspector as respects any period beginning not earlier than two years before the giving of the further notice (see s 222(5)(a)).[1] In *Griffin v Craig-Harvey* (1994), Vinelott J construed the two year period strictly and rejected the taxpayer's argument that the election may be made at any time during the period of ownership of a dwellinghouse. On the basis of the facts presented, there is no evidence to the effect that David had made an election within two years of acquiring the Surrey house. In the absence of such an election, s 222(5)(b) enacts that the Inspector of Taxes will decide which residence is the main dwellinghouse with a right of appeal to the Commissioners. Undoubtedly, the extent of occupation in a dwellinghouse is a significant factor.

On the assumption that the London house is treated as David's main residence, the relief available under ss 222–26 of the TCGA 1992 is in respect of the gain accruing on the disposal of the dwelling, including grounds of up to half a hectare (inclusive of the site of the residence), or such larger area as is required for the reasonable enjoyment of the residence, as determined by the Commissioners. Sound preliminary advice requires David to appeal to the Commissioners to determine whether the 'permitted' area of grounds ought to be extended to include the entire four acres (or if not, the relevant proportion) of grounds enjoyed by the London home. If the entire grounds is not fully within the 'permitted' area, a disposal of the grounds outside the permitted area involves a chargeable disposal (or more precisely, a part disposal). For the purpose of analysis, it is assumed that the entire four acres of garden is within the 'permitted' area.

In May 1998, David sold one acre of the garden to a neighbour. Since this area represents part of the garden of the London dwellinghouse, the gain on its disposal is exempt from capital gains tax. There is an *obiter* pronouncement from Brightman J in *Varty v Lynes* (1976). The sale of the house in June with a further two acres of land may attract partial relief which is restricted to the period of ownership during which the residence was occupied exclusively as David's only or main dwelling, inclusive of the last 36 months of ownership *in any event*. The period of ownership attributable to the letting of the property to students may *prima facie* result in reduction of s 222 relief on the ground that the gain for this period does not constitute occupation by David as his dwelling. However, s 223(4) extends s 222 relief to include a disposal of a dwellinghouse which has been 'wholly or partly' let as 'residential accommodation'. The gain attributable to the letting (time apportioned in accordance with the period of letting and the ratio of the property let) will be exempt from capital gains tax up to the lesser of £40,000 and the relief attributable to David's occupation. In *Owen v Elliott* (1990), the Court of Appeal construed the expression, 'residential accommodation' broadly to mean living accommodation as distinct from office accommodation. The expression is not restricted to premises let which are likely to be occupied as a home.[2] If David did not let part of the house as a separate dwelling, he may be able to claim the benefit of s 223(4). Material factors which will assist in determining the amount of relief available under s 223(4) are: the period of the letting; the gain attributable to the letting; and the gain attributable to the period of occupation.

In order to ascertain the proportion of the original allowable expenditure attributable to the one acre portion of the garden retained by David, but finally disposed of in July 1998 (that is, the acquisition cost of the land), the part disposal formula enacted in s 42 of the TCGA 1992 is required to be adopted.

The formula is $A/A + B \times C$, where A is the sale proceeds of the part of the asset sold, and B is the market value of the part retained, C is the aggregate of deductible expenditure (including indexation allowance up to April 1998)[3] on the whole asset.

The resulting expenditure is then used to calculate the gain accruing on the disposal of the one acre of land retained by David as outlined below.

In July 1998, David sold the remaining one acre of garden to a developer. The disposal of this asset is independent from the main residence in that the disposal is made after the time of disposal of the residence. In this event, the gain accruing from the disposal is chargeable, including the capital profit accruing while the garden was enjoyed as part of the house (see *Varty v Lynes*, where Brightman J stressed that the s 222 relief is only available in respect of land which the taxpayer occupies for his enjoyment with the residence). The disposal proceeds are reduced by the acquisition cost of the land (including indexation allowance up to April 1998) as mentioned above.

The removal contractors lost David's impressionist painting, worth £54,000 and damaged an Elizabethan table worth £12,000. Section 24(1) of the TCGA 1992 enacts that:

> ... the entire loss, destruction, dissipation or extinction of an asset constitutes a disposal, whether or not a capital sum by way of compensation or otherwise is received.

The reason for this provision is to permit the taxpayer to make a loss claim. Thus, the loss of the painting is deemed to be a disposal. If no compensation is received, the allowable expenditure is treated as the measure of the loss. When David receives the insurance moneys, he is treated, in theory, as making a disposal under s 22 of the TCGA of the capital sum which is derived from the asset. This remains the position whether or not the person paying the capital sum (that is, the insurance company) receives anything in return for the payment (see *Marren v Ingles* (1980)). The time of the disposal is the date when the capital sum is received (see s 22(2)). The view of the Revenue is that when both ss 24 and 22 overlap, there can only be one disposal, namely the destruction of the asset. The compensation money is treated as the consideration on that disposal. Applying this view the gain accruing to David on the disposal of the painting is the difference between the insurance moneys and the allowable expenditure, including indexation allowance.

Similarly, when David receives the insurance moneys for the damage to the table, a disposal or part disposal is effected under s 22 of the TCGA 1992. But David applies the entire capital sum in repairing the asset. In these circumstances, the taxpayer may elect to defer the charge to capital gains tax. If the election is made, David is required to deduct the compensation money from the acquisition cost and thus defer the charge to capital gains tax (see s 23 of the TCGA 1992).

The Surrey house is not the taxpayer's principal or main residence owing to the election made earlier. This house does not attract relief under s 222 of the TCGA 1992 unless its status was changed by David after he disposed of the London house. The installation of central heating may be construed as capital expenditure which enhances the value of the asset and is reflected in its value on the date of disposal (see s 38(1)(b)). The effect is that such expenditure is capable of being deducted in order to compute the gain. However, in *Oram v Johnson* (1980), the court decided that the time involved in the taxpayer improving and restoring his derelict cottage could not be valued and was not deductible in computing the gain. Expenditure means primarily 'monetary' expenditure or expenditure in 'money's worth'.[4] But the expenditure incurred in purchasing the central heating equipment is deductible under s 38(1)(b). It is necessary for David to isolate and quantify the amount of this expenditure.

The sale of the house in September 1998 constitutes an actual disposal of the asset. The sale proceeds are £90,000 together with the right to receive an additional amount subject to a contingency. In the circumstances, the condition precedent operated with the consequence that an additional amount of £20,000 is paid to David in December 1998. For capital gains tax purposes the date of disposal under a contract is when a contract of sale takes place and not at the date of completion, if this is later (see s 28(1) of the TCGA 1992). If the contract is conditional, the date of disposal occurs when the condition is satisfied (see s 28(2)). A conditional contract is one where, on construction, the condition is treated as a condition precedent to liability as opposed to a term of the contract (see *Eastham v Leigh London and Provincial Properties Ltd* (1971)). Moreover, s 48 provides that no allowance is made for the delay in the receipt of deferred consideration. Thus, the payment of the additional amount in December 1998 is treated as part of the consideration receivable in September 1998, the date of sale. Alternatively, if the amount of the additional consideration cannot be estimated at the outset (including the maximum figure), it cannot form part of the consideration but the right to it may be a separate asset (that is, a chose) acquired as part of the proceeds (see *Marren v Ingles* (1980)). The eventual receipt may constitute a disposal of the right and result in an additional charge to capital gains tax. It is submitted that, in the circumstances before us, the additional sum payable to David is capable of being valued in September 1998, albeit not precisely, by postulating the market value of the Surrey house with planning permission.

Notes

1   This time limit may be extended where the taxpayer was unaware of the need to nominate a main residence and his interest in each of them has no more than negligible capital value ESC D21.

2   This relief does not apply if the let portion of the residence forms a separate dwelling. The Revenue have stated that the taking of lodgers will not result in a loss of s 222 relief, provided that the lodger lives as part of the family and shares the living accommodation (SP 14/80).

3   Section 53(1)(A) of the TCGA 1992, introduced by s 122 of the FA 1998, freezes indexation allowance for non-corporate tax payers in respect of any item of allowable expenditure up to 1 April 1998.

4   In *Chaney v Watkis* (1986), the taxpayer's mother in law was a protected tenant living in a house owned by the taxpayer. He agreed to compensate his mother in law by paying her a sum equivalent to £9,400 if she vacated the premises which he intended to sell. He sold the premises and was able to strike a bargain with his mother in law to provide her with rent free accommodation if she released him from the contract to pay her £9,400. She agreed, and came to live in an extension to his own residence. The question in issue was whether the taxpayer was entitled to deduct £9,400 as an expense from the disposal of the house. The court held in favour of the taxpayer. Had the sum of £9,400 been paid to his mother in law, this amount would have been deductible. Likewise, an obligation in substitution of the obligation to pay a specified amount is of the same nature and is quantified.

Question 31

Eddie (aged 49) runs a small business as a jeweller in the West End of London. The business has been run by Eddie as a sole trader for some 20 years and, in December 1998, is worth (including goodwill) £500,000. Eddie wishes to transfer the business to his son, Sam (aged 25), at some stage. He is anxious to keep capital gains tax liability to a minimum.

Advise him as to potential capital gains tax charges, including any possibility of deferring or reducing the tax bill, in respect of the following options:

(a) before his 50th birthday he sells the business to his son, Sam, for £200,000;

(b) alternatively, when Eddie retires at the age of 51 he sells the business to Sam for its market value at that time.

Answer plan

The following points should be raised in response to this question:

- rebasing of assets owned on 31 March 1982;
- s 18 – disposals between connected persons s 286(2);
- s 17 – disposals and acquisitions in transactions otherwise than at arm's length;
- relief under s 165 – hold over relief in respect of gifts or sales at an undervalue of business assets;
- retirement relief – ss 163, 164 and Schedule 6 of the TCGA 1992.

Answer

Part (a)

Eddie (aged 49) would be unwise to transfer the business immediately to his son, Sam. Liability to capital gains tax will arise on such transfer. Admittedly, we have not been informed of the amount of allowable expenditure (as well as indexation allowance) Eddie has incurred. Since the business was built up over a period of some 20 years and, in particular, before 31 March 1982, Eddie will need to know the base cost of the assets employed in his business as at 31 March 1982. The assumption that is made is that the assets have been sold and immediately reacquired by the disponer on this date. Indexation allowance is given against the base value at this date (s 35 of the TCGA 1992). Assuming that the business is valued on the date of disposal at an amount greater than the allowable expenditure, the sale of the business to Sam constitutes an actual disposal. The value of the disposal is determined by substituting the market value of the business for the actual consideration payable by Sam.

There are two reasons for this view. Firstly, the disposal is effected between 'connected' persons. Section 18(2) of the TCGA 1992 enacts that an acquisition and disposal of an asset between connected persons 'shall be treated as ... a transaction otherwise than by way of a bargain made at arm's length'. Section 17(1) enacts that the acquisition and disposal of an asset in a transaction otherwise than at arm's length shall be deemed 'to be for a consideration equal to the market value of the asset'. The definition of a connected person appears in s 286. Section 286(2) enacts that a person is connected with his or her spouse or with a relative or the spouse of a relative. A relative is defined in s 286(8) as meaning 'brother, sister, ancestor or lineal descendants'. Sam as a relative is deemed to be connected to Eddie. Secondly, the sale by Eddie for £200,000 of an asset worth £500,000 may be construed as a sale at an undervalue if there is any element of bounty. The effect of such a sale, as enacted in s 17, is that it is a transaction 'otherwise than at arm's length'. A bargain not at arm's length generally refers to some element of connection or relationship between the parties which renders any bargain made between them being governed by other than market value considerations. It would be extremely difficult for Eddie to establish that the sale to Sam represents a full commercial transaction. Thus, the market value of £500,000 is required to be substituted for the actual sale proceeds.

However, some relief under s 165 of the TCGA 1992 may be available for Eddie in respect of this disposal to Sam. To gain the benefit of this relief Eddie will be required to isolate and value the items of business assets included in the transfer, for example, goodwill, plant and machinery, etc. Section 165 of the TCGA 1992 introduced a general 'hold over' relief limited to gifts and sales at an undervalue of business assets to any person, that is, individuals, trustees and companies. The effect is to postpone the liability to capital gains tax. The requirements as stated in s 165(1) are that the disponer makes a disposal of 'business assets' otherwise than at arm's length and a claim to relief is made by both the transferor and transferee (or where the transfer is made to the trustees of the settlement, the transferor alone is entitled to make the election).

The sale of the business by Eddie for £200,000 is a sale at an undervalue (as established earlier). Presumably, this sale price is reflected in the capital assets transferred by Eddie. In the absence of evidence to the contrary, it is assumed that Eddie disposed of business assets at an undervalue. But we have not been given the value of these assets. Section 165(7) enacts that if the actual consideration paid on the disposal exceeds the allowable capital gains tax deductions of the transferor, that excess is subject to a charge. It is only the balance of any gain (that is, the amount by which the consideration is less than the full value of the business asset) which may be held over. On the other hand, if the partial consideration is less than the allowable deductions, it is ignored. Accordingly, a capital loss cannot be created.

The assets within the claim are defined in s 165(2), as, *inter alia*, including any asset provided that throughout the period of ownership it is used for the purposes of a trade, profession or vocation carried on by the transferor. Whether an asset has been used for the purpose of the trade is a question of law. But non-business assets disposed of by Eddie will be subject to an immediate charge to capital gains tax at the market value of the asset at the time of the disposal.

There is no time period stipulated in the statute for the making of the joint election between Eddie and Sam. In this event, the usual six year period will apply. Moreover, there is no prescribed form for the election. It would appear that any notification in writing by the relevant parties will suffice. It would be prudent for Eddie and Sam to agree the amount of the 'held over' gain with the Revenue. This would involve valuations of the relevant assets.

The effect of the election, as enacted in s 165(4), is that the liability to capital gains tax on the disposal consisting of the notional consideration is postponed until the transferee disposes of the asset without making an election. The chargeable gain in respect of the element of bounty within the sale at an undervalue, shall be reduced by the amount of the 'held over' gain, that is, in the hands of Eddie the disposal attributable to the notional consideration shall be treated as giving rise to no gain and no loss.

But the disposal in respect of the monetary consideration shall be chargeable to capital gains tax. Likewise, in the hands of Sam the allowable expenditure in respect of the asset acquired is reduced by the amount of the 'held over' gain.

Part (b)

If Eddie retires at the age of 51 and disposes of the business to Sam for its market value at that time, he may be able to claim generous retirement relief under ss 163–64 and Schedule 6 of the TCGA. This relief is available to Eddie since all of the following conditions are satisfied:

• the disponer must be at least 50 years of age and have owned the property for a minimum period of one year prior to disposal;

• the disposal must be of chargeable business assets, that is, a disposal of a business or part of a business. In this case, Eddie will dispose of his entire business;

• the disponer must make a material disposal (see s 163(3)–(5)), that is, the individual is required to own the business for at least one year before the cessation of the business. The disposal of the asset may occur within a 'permitted period' after the cessation. This period is one year, unless the Revenue by notice in writing allow a longer period.[2]

The maximum amount of relief for the year of assessment 1998–99 is in respect of £625,000 of gains, that is, the aggregate of £250,000 and 50% of gains between £250,000 and £1 m. However, retirement relief is to be phased out over a period of five years, commencing 1999–2000. The phasing out is to be achieved by an even reduction of the relief of 20% for each year of assessment and its abolition from 6 April 2003. On the facts presented, it would appear that, subject to the amount of gains, Eddie is entitled to 60% of the retirement relief, subject to his date of birth and date of disposal. The relief is granted by reducing the aggregate gains on the chargeable business assets and will be given automatically to Eddie.

Notes

- Section 165 relief is extended to settlements. The requirements are modified in the case of business assets owned by trustees. The relevant business must be either that of the trust or of a beneficiary with an interest in possession in the settled property.
- The disponer entitled to retirement relief need not retire from the business.
- The alternative to the minimum age requirement of 50, is that the taxpayer is compelled to retire below that age for reasons of ill health (see s 163(1)).
- Retirement relief may also be given in the case of settlements with an interest in possession, provided that the beneficiary satisfies the appropriate conditions.
- Difficult questions arise as to whether an individual disposes of part of a business (within s 163) or of assets used in the business (outside s 163) (see *McGregor v Adcock* (1977); *Mannion v Johnston* (1988); *Atkinson v Dancer* (1988); *Pepper v Daffurn* (1993); *Jarmin v Rawlins* (1994); *Barrett v Powell* (1998)).

SECTION VI
CORPORATION TAX

CHAPTER 10

CORPORATION TAX

The Finance Act 1972 (FA) reformed the system of company taxation and introduced the imputation system. The key feature of this system is that a proportion of the company's corporation tax in the form of distributions, is imputed to the shareholders so as to satisfy their liability to the basic rate of income tax. Today, the lower rate of tax is deducted and the individual taxpayer's liability is satisfied up to the basic rate tax threshold. An individual who is liable to income tax at the higher rate will be required to pay tax on the difference between that higher rate and the lower rate.

When a company makes a qualifying distribution out of its profits, it deducts an amount equivalent to the lower rate of income tax, called advance corporation tax (ACT) and pays this to the Revenue. The company is entitled to deduct this ACT from its ultimate liability to mainstream corporation tax (MCT).

As part of the package for the 'modernisation' of the corporation tax system, radical changes were introduced. First, with respect to distributions paid after 5 April 1999, the rate of credit has been reduced to 10% of the sum of the distribution and the credit. This is equivalent to a tax credit fraction of one ninth of the distribution. Secondly, the right to repayment of the credit (where it exceeds the total tax liability) is withdrawn. The effect is that a UK company which is exempt from tax will no longer be able to claim payment of tax credits on distributions received. A person, other than a company, resident in the UK will only be entitled to claim relief for tax credits on distributions received so far as they are charged to tax. The effect of this is that charities and individuals who have allowances to set against income in the form of distributions will not be able to claim payment of the tax credits: see s 231 of the Income and Corporation Taxes Act 1988 (TA) (as amended by s 30 of the Finance Act (No 2) 1997 (FA)). Thirdly, ACT is to be abolished on all distributions paid on or after 6 April 1999: see s 31 of the FA 1998. The effect is that no dividend paid after 5 April 1999 will give rise to a franked payment. Fourthly, no franked investment income (FII) received by a company after 5

April 1999 can be used to frank distributions made by the company. Fifthly, surplus ACT in respect of post-5 April 1999 distributions will be subject to a system of 'shadow ACT'. The idea here is that companies would calculate the ACT that they would have paid on distributions, apply the usual ACT offset rules and, to the extent that further ACT could have been offset ('eligible surplus ACT'), reduce the MCT otherwise payable by reference to the eligible surplus ACT: see s 32 of the FA 1998.

Corporation tax is charged on the profits of a company resident in the UK. A company for these purposes means any body corporate or unincorporated association but does not include a partnership or local authority.

Profits mean income and chargeable gains. Profits accruing to the company in a representative or fiduciary capacity are excluded.

Corporation tax is charged by reference to a 'financial year' ending 31 March. A financial year means a year commencing on 1 April and ending on the following 31 March. Tax is charged on the profits made in the company's 'accounting period', that is, a period not exceeding 12 months for which the company makes up its accounts. Corporation tax is charged on a current year basis. If an accounting period straddles more than one financial year the profits must be apportioned to correspond to the relevant financial years.

The rate of corporation tax for the financial year 1998 is 31%. Small companies pay tax for the financial year 1998 at the rate of 21%. There is taper relief for companies with profits exceeding £300,000 but not exceeding £1.5 m during the financial year 1998. Corporation tax is payable within nine months after the end of the accounting period for which it is assessed.

Self-assessment for companies has been introduced in respect of accounting periods ending after 30 June 1999. Companies will be required to make a self-assessment in their return which may be subject to selection for review by the Revenue. Corporation tax self-assessment (CTSA) applies to corporation tax payable as well as amounts chargeable as if they were corporation tax, for example, tax on close company loans to participators: see s 117 and Schedule 18 of the FA 1998.

When a company pays a charge on income in an accounting period, it is entitled to deduct the charge from its profits for corporation tax purposes unless:

(a) the charge is treated as a distribution; or

(b) the sum is charged to capital; or

(c) the charge is not ultimately borne by the company; or

(d) the charge is not made for valuable and sufficient consideration (except covenanted donations in favour of charities which are capable of exceeding three years).

A charge on income is any payment of annuities or other annual payments. By virtue of of the FA 1996, interest payments are no longer treated as charges on income but are treated as business expenses deductible in computing the profits of the company.

The income of a company is computed in accordance with income tax principles as though accounting periods were years of assessment. Similarly, chargeable gains are computed in the same way as for capital gains tax. The total profits of the company are arrived at by aggregating the company's income with its chargeable gains. Capital allowances may be deducted as trading expenses and if this produces a loss, it may be relieved by one of the methods available.

If a company receives distributions from another company the distributions are not liable to corporation tax in the hands of the recipient. The company receiving the distribution is entitled to a tax credit, which coupled with the distribution is called franked investment income (or FII). FII may be used *inter alia* to frank distributions made by the company. As from 6 April 1999, no UK company will be required to pay ACT on qualifying distributions and no FII attributable to a distribution made after this date will be available to frank any distributions: see s 31 of the FA 1998.

Companies may combine their resources by forming a group. There are a variety of advantages to be gained from group association. For accounting periods beginning before 6 April 1999, companies may elect to treat qualifying distributions made by one company to another without payment of ACT. Such income is known as group income. Moreover, a company in a group may surrender ACT to another company in the same group and the transfer of assets within a group may be effected without a liability to capital gains tax. If a company has a trading loss or capital allowances which it cannot set off against its own profits, it may surrender the relief to another company within the same group.

Close companies: a close company is a company under the control of:

- five or fewer participators; or
- participators who are directors.

This definition looks deceptively simple but on closer examination is capable of challenging some of the most accomplished tax lawyers.

The effect of close company status is that loans to participators or their associates require the company to pay a sum equal to ACT on the amount of the loan or advance. This amount is not credited against the company's liability to MCT. The tax is repayable when the loan is repaid. Furthermore, the legislation adopts an extended meaning of distributions to include benefits in kind provided to participators and their associates. If the company is a 'close investment holding company', the small company's rate of corporation tax will not be applicable to the profits of the company. If a close company makes a transfer of value, this is deemed for inheritance tax purposes to be a transfer made by all the shareholders in the company in proportion to their shareholding. If the shareholders fail to pay inheritance tax on such transfers, the company becomes liable.

Question 32

Able, who owns 20% of the shares in Money Ltd is an employee of the company. The remaining shares are owned equally by three other directors and Fred, who is not connected with any of the directors and does not work for the company.

On 1 May 1998, the company made an interest free loan of £80,000 to Able for use for his own private purposes. Able repaid £60,000 of the loan on 31 January 1999, and the company waives the balance of the loan on 1 March 1999.

In June 1998, the company provided Fred and his wife an 'all expenses paid' holiday in the Caribbean at a cost of £4,000.

Both Able and Fred are higher rate taxpayers.

Money Ltd prepares its accounts to 31 December.

You are required to:

(a) explain the corporation and income tax implications of the loan to Able;

(b) explain the corporation and income tax consequences of the provision of the holiday for the benefit of Fred.

Answer plan

A suitable answer should include the following:

- close company definition;
- corporation tax effect of the loan to Able – ss 419, 420 of the TA 1988;
- income tax consequences – s 160 of the TA 1988;
- corporation tax consequences of receiving repayment of loan;
- income tax consequences of waiving the loan – s 421 of the TA 1988;
- corporation tax consequences of providing benefits in kind to participators – s 418 of the TA 1988;
- income tax consequences of participator receiving benefits in kind.

Answer

Part (a)
Corporation and income tax implications of loan to Able

A close company is defined in s 414(1) of the TA 1988 as, *inter alia*:

> One which is under the control of five or fewer participators, or of participators who are directors.

'Control' is defined in s 416(2) of the TA 1988 in terms of ownership of share capital (including income on distribution or assets on a liquidation) and voting rights. Thus, Able and at least two other shareholders own more than 50% of the voting power and/or share capital of Money Ltd. They therefore control the company. A 'participator' is defined in s 417(1) of the TA 1988 in terms of having a financial interest in the company. Shareholders undoubtedly possess such interest.

Applying the above definition to the circumstances raised in the problem, it seems reasonably clear that Money Ltd is a close company. This assessment is supported by the test of control by five or fewer participators or the control of its directors (three directors of the company).

The effect of close company status is to counteract the ease with which such companies, but for special provisions to the contrary, may avoid or minimise corporation tax on its profits by manipulating the company's affairs. Accordingly, special provisions have been enacted to counter the disguise of special loans and non-commercial expenses of the company as distributions.

Loan to Able

Sections 419 and 420 of the TA 1988 enact that a close company which, otherwise than in the ordinary course of business, makes a loan to an individual who is a 'participator' in the company, is assessed on an amount equal to such proportion of that loan as corresponds to the rate of advance corporation tax (ACT) for the financial year in which the loan was made.[1] The amount of the loan is not treated as a distribution of profit by the company and the ACT assessable on the company is notional in the sense that the company is not entitled to set off this amount of tax from its liability to mainstream corporation tax (MCT). The amount assessed on the company is payable as if it were corporation tax chargeable for the accounting period in which the loan was made.

Thus, Able, a participator, receives a loan of £80,000 from Money Ltd, a close company, on 1 May 1998 and the company makes up its accounts to 31 December. The company is assessed to tax on 20/80 of the amount of the loan of £80,000, that is, £20,000.

This tax is due and payable within 14 days following the end of the accounting period in which the loan was made, that is, 14 days following 31 December 1998. Money Ltd is under an obligation to notify the Revenue of the details of the loan within 12 months from the end of the accounting period in which it was made. In *Joint v Bracken Developments Ltd* (1994), the court held that interest under s 88 of the Taxes Management Act 1970 (TMA) was payable by a company for failing to notify the Revenue of its liability to tax in respect of a loan to a participator.

Income tax consequences of receiving the loan

An employee who earns £8,500 per annum or more and receives an interest free loan 'by reason of his employment' is taxed on the cash equivalent of the benefit of the loan (see s 160 of the TA 1988). We are not told of Able's earnings but he is a higher rate taxpayer and thus earns more than £8,500 per annum. The expression, 'by reason of his employment', is defined in Schedule 7, Pt 1 of the TA 1988 as, *inter alia*, a loan made by an employer. The cash equivalent of the loan is the amount of interest which would have been payable had interest at the official rate been payable on the loan (less the amount of interest actually paid). The methods of calculation are stated in Schedule 7, paras 4 and 5. Thus, Able may be liable to income tax on the benefit of receiving an interest free loan from Money Ltd.

Corporation tax consequences of partial repayment of loan: Able repays part (£60,000) of the loan in January 1999. The effect of this repayment is that Money Ltd is entitled to recover from the Revenue an equivalent amount of ACT on the part of the loan repaid, that is, 60/80 of £20,000 = £15,000. This relief is granted to the company on a claim made within six years from the end of the financial year in which the repayment was made (see s 419(4) of the TA 1988).

Waiver of the remainder of the loan

On 1 March 1999, Money Ltd waives the balance of the loan, that is, £20,000. Section 421 of the TA 1988 provides that where a loan charged under s 419 is wholly or partly written off or released, the borrower is treated as receiving an amount equal to the amount of the debt released, grossed up at the lower rate of income tax.[2] The notional lower rate of tax is neither assessed to tax or repayable, but higher rate of tax may be payable (less a credit for the lower rate of tax as deducted) on the gross amount of the notional income as if it were dividend income. In other words, when the company writes off the balance of the loan, the borrower suffers similar consequences as if the loan were a distribution, but is unable to claim repayment of the 'tax credit' or to use the notional income to cover charges.

The company receives no credit against its corporation tax liability for the sum paid to the Revenue by Able.

For 1998–99, Able is treated as receiving £25,000 of income in the year of assessment of release, that is, the amount of the loan waived (£20,000) in addition to a (non-refundable) 'credit' of the amount of tax at the lower rate (20%) or 100/80 x £20,000. This gross sum is aggregated with Able's other income and higher rate tax is assessable on his taxable income, that is, 40% tax is payable on the gross income but a deduction of the lower rate of tax is made.

Where the borrower is both a participator and an employee of the company such as Able, and the waiver of the loan is chargeable to income tax under s 421 of the TA 1988, the Revenue does not seek to assess the employee under the beneficial loan provision under s 160(2) of the TA 1988.

Corporation and income tax implications of benefit to Fred: The provision of the holiday for Fred: s 418 of the TA 1988 provides that close companies are treated as making distributions when they incur expenses in providing benefits in kind for a participator. This rule does not apply to benefits in kind which are assessable to income tax under ss 153–68 of the TA 1988. Fred is not an employee of Money Ltd and is not subject to income tax under ss 153–68 of the TA 1988, but is a participator within the definition earlier stated and falls within s 418 of the TA 1988. The effect is that Money Ltd is treated as making a distribution of the amount of the expense incurred in providing the benefit to Fred. The ACT deducted by the company is payable to the Revenue 14 days from the end of the relevant quarter and may be set off against its liability to MCT.

Thus, the holiday payment of £4,000 will attract ACT of £1,000 which may be set off against Money Ltd liability to MCT for the accounting period ending 31 December 1999.

The income tax consequences of Fred receiving the holiday benefit is that he is chargeable to income tax on the gross income, including the tax credit. Fred will be treated as having received a gross sum of £5,000 with a tax credit of £1,000 for the year of assessment 1998–99. He will be liable to higher rate income tax on this amount.

Notes

1　In respect of loans or advances made on or after 6 April 1999, the amount of tax payable by the company shall be 25% of the loan or advance.

2　Where the writing off or release of the loan takes place after 5 April 1999, the amount is deemed to have been received after deduction of tax at the Schedule F ordinary rate.

Question 33

Part (a)

The definition of a close company is deceptively simple but involves a tortuous process of wading through a maze of statutory principles. One reliable approach is to assume that the majority of private companies are close, it is only a matter of proving it.

Do you agree?

Part (b)

Peach Ltd is a UK resident company with the following list of shareholders:

Shares (one vote per share)	
Mr A Abraham, Chairman	3,000
Mr B Abraham	1,000
Mr B Blood, Managing Director	1,000
Mr C Collier, Director	1,000
Mr D Devon, Director	1,000
Mr E Everett, Director	1,000
Mr F Fender, Director	1,000
Mr G Goddin, Secretary	4,000
Mr H Goddin	1,000
Mrs I Ivy	1,000
Mrs J June	1,000
Other small shareholders	14,000
	30,000

Mr B Abraham is the son of A Abraham. Mr H Goddin is the son of G Goddin (the company secretary) and the brother of Mrs Ivy and Mrs June. The company's shares are not quoted on the Stock Exchange and the company has no associated companies.

Examine whether Peach Ltd is a close company.

Answer plan

Part (a)

You should give definitions of the following:

- close companies;
- control;
- participator;
- associate;

- director;
- exceptions.

Part (b)

This deals with the status of Peach Ltd – whether it is a close company or not. You should:

- aggregate the shares attributable to each individual with his associates to ascertain whether Peach Ltd is controlled by five or fewer participators;
- aggregate the shares attributable to directors with their associates to ascertain whether Peach Ltd is controlled by directors/participators;
- consider whether any exclusions are applicable.

Answer

Part (a)

The statement posed is accurate in that the definition of a close company looks deceptively simple, but on further examination the formula involves a web of definitions of ancillary concepts. It is true that the vast majority of private companies are close and the only relevant task for the analyst is to determine which aspect of the definition is satisfied by reference to the facts of any given situation.

The expression, 'close company' is defined in some detail in ss 414 and 415 of the TA 1988. A close company is defined as a company resident in the UK:

- which is under the control of five or fewer participators; or
- which is under the control of any number of participators who are directors of the company; or
- in respect of which, more than 50% of its assets could be distributed on a notional winding up between five or fewer participators or director participators.

Within this definition, there are clearly a number of terms that require further clarification.

Control

This term is defined in s 416 of the TA 1988. A person has control of a company if he is able to exercise, or is entitled to acquire control, whether directly or indirectly, over the company's affairs. Control is established if a person is entitled to acquire:

- more than 50% of the share capital or issued share capital or voting power of the company; or
- such part of the issued share capital as would entitle him to receive more than 50% of the income of the company if it were distributed amongst the participators, ignoring the rights of loan creditors; or
- such rights as would on a winding up of the company, or in any other circumstances, entitle him to more than 50% of the assets of the company available for distribution among the participators.

In order to determine whether a person has control of a company, the rights and powers of the following classes of persons are required to be aggregated: nominees, associates, nominees of associates and companies of which the person or his associates has or have control.

Participator

Section 417 of the TA 1988 defines participators as persons having a share or interest in the capital or income of the company and includes:

- any person who possesses, or is entitled to acquire share capital or voting rights in the company;
- any loan creditor of the company such as debenture holders, but excluding any bank which lends money, in the ordinary course of business, to the company; and
- any person who possesses, or is entitled to acquire a right to receive, or participate in distributions of the company, or any amounts payable by the company by way of premium on redemption of any loan; and
- any person who is entitled to secure that any income or assets of the company will be applied directly or indirectly for his benefit.

Associate

Section 417 of the TA 1988 provides that:

(a)   Any direct relative, that is, spouses, parents and remoter ancestors, children and remoter issue, brothers and sisters.

Relatives excluded for this purpose include sons and daughters in law, issue of brothers or sisters, relatives of spouses, brothers or sisters in law and uncles and aunts:

- business partners;
- the trustees of any settlement made or entered into by the participator or any of his direct relatives, whether living or dead;
- the trustees or personal representatives interested with the participator in any shares or obligations of the company which are subject to any trust or part of any estate of a deceased person. In *Willingdale v Islington Green Investment Co* (1972), one of three executors of a deceased shareholder in a close company was a participator. The court decided that the other executors were his associates:

(b)   Where the participator is a company, an associate is any other company interested in the shares or debentures of that company.

Director

Section 417 of the TA 1988 provides that any person occupying the position of director by whatever name called is a director, in addition to any person on whose instructions or directions the directors are accustomed to act, and the manager of a company, either alone or with his associates, if he (or they) holds or controls 20% of its ordinary share capital.

Ordinary share capital is defined as meaning all issued share capital by whatever name called, other than capital having a right to dividend at a fixed rate, with no other right to share in the profits of the company. It follows that participating preference shares are classified as 'ordinary share capital' for this purpose.

A person is not a director merely because the directors act upon his professional advice. To be a director, he must be in the habit of directing company policy and company affairs.

Quoted companies which are not close

Even though a company may satisfy the criteria for control contained in the basic definition, it may nevertheless not be a close company if certain conditions prevail. These are as follows:

- if shares in the company carrying not less than 35% of the voting power have been allocated, or acquired unconditionally, and are beneficially held by the public. Shares entitling the holder to a fixed rate of dividend are ignored; and

- such shares have within the last 12 months, been the subject of dealings on a recognised Stock Exchange, and quoted in the Official List.

Shares are not held by the public if (*inter alia*) they are held by a director of the company or his associates. Similarly, the exception from close company status does not apply when the principal members (that is, the five members who hold the greatest voting power in the company, but excluding any who hold less than 5% of the voting power) possess more than 85% of the total voting power.

To ascertain whether a UK resident company is close or not, the multiple associated definitions of a close company may be summarised in the following steps:

(1) identify the shareholders in a company and aggregate the shareholding of associates;

(2) if five or fewer participators control more than 50% of the votes in the company, the company is close, if not, proceed to stage (3);

(3) consider whether the company is director/participator controlled, irrespective of the number of directors. Identify the persons who are directors, including those who are not called directors but qualify by holding 20% of the ordinary share capital. If at least 50% of the votes are held by such directors, the company is close;

(4) if the company is still not close, consider whether control can be established by five or fewer participators under the winding up hypothesis;

(5) if the company is close, consider whether it may be exempted under one of the statutory exceptions.

Part (b)

The issue in this question is whether Peach Ltd is a close company. It is necessary first to link all the shares attributable to a participator including his associates.

B Abraham is the son of A Abraham and therefore their shares may be linked. Their combined holding is 4,000 votes and are treated as belonging to one person.

Mr H Goddin is the son of G Goddin and the brother of Mrs Ivy and Mrs June. Their aggregated holding of 7,000 votes is treated as held by one participator.

The question of whether there are five or fewer participators may be answered by quantifying the votes of the five largest shareholders, including their associates. These are:

A Abraham and associate	4,000 votes
G Goddin and associates	7,000 votes
B Blood	1,000 votes
C Collier	1,000 votes
D Devon	1,000 votes
Total	14,000 votes

50% of the votes in Peach Ltd is equivalent to 15,000.

Accordingly, Peach Ltd is not controlled by five or fewer participators.

The next stage is to consider whether the company is director/participator controlled. This analysis requires all the votes of directors/participators, including their associates, to be aggregated.

Mr G Goddin is the Company Secretary and therefore holds a managerial post. He has a combined holding, together with his associates, of 7,000 votes. This is greater than 20% of the ordinary share capital of the company. He is deemed to be a director.

The directors' holdings are:

A Abraham and associate	4,000 votes
B Blood	1,000 votes
C Collier	1,000 votes
D Devon	1,000 votes
E Everett	1,000 votes
F Fender	1,000 votes
G Goddin and associates	7,000 votes
Total	16,000 votes

The directors/participators are treated as controlling the company and therefore the company is close.

We are told that the company is UK resident, has no associated companies and the shares are unquoted. Accordingly, none of the exceptions is relevant.

Question 34

George is the owner of shares in Britco Ltd. The company draws up accounts up to 31 March each year. The accounts of the company for the year ending 31 March 1998 show an income profit of £600,000 and capital gains of £100,000. In February 1998, Britco receives £80,000 dividends from Litco Ltd, a company in which it holds shares. On 1 December 1997, Britco Ltd pays out a dividend of £40,000, of which George receives £400 in respect of his shareholding. In addition to his dividend income, George receives a salary of £50,000 per annum as Director of Britco.

Advise:

(a) Britco as to its liability to corporation tax, indicating when the tax is payable; and

(b) George as to his liability to income tax.

Answer plan

Your answer should discuss the following:

- definition of profits for corporation tax purposes;
- rate of MCT;
- tapering relief;
- date of payment of MCT;
- ACT;
- dual effect of ACT – set of against MCT, tax credit to George;
- FII;
- FII used to frank qualifying distributions;
- George's salary and Schedule E;
- dividend received by George liable to tax under Schedule F.

Answer

Part (a)

The effect of ss 6 and 8 of the TA 1988 is that 'the profits of companies are chargeable to corporation tax'. Section 832 of the TA 1988 defines a company as including not only a body corporate but also unincorporated associations. Britco Ltd is a body corporate and liable to corporation tax on its profits.

The profits of a company are defined in s 9 of the TA 1988 as including:

- income computed under the same Schedules and Cases as apply for income tax purposes;
- together with the chargeable gains accruing to the company during its accounting period.

Britco receives £600,000 of income profits and £100,000 of capital gains during its accounting period ending 31 March 1998. Thus, the net profits of Britco for the financial year 1997 is £700,000. The corporation tax rate varies with the amount of profits liable to corporation tax. The standard rate of MCT is set at 31%. But, for small companies, it is 21%. A small company is a company with profits not exceeding £300,000. If the profits exceed £300,000[1] (lower relevant maximum amount), but do not exceed £1.5 m (upper relevant maximum amount), a form of tapering relief is available (see s 13 of the TA 1988). Profits for the purpose of tapering relief include not only the taxable profits, but also FII (see s 13(7) of the TA 1988). The relief is computed by applying the following formula:

Taxable profits at 31% less $1/40$ x (M – P) x I/P, where M is the upper relevant maximum amount; P is the amount of the profits (including FII, see below); and I is the amount of basic profits (that is, liable to MCT).

The computation is presented thus:

MCT on £700,000 at 31% =	£217,000
Less tapering relief	
1 / 40 x (£1.5 m – £800,000) x £700,000/£800,000 =	£15,312
MCT payable	£201,688

Strictly speaking, Britco is required to make a claim for tapering relief. This may be done formally by letter to the Revenue. Although the Revenue have accepted informal notification by way of a tax computation accompanying the accounts. No time limit is specified, accordingly, the claim may be made within six years from the end of Britco's accounting period.

Date of payment of MCT

Britco is charged to corporation tax on a current year basis on its profits (excluding FII) computed within the financial year. When the accounting period does not coincide with the financial year the profits are required to be apportioned on a time basis. In the present case, Britco's accounting period coincides with the financial year ending 31 March 1998. The company is required to pay its MCT within nine months from the end of its accounting period, that is, within nine months from 31 March 1998. Under the pay and file system, a company is required to pay its MCT within the time period mentioned above and file its return in the statutory format within 12 months after the accounting period ends, subject to penalties for failure to comply with the return requirements.

Advance corporation tax

When Britco Ltd makes a qualifying distribution of £40,000 (that is, a dividend payment) to its shareholders on 1 December 1997, the company becomes liable to Advance Corporation Tax (ACT). The rate of ACT varies from financial year to financial year. For this period (1997–98), the rate is 20% of the gross distribution, which amounts to one quarter of the net amount of the distribution, that is, the lower rate of income tax. The amount of ACT payable by Britco Ltd is £10,000 and, subject to any relief available to the company, is payable within 14 days from the end of the quarter (return period) in which the payment was made. The end of each return period or quarter is as follows: 31 March; 30 June; 30 September; 31 December.

The relevant amount of ACT is payable to the Revenue within 14 days following 31 December.

The gross distribution (tax credit plus the net distribution, or £50,000) is known as a franked payment.

Franked investment income

In February 1998, Britco receives £80,000 in respect of dividends from Litco Ltd. Since Litco would have had to account to the Revenue for ACT in respect of the dividends declared, Britco Ltd does not have to pay tax on the gross dividend. Indeed, Britco is entitled to a tax credit of one quarter of the net distribution, that is, £20,000. The credit plus the distribution in the hands of Britco Ltd is known as franked investment income (FII).

The principal use of the credit within FII is to frank distributions made by Britco, that is, the credit may be used to set off ACT payable by Britco. In other words, where a company receives FII, it will be exempt from liability to ACT in respect of qualifying distributions made within the accounting period, to the extent that the franked payment is equal to or is less than the FII (see s 241 of the TA 1988). In Britco's case, its franked payment of £50,000 is less than the FII received. Thus, Britco Ltd may reclaim the ACT paid to the Revenue in January 1998 (see s 20(2) of the TA 1988). The surplus FII is carried forward to future accounting periods and treated as FII in that accounting period.[2]

Set off of ACT against MCT

Britco Ltd is entitled to deduct the ACT paid in its accounting period from its MCT liability on its profits. The effect of such set off is that the company's liability to MCT is discharged to the extent of the claim (see s 239 of the TA 1988). Thus, Britco's MCT liability, as computed above, is adjusted by the amount of ACT paid in the period as follows:

MCT payable but for a distribution	£201,688
Less ACT paid in the accounting period	£ 10,000
MCT payable after distribution	£191,688

Part (b)

Income tax liability of George

As a director of Britco Ltd, George receives a salary of £50,000. This amount is chargeable to income tax under Schedule E (see s 19 of the TA 1988). The income tax is collected under the PAYE system. It would appear from the scale of the emoluments that George is a higher rate taxpayer paying tax at the rate of 40% for the year of assessment 1994–95.

When George receives the dividend of £400 during the year of assessment 1994–95 he will be liable to income tax under Schedule F on the gross amount of the distribution (£500). But George is entitled to a tax credit of a sum equivalent to the lower rate of income tax in force at the date of the distribution, that is, one quarter of the net dividend – £100. The tax credit may be used to set off against George's liability to income tax. Since George's marginal rate of income tax is 40%, a further assessment of income tax of 20% is payable by him in respect of the dividend.

Notes

1 These limits are reduced for accounting periods of less than 12 months and by reference by the number of associated companies (see s 13(4)–(6)).

2 As an alternative to carrying forward surplus FII and at the same time acquiring immediate relief for surplus FII, the

company may claim to have the tax credit within the surplus FII released for immediate use. The surplus FII is treated as if 'it were a like amount of profits chargeable to corporation tax' (notional profits) and available for set off against the following:

(a) trading losses arising in the same accounting period;

(b) surplus charges on income brought forward or in the current accounting period;

(c) surplus expenses of management brought forward or in the current accounting period;

(d) capital allowances granted against total profits (not only trading profits) brought forward or in the current accounting period.

Question 35

London plc owns the entire issued share capital of a number of trading companies and one property investment company. London plc also owns 80% of the issued share capital of one other trading company, London Electronics Ltd. All the companies are resident in the UK.

The property investment company, London Properties Ltd, owns the freehold and leasehold properties from which the subsidiary companies trade. All property acquisitions and sales on behalf of the group are carried out by this company.

London Properties Ltd receives rental income assessable under Schedule A from the other members of the group. The company has no other assessable income. Property disposals by this company have in the past given rise to capital gains tax. No corporation tax charges have arisen due to the availability of rollover relief. There are no capital losses which have been brought forward that are available to this company.

In January 1996, the board of directors of London plc decided that a new office block should be constructed to house the headquarters of the group. A site for development was acquired and construction for London Properties Ltd commenced in July 1996. The group encountered unexpected trading problems soon after the commencement of construction works. It became apparent that the new development would be an unbearable strain on the financial resources of the group. The board of directors decided that, on completion, the office block would be let to a third party and a purchaser for the building would be sought. By April 1998, the property was fully let.

A merchant bank, City plc, which has no connection with the London group, has indicated that it would be prepared to purchase the office block for £5 m. The building is to be used as the administrative headquarters of City plc. The suggested price exceeds the cost of the property by £2 m. The offer has not at this time been accepted.

London Properties Ltd has agreed, subject to contract, to sell an additional investment property to City plc. The proceeds of sale will be £7 m. A capital gain of £3 m will arise. A mortgage over the property for £3 m is held by Zania Bank plc. As part of the transaction, City plc will be prepared to take over responsibility for the mortgage on the property.

Three members of the group have unrelieved capital losses brought forward:

London Information Services Ltd joined the group in 1986. A capital loss of £500,000 arose on the sale of goodwill in 1996.

London Engineering Ltd was acquired by the group in 1993. At that time, the company had agreed capital losses of £600,000.

The investment in London Electronics Ltd was acquired by the group in 1994. At that time, the company had agreed capital losses of £1.5 m.

During the next three years London Properties Ltd is expected to incur expenditure in excess of £10 m on industrial units to be used by London Electronics Ltd. The group does not expect to incur any further capital expenditure in the foreseeable future:

(a) explain the taxation consequences of the sale of the office block by London Properties Ltd to City plc;

(b) explain the taxation consequences if, prior to acquisition by City plc, the investment property is sold to London Electronics Ltd, London Engineering Ltd and London Information Services Ltd as joint tenants.

Answer plan

Your answer should include discussion of:

- Schedule A income;
- capital asset or trading stock;
- badges of trade;
- s 776 of the TA 1988 and Schedule D Case VI;
- intra-group transfer s 171 of the Taxation and Chargeable Gains Act (TCGA) 1992;
- *Furniss v Dawson* (1984);
- set off of gains against losses – Schedule 7A to the TCGA 1992;
- roll over relief under ss 152–59 of the TCGA 1992.

Answer

Part (a)

One of the first issues to consider is the status of the transaction concerning the office block in the hands of London Properties Ltd. Admittedly, the company owns all the freehold and leasehold properties from which the subsidiaries trade. These properties are held by London Properties Ltd as capital assets of the group. The site on which the office block has been built, was acquired in 1993. The question in issue is whether the site was acquired as a capital asset or as a trading transaction. This is question of mixed law and fact. Major factors to be taken into account are:

The rental income received by London Properties Ltd from the letting of the office block to City Ltd, is assessable under Schedule A to corporation tax. The company is entitled to deduct expenditure of maintenance, repairs, insurance and management. Where the office block and the other properties let by London Properties Ltd are managed as one estate, all expenditure may be deducted from any rent accruing within the estate.

The new development has not been used for the purpose of the trade of any member of the London group. Moreover, the decision to let and subsequently sell the building was taken during the course of the construction of the building. These are factors which may support a case that the company was trading.

It is necessary to consider the extent to which the badges of trade may assist in determining the status of the transaction.

The decision to acquire the site and develop it for use as an office block to house the headquarters of the group is consistent with a capital asset. The decision to sell the property was only taken because of the financial difficulties experienced by the group. In *Taylor v Good* (1974), the court decided that a large country residence purchased by the taxpayer at an auction for a bargain price was a capital asset. The asset was not converted into trading stock when the taxpayer applied for and obtained planning permission before selling the same to a property developer for a profit. The same principle was applied in *Kirkham v Williams* (1991), where a plant hire contractor purchased a site and used part of it as an office and warehouse. He obtained planning permission to build a large dwelling house on the site. On completion of the construction, he sold the site and carried on business from other premises. The court held that the profits were of a capital nature. Similarly, in *Simmons Properties Ltd v IRC* (1980), the House of Lords decided that the taxpayer's intention at the time of the acquisition was of paramount importance and a capital asset was not converted into trading stock. Contrast *Iswera v Ceylon CIR* (1965), where the taxpayer, wishing to live near his children's school, bought the only land available to him on which to build a house. The site was too large and he sold part of it. The court held that the transaction was an adventure in the nature of a trade. In *Turner v Last* (1965), a farmer was taxable on the profits under Schedule D Case I when he sold two plots of land with planning permission.

Another factor is that no similar trading transaction had been entered into in the past by the company. This evidence points to a capital profit.

Moreover, the building was not altered in any significant way in order to comply with the requirements of the merchant bank, City Ltd. This factor points to a capital asset.

Notwithstanding the arguments presented above to suggest that the profits are of a capital nature, it is still possible for the

Revenue to establish that the profits may be assessable to corporation tax under Schedule D Case VI by virtue of s 776 of the TA 1988. This anti-avoidance provision treats capital sums as though they were income profits. The section is applicable where the following conditions are satisfied.

Either:

(1) (a) the land is acquired with the sole or main object of realising a gain from the disposal of the land (s 776(2)(a)); or

(b) land is held as trading stock (s 776 (2)(b)); or

(c) the land is developed with the sole or main object of realising a gain on its disposal following development (s 776(2)(c)); and

(2) a gain of a capital nature is obtained; and

(3) the gain is obtained from the disposal of the land; and

(4) the gain must be obtained either:

(a) by the person who acquired, held or developed the land or by or through any connected persons; or

(b) as a result of a scheme or arrangement which has allowed a gain to be realised by an indirect method by any person who is a party to or concerned in the arrangements or the scheme.

This is an extremely wide provision and detailed discussion is not warranted in this question. It was the intention of the group to dispose of the property at a profit. On the other hand, it is arguable that the group only continued with the project after it developed financial difficulties and considered that by completing the development it would be possible to recover some of its costs. There is a clearance procedure under s 776(11) and, unlike other clearance procedures, the application is made to the local tax office. This encourages the local officials to issue a blanket refusal without giving reasons.

If the profit arising from the sale of the development constitutes a chargeable gain, roll over relief (under ss 152–59 of the TCGA 1992) will not be available to defer the capital gains liability. The office block has never been used for a qualifying trade by any of the subsidiaries of the group.

Part (b)

The sale of the investment property by London Properties Ltd to London Electronics Ltd, London Engineering Ltd and London Information Services Ltd as joint tenants may constitute an intra group transfer and fall within the provisions of s 171 of the TCGA 1992. The effect of this transaction is that no liability to corporation tax on the capital gain will exist. The sale is deemed to take place for a consideration that gives rise to 'no gain and no loss'. The effect of this provision is that the members of a group are treated as one and the different trades of each member are treated as one. Provided that the asset does not leave the group or any of the relevant subsidiaries does not cease to be a member of the group, the gain accruing on the disposal is not chargeable.

It is the policy of the Revenue not to seek to apply the *Furniss v Dawson* (1984) principle where assets are transferred between group members in order to take advantage of accrued capital losses. In any event it would be difficult for the Revenue to argue that there is a pre-ordained series of transactions because, at present, the sale of the property has not been agreed.

Capital losses brought forward by London Engineering Ltd and London Electronics Ltd will not be available to reduce any gain arising on the sale of that company's interest in the property due to the provisions of Schedule 7A to the TCGA 1992. This provision was introduced to restrict the practice of acquiring tax loss companies for the purpose of utilising its losses to set off gains made by companies within the group, as a prelude to disposals outside the group. Where the losses originate from a company which joined the group on or after 31 March 1987 the right to utilise the loss is severely restricted. The capital losses brought forward by London Information Services Ltd will be available to reduce future gains arising in the group, since it joined the group before 31 March 1987.

If the joint tenants occupy the building for the purpose of their trades, roll over relief will be available on a subsequent sale outside the group. The reason being that the companies will have occupied the building throughout their ownership for the purpose of their trades. The previous use within the group is irrelevant.

Question 36

But for the introduction of the imputation system, distributions made by companies would not have been deductible in computing the company's liability to corporation tax. The effect would have been that the company's profits would have suffered tax twice: once in the hands of the company and once in the hands of the recipient of the distribution.

Explain how the imputation system operates and describe the extent to which the system alleviates a double charge to tax.

Answer plan

Good answers will provide discussion of the following:

- outline of the classical system;
- corporation tax assessed on the profits of companies;
- income tax assessed on distributions without tax credit for paying company;
- outline of imputation system;
- corporation tax (MCT) assessed on company's profits, whether distributed or not;
- deduction of ACT when making qualifying distributions;
- ACT may be deducted by company from its liability to MCT;
- recipient of distribution entitled to tax credit, equivalent to lower rate of tax;
- taxation consequences of making a non-qualifying distribution.

Answer

The classical system of taxation of companies, introduced by the FA 1965, charged the profits of companies neither to income tax nor capital gains tax but only to corporation tax. This rule is similar to the imputation system of taxation of the profits of companies, introduced by the FA 1972. The major difference between the two systems is that the classical system treated companies and its shareholders as separate entities. Corporation tax at the rate in force was levied on the profits of companies. Distributions made by companies suffered income tax at the current standard rate without allowing the company to deduct the income tax from its liability to corporation tax.

As an illustration of the classical system assume a corporation rate of 40% and income tax rate of 30%.

If a company distributed none of its profits, the tax charge on the company was 40%. If the company distributed all its profits the total tax charge was 70% (40% in the hands of the company and 30% in the hands of the shareholders).

Under the classical system, dividends were treated in substantially the same way as annuities or annual payments paid out of profits or gains not brought into charge to income tax. Each shareholder included the grossed up amount of the dividend payment in his return of total income.

Companies could not deduct the income tax paid on dividends or other distributions in computing profits chargeable to corporation tax. Accordingly, the profits of companies were, in a sense, taxed twice – once at the corporation tax rate in the hands of the company and again at the income tax rate when the profits were distributed to its shareholders.

One criticism that was levelled at this system was that it encouraged companies to retain profits in order to avoid income tax on distributions. However, in the case of close companies, there were provisions designed to counteract such withholding of distributions when the retention of profits was not justified by the commercial needs of the company.

Another criticism of the old system was that it treated the company and its shareholders as separate entities which was juristically correct but commercially unrealistic.

The main features of the imputation system are as follows:

(a) a company pays corporation tax (MCT) on its profits, whether distributed or not, at the prescribed rate. For 1995–96, this is 33%. For small companies (profits not exceeding £300,000) the rate is 25% for 1995–96. There is tapering relief available when the company's profits exceed £300,000, but do not exceed £1.5 m.

If the company's accounting period does not coincide with the financial year the profits of the accounting period are required to be apportioned on a time basis.

(b) When a company makes a qualifying distribution (for example, a dividend), it does not deduct Schedule F income tax as was the position under the classical system. Instead, the company deducts Advance Corporation Tax (ACT) of an amount equivalent to the lower rate of income tax (20% of the gross distribution or one quarter of the net distribution for 1995–96). The ACT is paid to the Revenue within 14 days from the end of the quarter in which the distribution was made.

There is a limit as to the amount of ACT which may be set off against the company's liability to MCT. The maximum ACT set off is the amount of ACT which would have been paid if the dividend declared together with ACT thereon equalled the profits of the year. In reality for 1995–96 this amounts to 20% of the profits. For small companies taxed at 25%, the effective rate of MCT will be reduced to 5%. For other companies, the effective rate is 33% less 20% for 1995–96.

The ACT paid in an accounting period which exceeds the prescribed limit (called surplus ACT) may be carried back and set against the company's liability to MCT (subject to limits) in the preceding six years, taking the most recent period first. Alternatively, the surplus ACT may be carried forward without time limit and set against MCT on future profits.

(c) ACT deducted by the company in respect of distributions made in an accounting period, is available for set off against the company's corporation tax liability on its profits, both income and capital, for the period.

For example, a company with profits of £100,000 in an accounting period pays corporation tax at the rate of 25% to the Revenue. This amount of £25,000 is payable within nine months from the end of the accounting period. If the company pays a dividend of £16,000 to its shareholders, it pays £4,000 (1/4 x £16,000) of ACT to the Revenue within 14 days of the end of the quarter. The company is then entitled to claim a set off of the ACT against its MCT. Thus, the company's liability to MCT is reduced to £21,000 (£25,000 – £4,000).

(d) An individual resident in the UK who receives a qualifying distribution is liable to income tax under Schedule F. He receives a tax credit, equivalent to the amount of ACT deducted by the company. His liability to income tax under Schedule F is in respect of the aggregate of the net distribution and the tax credit. The tax credit for income tax purposes satisfies his liability to lower rate (20% for 1995/96 year of assessment) and basic rate income tax (25% for 1995–96). If the shareholder is not liable to income tax because his personal allowances are equal to or greater than his income for the year of assessment, he is entitled to reclaim from the Revenue only the lower rate of tax in respect of the dividend. But, if he is liable to income tax at the higher rate (40% for 1995/96), he is required to pay the difference between the higher rate of tax and the lower rate of tax to the revenue.

For example, during the year of assessment 1995–96 an individual receives a dividend of £400 with a tax credit of £100. He is required to 'gross up' the net dividend with the amount of the tax credit in order to ascertain his liability to higher rate tax. His liability to lower and basic rate tax is discharged.

If he is not liable to income tax during this year of assessment he is entitled to reclaim the tax credit from the Revenue.

If he is liable to income tax at the basic rate his liability to tax in respect of the dividend is discharged.

If he is liable to tax at the higher rate of tax (40% for 1995–96) he is required to pay the extra tax subject to a deduction in respect of the tax credit, that is, he is required to pay an extra 20% in respect of the dividend.

(e) An individual resident in the UK who receives a non-qualifying distribution (such as the issue of bonus redeemable shares or securities) is not liable to basic rate income tax, but is liable to higher rate income tax subject to a deduction of the basic rate of tax. When the shares are redeemed, the redemption value of the shares will be treated as a qualifying distribution with the consequence that if he is liable to income tax at the higher rate, a deduction will be made for any higher rate tax paid on the non-qualifying distribution. In short, he will be liable to pay an additional higher rate of income tax provided that the higher rate tax has increased between the date of the issue of the shares and the date of redemption.

The current system of imposing tax on companies is called an 'imputation' system because part of the company's liability to corporation tax is imputed to the members, and is treated as satisfying their basic rate income tax liability. Effect is given to this imputation by conferring a tax credit on the member in respect of each distribution made to him. The system removes the bias against distributed profits, for its effect is that a company pays corporation tax at a flat rate on all its profits whether distributed or not.

Question 37

Part (a)

> In applying the concept of residence to a company, we ought ... to regard that the real business is carried on where the central management and control actually resides. [*Per* Lord Loreburn LC in *De Beers Consolidated Mines Ltd v Howe* (1906).]

Explain the above statement and indicate whether today it is an accurate test of residence of a corporation.

Part (b)

What is a 'company' for corporation tax purposes?

Answer plan

The following issues should be considered:

- Lord Loreburn's test of residence in *De Beers Consolidated Mines v Howe* (1906) of central management and control;
- significance of board meetings;
- dual residence;
- residence of subsidiaries;
- s 66 of the FA 1988 – incorporation in the UK;

- s 832 – definition of a company;
- ways of becoming a corporate association;
- unincorporated associations – definition.

Answer

Part (a)

Prior to the introduction of a supplementary test for residence of corporations by Parliament in 1988, there was no statutory definition of residence of a corporation. The test of residence as laid down by Lord Loreburn in the *De Beers* case (1906), focuses on the identification and location of the central management and control of the company. This test has been treated as 'precise and unequivocal' by Lord Radcliffe in *Unit Construction v Bullock* (1960).

In the *De Beers* case, the company was registered in South Africa. The diamond mines which the company worked were also situated in this country. The diamonds were sold through a London syndicate. Directors meetings were held both in South Africa and the UK. The majority of the directors resided in the UK. The company's contention that the place of incorporation determined its residence was rejected by the Commissioners who held that the company was resident in the UK. It was in the UK that the directors controlled and managed the chief operations of the company. The House of Lords upheld the decision of the Commissioners.

The type of control which is important is that of directors rather than the shareholders. The shareholders may, by virtue of their votes, control the company, they may compel the directors to do as they wish and account to them, but it does not follow that the shareholders manage the company. Thus, the question of residence is one of management control of the company. The place of central control and management involves actual control and not merely the place where control should properly be exercised. The notion of central management and control is, in broad terms, directed at the highest level of control of the business of a company. This is a question of fact and is to be distinguished from the place where the main operations of a business are to be found. In *Calcutta Jute Mills Co v Nicholson* (1876), a company registered in England carried on business of spinners and manufacturers of jute with mills in India. Its directors' and shareholders' meetings were held in England. It was decided that the company was resident in the UK.

It follows that factors which together are decisive in one instance may individually carry little weight in another. Importance may be attached to the place where the company's board of directors meet. There are instances of the board of directors meeting in the same country as that in which the business operations take place, and central management and control would clearly be located in that one place. There are also instances where the central management and control may be exercised by directors in one country though the actual business operations may be located elsewhere under the management of local directors.

But the location of board meetings, although important in the normal case, is not necessarily conclusive. In some cases the central management and control may be exercised by a single individual, for example, a Chairman or Managing Director who has a dominant shareholding or is given special powers by the articles of association. In general, the place of directors' meetings is significant insofar as those meetings constitute the medium through which the central management and control is exercised. If, for example, the directors of a company were engaged collectively and actively in the UK in the complete running of a business which was wholly in the UK, the company would not be regarded as resident outside the UK merely because the directors held formal board meetings outside the UK. In *American Thread Co v Joyce* (1913), a UK company manufactured cotton thread in America. Three of its seven directors were required to reside in America and formed a committee to direct its current affairs. Regular meetings of the directors were held in America but extraordinary meetings were held in London to deal with certain important matters. The House of Lords held that the company was resident in the UK.

Moreover, the central control and management may be exercised in more than one country. In this event, the company will be treated as having multiple residences in the countries in which it is controlled. If a substantial degree of control is exercised in the UK the company will be treated as resident in the UK. In *Swedish Central Railway Co v Thompson* (1925), the company had been incorporated in the UK to obtain the concession for and then build a railway line in Sweden. The company had in 1900 leased the railway to a Swedish company in return for an annual rent. In 1920, articles of association of the company were altered to remove the central management and control of the company to Sweden and the Revenue admitted that the company was now controlled and managed from Sweden. The Special Commissioners concluded that the company was managed from Sweden and the UK. This decision was upheld by the House of Lords. The place of registration, in addition to the place where certain administrative duties were performed, were significant factors in deciding whether the company was resident in the UK. In *Egyptian Delta Land and Investment Co v Todd* (1929), the company was incorporated in 1904 in the UK for the purpose of dealing in and developing land in Egypt. In 1907, most of its functions were transferred to Egypt. All that remained in London was a registered office, a register of members and a register of bearer warrants. There was a London secretary of the company who dealt with occasional correspondence and filed the annual returns. These were administrative matters which satisfied the Companies Acts requirements. The Special Commissioners decided that the *Swedish Railway Co* case could be distinguished on its facts and concluded that the company was not resident in the UK. This decision was upheld by the House of Lords. The mere satisfaction of the Companies Acts requirements *per se* is not sufficient to constitute residence in the UK.

In determining the residence of a company and, subject to statutory provisions to the contrary, the Revenue adopt the following approach:

(a) they first try to ascertain whether the directors of the company in fact exercise central control and management;

(b) if so, they seek to determine where the directors exercise this central control and management (which is not necessarily where they meet);

(c) in cases where the directors apparently do not exercise central control and management of the company, the Revenue then look to establish where and by whom it is exercised.

The same principles are applied in determining the residence of companies incorporated and carrying on business abroad which are subsidiary companies of a company resident in the UK. If the board of the subsidiary company meets abroad and effectively controls the business of that company, then it will not be resident in the UK. Alternatively, if the business of the subsidiary is in fact managed and controlled in the UK by the board of the parent company, then the subsidiary company will be resident in the UK, even though its articles of association require its board to meet in the country of incorporation. In *Unit Construction v Bullock* (1960), three subsidiary companies had been incorporated and registered in Kenya. Their articles of association placed the management and control of the business in the hands of directors and provided that meetings might be held anywhere outside the UK. Two years later, the Kenyan companies incurred substantial losses and the parent company took over management and control of the subsidiaries in an attempt to save its investment. All decisions of major importance were thereafter taken by the parent company. The House of Lords held that the Kenyan companies were resident in the UK. Likewise, if the decisions of the board of the subsidiary companies are held abroad but are subject to overriding control by a committee of the board which meets in the UK, the company will be resident in the UK (see *American Thread Co v Joyce*).

In addition to the above case law approach, a second criterion for determining residence of a company was enacted in s 66 of the FA 1988. As from 15 March 1988, a company incorporated in the UK is treated as resident here for tax purposes. Such a company may also be resident in another country where its central management and control is exercised. Moreover, companies incorporated in the UK before 15 March 1988 and carried on its business before this time, will become resident in the UK as from 15 March 1993. This change does not mean the abolition of the old case law test of control. The case law test remains important in two circumstances, namely:

(a) where the company is incorporated in a country outside the UK; and

(b) where the company was incorporated in the UK before 15 March 1988 and the issue arises before 15 March 1993.

Part (b)

The effect of ss 6(1) and 8(1) of the TA 1988 is that the profits of companies are chargeable to corporation tax and a company resident in the UK is liable to corporation tax on all its profits, wherever arising. A non-resident company is liable to corporation tax only if it trades in the UK through a branch or agency and its liability will then be restricted to the chargeable profits from that branch or agency (s 11 of the TA 1988). It follows that a non-resident company trading in the UK but not through any branch or agency, cannot be assessed to corporation tax but will be subject to UK income tax.

Section 832 of the TA 1988 defines a company as any body corporate or unincorporated association but excluding a partnership or local authority.

A company may be incorporated by Royal Charter, under a special Act of Parliament or under the Companies Act 1985. The effect of incorporation is that the company is treated as an entity distinct from its promoters and shareholders.

An unincorporated association has been defined as 'two or more persons bound together for one or more common purposes by mutual undertakings, each having mutual duties and obligations, in an organisation with rules which identify in whom control of the association and its funds rests', *per* Lawton LJ in *Conservative and Unionist Central Office v Burrell* (1982), the Court of Appeal held that the Conservative Party Central Office was not chargeable to corporation tax as the organisation was not an unincorporated association. Whether an organisation satisfies this test or not is a question of law. In *Blackpool Marton Rotary Club v Martin* (1988), the court held that a Rotary Club founded in 1972, which raised funds for charities and also acted as a social club for its members, was an unincorporated association and liable to corporation tax on its bank interest.

If an unincorporated association has members who are bound together for business purposes it will be treated as a partnership under the Partnership Act 1890 and liable to income tax. A partnership is excluded from corporation tax by virtue of s 832 of the TA 1988.

Question 38

Jonathan intends to commence a supermarket business. His wife, Margaret, is willing to assist him by devoting as much of her time as is reasonably necessary to make the business a success, but is reluctant to contribute financially to the venture. Jonathan has limited resources and is considering the various mediums of business available to him. In particular, he wishes you to advise him on whether to commence the business operation as:

(a) a sole trader; or

(b) partnership with his wife, Margaret; or

(c) a limited company.

Advise him.

Answer plan

Your answer should consider the following points:

- raising capital and fragmentation of business;
- maximum number of participants in business;
- charges on business assets and floating charges;
- separate entity as a company;
- effect of death of founding member of business;
- formal requirements of trading entity;
- rates of taxation of different trading entities;
- dates of payment of tax;
- loss relief of different trading entities;
- methods of reducing profits available to companies;
- rates of taxation on capital gains;
- 'double taxation' on sale of company assets.

Answer

One of Jonathan's primary concerns will be his ability to raise capital. As we have been told, he has limited resources to start the business. It will be necessary for him at a very early stage to make a calculation of the amount of capital he will need in order to commence the business. In particular, he will need to ascertain the cost of suitable premises (possibly converting existing premises), running costs of the business and machinery needed for the trade.

Having carefully estimated his initial costs, Jonathan will then be required to raise the necessary finance from banks and other finance institutions. It is here that the trading medium of the company may have an advantage over the other methods of trading. The company is able to provide assets (shares) which are easy to transfer and divide into many parcels. Large numbers of shares may be easily divided between friends and family for consideration. However, a sole trader or partnership suffers the disadvantage of not being capable of such widespread diversity. The maximum number of persons who may be members of a partnership is 20: see s 716 of the Companies Act 1985.[1] Margaret may also join the firm, but she has already indicated that she is unwilling to contribute funds to the business. Thus, she may be treated as a salaried partner not responsible for contributing to the capital, not sharing in the profits of the business and not being responsible for the losses.

Allied to the above as an attraction for trading as a company is the ease with which a charge may be attached over the assets of the company. In respect of all three mediums of trading, a fixed charge may be attached to specific assets of the business. This may have the effect of restricting the trader's activities and flexibility. But a company has a distinct advantage over the other mediums of trading by the imposition of a floating charge over the assets of the company. A floating charge is an equitable charge over assets of a particular description owned by a company from time to time, that is, the company's circulating capital. It is not possible to impose a fixed charge on the stock of the company for this will prevent the company from dealing with its stock. But it is possible to impose a floating charge over the stock of the company, in which case the charge will 'float' over whatever stock the company acquires from time to time.[2] The advantage of the floating charge to the company is that the company is left free to deal with the business assets as it sees fit, subject to the limitations imposed by the terms of the charge.

The company has the distinct advantage over the other mediums of trading by virtue of its separate legal entity. The company is treated as a distinct entity, different from the promoters of the company as well as the shareholders. The shareholders' liability is restricted to the amount they agreed to subscribe to the business and cannot be increased beyond this amount, except with their consent (see s 16 of the Companies Act 1985). Once this limit has been reached, the company's liability does not affect the shareholders. On the other hand, the sole trader's and partner's liability extend to these individuals' private fortunes.

A company never dies, it may only be liquidated. The death of a shareholder does not affect the business, but the death of a sole trader or partner has the effect of terminating the trade. The reason for this rule is that the assets of the business are vested in the sole trader or partner.

A company suffers from a greater deal of formality and rigidity when compared with the other mediums of trading. The expense of formation (including 'off the peg' companies) of a company is probably the same as a professionally drafted partnership agreement. A company is under an obligation to file annual returns and to submit annual audited accounts to the Registrar of Companies. The company is required to have at least one director and a secretary. Changes in the internal running of the company requires changes in the articles of the company. These require a special resolution, that is, 75% majority of shareholders. The activities of a company are limited to the specific purpose(s) as set out in its memorandum. Conduct beyond such powers is *ultra vires* and void. However, the modern tendency is to draft extremely wide objects clauses so as to avoid restricting the company's activities. The Companies Act 1985 has greatly modified the *ultra vires* doctrine. Sole traders and partnerships are, of course, not subject to such rule. Moreover, a company's affairs are subject to a great deal of publicity detailed in its annual accounts which is available to the public. The affairs of a sole trader and partnership may be kept secret.

Companies pay corporation tax on its profits (both income and capital) at a flat rate of 21% or 31% depending on its size. Small companies pay corporation tax at the rate of 21%. A small company for the financial year 1998, is one with profits not exceeding £300,000. Certainly in the early years, Jonathan's company (if he decides to incorporate the business) is more likely to be a small company. If the profits exceed £300,000 but do not exceed £1.5 m, the company is entitled to taper relief. Alternatively, a sole trader or partner in a business pays income tax at a top rate of 40% if the individual's taxable income exceeds £27,100 for 1998–99.

The dates of payment of tax vary with the type of business. A company pays corporation tax on the current year basis, within nine months from the end of the company's accounting period. A new business is assessed to income tax on the current year basis and tax is payable in two equal installments, the first is due on 31 January in the tax year and the other is due on 31 July following the end of the tax year.

Greater flexibility is accorded to a trader or partner in respect of loss relief as compared to a company. The unincorporated trader is able to set his trading losses against his capital gains in the year of the loss and one following year. He may also set off his losses against his other income of the year in which the loss arises and of the preceding year. There are special reliefs enacted under s 381 of the TA 1988 in respect of the early years of trading. Whereas a company does not enjoy such a degree of flexibility as an unincorporated trader. Companies may set their losses against capital profits but otherwise are required to set off its losses against its profits in the future.

There are a variety of ways in which a company may reduce its profits and thus its liability to corporation tax. Directors' remuneration is deducted from the profits of a company and therefore reduces the net profits liable to corporation tax. Such award of remuneration could be used by the company to control its profits and in appropriate cases to restrict its rate of tax, that is, to keep it below £300,000. The directors are, of course, liable to income tax under Schedule E in respect of their income. The company is required to deduct income tax under the PAYE system. Perhaps, both Jonathan and Margaret may be appointed directors with an appropriate number of shares in the company. With respect to a partnership, all the income profits of the partnership are apportioned between the partners and taxed as their income.

When the company makes a qualifying distribution it is required to deduct ACT equivalent to 20/80 of the amount of the net distribution. This ACT may be set off against the company's liability to corporation tax and a repayment or discharge from corporation tax is achieved. The individual recipient of the distribution will be liable to a higher rate of income tax under Schedule F on the gross amount of the distribution but is entitled to a tax credit (of 20% of the gross amount of the dividend) in respect of the tax deducted. The tax credit discharges the individual's liability to basic rate tax. If the recipient is not liable to income tax, he is entitled to reclaim the credit. It must be stressed that most private companies are close companies and most benefits in kind received by participators are treated as distributions by the company with the effect as described above. In addition, loans made by close companies to participators (and companies are prohibited from making loans to its directors: see Companies Act 1985) subject the company to liability to pay ACT which will be refunded when the loan is repaid. The shareholder will suffer Schedule E income tax liability on the loan. Since the sole trader and partnership are treated as the same entities with profits liable to income tax, the issue arises as to whether the expense is deductible by the business.

Capital gains are included in the profits of the company and are subject to corporation tax at the relevant rates. An individual, however, is entitled to an annual relief (of £6,800 for the year 1998–99), but the gain is added to his marginal income tax rate for the year of assessment with a top rate of 40%. Although the company does not receive an annual relief from capital gains tax, the highest rate of corporation tax is 31%. A significantly lower limit compared with individuals.

Retirement relief is available in the case of a disposal of shares provided that the company is a trading company and a personal company and the disposal is by a full time working director who has attained the age of 50 (for 1998–99). In *Palmer v Maloney* (1998), the court decided that a person who devoted 85–90% of his time to the affairs of a company in which he was a major shareholder was not enough. The conditions of the relief are more generous in respect of sole traders and partners.

A company suffers a form of double taxation when it sells an asset. It pays corporation tax on its profits, including the sale proceeds. In addition, the value of its shares increases and a further liability to corporation tax arises on the disposal of those shares, whereas, the sole trader or partner will pay capital gains tax in respect of disposals of such assets.

It is generally difficult to lay down any hard and fast rules as to which business medium will be suitable to Jonathan. A vast number of factors must be considered. A primary issue of importance is the significance of limited liability. On balance, if the business envisaged is large, the medium of the company may be advisable, but if a modest undertaking is contemplated a partnership or sole trading may be appropriate.

Notes

1 An exception is made in respect of certain professions, including those of solicitors and accountants.

2 In *In re Yorkshire Woolcombers Association Ltd* (1903), the characteristics of a floating charge were stated by Romer LJ as:

   (a) an equitable charge on a class of assets, present and future;

   (b) the class is one which, in the ordinary course of business, changes from time to time;

   (c) until some step is taken by or on behalf of those interested in the charge, the company may carry on its business in the ordinary way.

Question 39

Outline the merits of companies affiliating themselves into groups.

Answer plan

A good answer will deal with the following matters:

- definitions of a group;
- joint election in respect of the payment of dividends to 51% group member;
- the surrender of surplus ACT to a claimant company within a 51% group;
- transfer of assets between members of a group;
- group relief;
- replacement of business assets by group members.

Answer

Generally, individual companies joining together as a group of companies are treated separately for corporation tax purposes. Each company is taxed separately and the group is not treated as one unit. However, there are a number of taxation privileges associated with group identity. These are as follows:

- dividends and other income payments between members;
- the surrender of ACT to subsidiary members of a group;
- transfers of assets between members;
- the surrender of losses;
- replacement of business assets by group members.

The concept of a 'group of companies' varies with the nature of the relief that is claimed and the context in which the issue arises. There are provisions which relate to 51% or 75% or 90% subsidiaries. The group relationship between companies is determined by control or ownership of shares in another company. Thus, if company A owns 100% of the shares in company B which owns 90% of the shares in company C, then A, B and C form a group. If company C owns 40% of shares in company D, D is not a member of the group.

Where a dividend (but not other distributions) is received by a member of a 51% group from another member of the group, the dividend is treated as group income. On a joint election by both the paying and recipient companies, the paying company will not be liable to pay ACT on the dividends. Likewise, the recipient company may not claim a tax credit (see s 247 of the TA 1988). Accordingly, the dividend is not included as 'franked payments' made by the paying company or FII of the recipient company. The individual companies within the group are treated as a single unit if the election is made. Likewise, if the same conditions are satisfied the companies may jointly elect that charges on income be paid by one group member to another without deduction of income tax.

A UK resident company may surrender all or part of any surplus ACT attributable to dividends paid by it during an accounting period to a subsidiary member of a 51% group: see s 240 of the TA 1988. The recipient company must be a subsidiary during the whole of the accounting period for which the ACT was paid. If these conditions are satisfied the subsidiary is treated as if it had made a distribution which attracted the ACT. The ACT may be offset against the subsidiary's current liability to tax or carried forward, but it cannot be carried back. The claim to surrender ACT must be made within six years following the end of the accounting period in which it was made.

A disposal of an asset by a group member to another company within a '75% group' is treated as giving rise to 'no gain and no loss' (see s 171 of the TCGA 1992). The effect is that the real gain arising in respect of the transaction is postponed until the asset is transferred outside the group or until the company owning the asset leaves the group (see s 178 of the TCGA 1992). If the recipient company appropriates the asset as trading stock it is required to make an election:

- either to treat the appropriation as taxed as a disposal at market value; or
- to convert the gain into a trading profit less the amount of the gain and postpone the liability to pay tax until the asset is sold.

In *News International v Shepherd* (1989), the court decided that the acquisition of a tax loss company which acquired an asset from the parent did not constitute a composite transaction within the *Furniss v Dawson* (1982) principle. As a result of the *Shepherd* decision, s 88 and Schedule 8 to the FA 1993 were passed which introduced a new s 177A and Schedule 7A to the TCGA 1992. The objective of these provisions is to counteract the tax planning practice of purchasing capital loss companies. But the provision extends to companies acquired with unrealised capital losses. In summary, the statute introduced restrictions on the set off of pre-entry losses. Bought-in, realised or latent losses may only be set against gains accruing to the acquired company before it joined the group, gains accruing on assets it or an associated company acquired before then, and gains accruing on assets used exclusively in a trade started before then.

All trades carried on by members of a 75% group are treated as a single trade for the purpose of applying the rules relating to the replacement of business assets (see s 175 of the TCGA 1992). It has been the Revenue practice to regard this as permitting a gain arising on an asset owned by one member to be rolled over into the cost of an asset acquired by another member. Section 48 of the FA 1995 introduced a new s 175(2A) which provides that if the disposal of the old assets is by one member of the group and the acquisition of the new assets is by another member, roll over relief applies as if the two companies were the same person.

Group relief is available to 75% members of a group. Group relief is a means of transferring the benefit of certain corporation tax reliefs from one member of a group (the surrendering company) to another group member (claimant company). This might be done for a variety of reasons. The main reason, in practice, is that normally the surrendering company has such enormous trading losses that it cannot see any hope of getting them relieved against its own income in the future. The types of relief available are:

(a) trading losses made by the surrendering company in its current accounting period. Trading losses brought forward are ignored;

(b) capital allowances of the surrendering company given by way of discharge or repayment of tax and are available for set off against a specified class of income, for example, allowances on industrial buildings and structures subject to a lease are to be given primarily against Schedule A income or allowances on machinery and plant leased otherwise than in the course of the trade. Insofar as the allowances exceed such income for an accounting period they may be surrendered;

(c) if the surrendering company is entitled to a deduction for management expenses, the amount that may be surrendered is so much as exceeds the 'profits' accruing in that accounting period. In computing the 'profits' of the accounting period, losses, capital allowances and management expenses brought forward are ignored;

(d) the amount by which charges on income that are paid in an accounting period of the surrendering company exceed its 'profits' in that accounting period may be surrendered to the claimant company. The 'profits' of the surrendering company are computed without regard to any deduction of losses, capital allowances or management expenses brought forward.

A special method of computing the profits of the company against which group relief may be allowed. Group relief shall be allowed as a deduction against the claimant's total profits for the period as reduced by other relief (trading losses, capital allowances given against profits and charges on income), but before any relief derived from a subsequent accounting period, namely, relief for a trading loss carried back from a later accounting period, capital allowances available against a specified class of income and terminal loss relating to a subsequent accounting period. In short, group relief takes priority over any relief which is carried back from a subsequent accounting period.

It is not necessary to make a payment for group relief but if one is made, it is ignored in computing the profits and losses of both companies for tax purposes.

In conclusion, it may be said that several companies joining together to form a group makes good commercial sense. An obvious disadvantage is that the group is likely to lose the tapering relief available to medium sized companies. The upper and lower limits are reduced by the number of associated companies. The effect is that lower limits are applicable to associate companies. Two companies are associated if they are under common control or if one has control of the other.

SECTION V
INHERITANCE TAX

CHAPTER 11

INHERITANCE TAX

Inheritance tax is one of the taxes charged on the movement of capital, being essentially a tax on the transfer of capital. Inheritance tax had its early origins in estate duty, a tax charged on the property of a deceased person on his death. This duty was later replaced by capital transfer tax (CTT) in 1975, which unlike estate duty, also taxed transfers of capital made by a person during the disponer's lifetime and on death. CTT later gave way to inheritance tax (in respect of transfers which occurred on or after 18 March 1986), a tax, which like estate duty, imposes a charge on the property of a person on his death, but which also, like CTT, imposes a charge on life time transfers. Inheritance tax differs from CTT in one important respect – unlike CTT, most life time transfers are not immediately chargeable, and, indeed, may never be chargeable. Some of these are potentially chargeable and will become chargeable if the donor or transferor dies within seven years of the transfer. These types of transfer are referred to as potentially exempt transfers (PETs). In effect, therefore, inheritance tax is a charge on transfers made (or deemed to be made) by a person on the occasion of that person's death, or in the seven year period immediately preceding death. The principal legislation is the Inheritance Tax Act 1984 (IHTA), which originally was the Capital Transfer Tax Act 1984. There are a number of different rates of tax on *chargeable* transfers. First, there is a nil (0%) rate for transfers of value up to a certain specified amount (this amount varies from year to year – for example, for the 1998–99 year of assessment, this amount is £223,000). Secondly, there is a 'life' rate for chargeable dispositions made during the transferor's lifetime (in 1998–99, this is 20%). Thirdly, there is the normal (or 'death') rate, in respect of chargeable transfers occurring on the death of the transferor (in 1998–99, this is 40%: see, generally, s 7 of the IHTA 1984). Tapering relief is available in respect of chargeable transfers made longer than three but less than seven years prior to the transferor's death (s 7(4) of the IHTA 1984).

Definitions

As indicated earlier, inheritance tax is chargeable on the movement (or a transfer) of capital. The actual charge is to be found in s 1 of the IHTA 1984 which provides that inheritance tax shall be charged on the *'value* transferred by a *chargeable transfer'* (emphasis added). A chargeable transfer is defined as a *'transfer of value,* made by an *individual'*, and which is not an exempt transfer (s 2(1) of the IHTA 1984; emphasis added). For these purposes, a transfer of value is a *disposition* made by a person (the transferor) which results in the reduction of the value of that person's estate. The value transferred by the transfer is the amount by which the transferor's estate is reduced on account of the transfer (s 3(1) of the IHTA 1984). For the purposes of the Act, a person's estate is the aggregate of all the property to which he is beneficially entitled, except that a person's estate during his lifetime does not include 'excluded property' (s 5(1) of the IHTA 1984). *Excluded property* is defined in s 6; it includes for example, property situated abroad if the owner is an individual who is not domiciled in the UK. Some dispositions are treated as not being transfers of value (see, generally, ss 10 *et seq* of the IHTA 1984).

As the preceding statements reveal, the concept of a person's estate is an important feature of the inheritance tax scheme. Generally, the tax attaches to the amount by which a disposition causes a reduction in the value of the transferor's estate. What this means is that the relevant issue is the loss to the transferor, and not the gain of the recipient (that is, the amount by which the recipient's estate is increased on account of the transfer) – and there may be wide discrepancies in these. For example, if a person with a 51% holding in a company gives away a 2% holding, his estate would thereby lose much more (a controlling interest in the company, whatever that may be worth) than the recipient would gain (a mere 2% holding). The issue of the reduction in the transferor's estate also comes into play in cases where (as is normally the case) the burden of the tax is to be borne by the transferor or his estate. In such situations, the reduction in the estate will be the value originally transferred (as defined) in addition to the tax that will be chargeable on that transfer (s 5(4)).

Exemptions

A transfer of value is either chargeable or exempt. As indicated earlier, s 2(1) of the IHTA 1984 provides that a transfer is chargeable if it is not exempt. The Act (from s 18 onwards) contains a wide variety of transfers which are declared to be exempt. Among these are inter-spousal transfers (s 18), small gifts (s 20), gifts to charities (s 23) and to qualifying political parties (s 24), etc. Somewhere in between the chargeable and the exempt transfer is the potentially exempt transfer (PET). This is defined as a transfer of value which is made by an individual on or after 18 March 1986, which would otherwise be a chargeable transfer, and which constitutes a gift to another individual, or to an accumulation and maintenance trust or a disabled trust (s 3A(1)). A PET is normally presumed, at the time when it is made, to be exempt (s 3A(5)), and references to chargeable transfers do not normally include references to PETs (s 3A(6)). A PET will indeed be exempt if it is made seven years or more before the death of the transferor – but if the transferor dies within seven years of the transfer, the PET becomes a chargeable transfer (s 3A(4)).

Death

In many cases, the death of the transferor will be the event that will trigger a charge to inheritance tax. Section 4(1) of the IHTA 1984 treats the death of a person as a transfer of value by that person of an amount equal to the value of the person's estate immediately before the death. Apart from this deemed transfer of the whole of the deceased's estate, death also has other consequences. The first is that any PET which was made within seven years of the death becomes chargeable. The second is that chargeable transfers made during the life of the transferor, but within seven years of his death, become liable to a supplementary charge at death rates, subject to tapering relief where the death occurs more than three but less than seven years of the transfer.

Question 40

Baroness Kludge of Longton is a wealthy Staffordshire businesswoman aged 60. In order to try to reduce the amount of inheritance tax payable in the event of her death, she has made a number of transactions. One involves gifts of three of her country estates. The first, an estate in Shropshire, worth £150,000, was donated to 'Save our Frogs', a local charity, for the purpose of rearing endangered amphibians. The second, an estate in Stafford, worth £120,000, was given to the *Staffordshire Bugle*, a local newspaper, which had employed her grandfather 60 years ago. The third, worth £100,000, was given to Lancelot, her butler of many years. She has an agreement with Save our Frogs and the *Staffordshire Bugle* to lodge in the relevant estates whenever she is 'in the area'. She has also made a gift of her house in London, worth £450,000, to her estranged husband, Baron Kludge, 'in appreciation of the good times we had together', and a gift of £2,000 to James Kludge, the Baron's 16 year old son from a previous marriage, who she is very fond of. After two years of desperate effort, her estate agents have recently managed to dispose of her mansion in the Welsh valleys, worth £200,000, for a sum of £125,000. They had just succeeded in convincing her that, given the 'slowness of the housing market and current interest rates', it was impossible to obtain a higher price.

Assuming that her cumulative total of chargeable transfers is £140,000, advise Baroness Kludge as to the inheritance tax implications of these transactions.

Answer plan

This question involves a large number of issues. Some issues relate to gifts to charities, gifts subject to reservations, and inter-spousal transfers, and others involve general questions about the types of activity which would amount to transfers of value. There are also general questions about exempt and potentially exempt transfers (PETs). It is best to address these issues chronologically, and if possible, separately, so as not to mix up the issues or miss any point. However, some of the activities (for example, the gifts of the country estates) are related, and could be discussed together.

Answer

In order to advise on the possible inheritance tax implications of Baroness Kludge's activities, we need first to examine briefly the scope of the tax. According to s 1 of the IHTA 1984, inheritance tax is charged on the values transferred by chargeable transfers, which are defined by s 2(1) as non-exempt transfers of value made by individuals. Transfers of value are 'dispositions' which reduce the value of the transferor's estate (s 3(1)). Therefore, in order for the Baroness' activities to have any inheritance tax implication at all, they must have amounted to transfers of value which are not exempt transfers. We will examine each of her activities in the general context of this theme.

We will first consider the gifts of her country estates. Each of these would amount to a 'disposition'. Even though the term is not defined in the IHTA, it would seem wide enough to include any activity whereby an interest in property is passed from one person to another. Clearly, these dispositions would result in a reduction in the value of the Baroness' 'estate' (which means the aggregate of all the properties to which she is beneficially entitled (s 5(1)). Thus, each of these gifts would *prima facie* amount to a transfer of value (there may however be other factors, to discussed later, which may negative this conclusion). If these are transfers of value, are they 'chargeable' transfers? The clear provision of s 2(1) is that they would be chargeable unless they are 'exempt'. This leads us to an examination of the question whether any of them is exempt.

The gift to Save our Frogs may possibly be exempt under the 'gifts to charities' rule. Section 23(1) provides that a transfer of value is exempt to the extent that the value transferred by it is attributable to property which is 'given to charities'. For this purpose, property is 'given to charities' if, *inter alia*, it becomes the property of charities. Since we are told that the estate was 'donated' to Save our Frogs, it would seem that the estate has thereby become the property of that charity, and that the gift would consequently be exempt. There is, however, a restriction in s 23(4) which may be applicable in this case. The sub-section provides that the exemption will not apply in relation to any property if the property is land or a building and is given 'subject to an interest reserved or created by the donor' which entitles him to occupy any part of the land/building otherwise than at a proper rent. In this case, Baroness Kludge has an 'agreement' with Save our Frogs, which would entitle her to 'lodge' at the estate when she is in the area. It would seem that her lodging at the estate would fall within the term 'occupy' in s 23(4) and, since there is no indication from the facts that a commercial rent is payable for such a lodging, it appears that she has created or reserved an interest of occupation in the estate. Questions arise as to whether this interest is one that would 'entitle' her to occupy, or merely be one that permits her to occupy, and whether this would be material. It is submitted that permission and entitlement are two very different things and that the difference would be material here. Therefore, if the 'agreement' referred to were binding, then the exemption would not apply – but, if it merely involved permission (even if invariably given), then it is submitted that the exemption would not be lost. In this question, it is not possible to decide the matter definitively, but it would appear that the gift is absolute, and that the 'agreement' to lodge only implies permission. Thus, the exemption in s 23 would appear to be available.

In spite of the conclusion just reached, there is another factor which may affect the inheritance tax position of the gift to Save our Frogs, and, of the gift to the *Staffordshire Bugle*. This concerns the 'gifts with reservation' rules. The governing provision is s 102 of the FA 1986. The section applies where an individual disposes of property by way of gift, and either possession and enjoyment of the property is not *bona fide* assumed by the donee at or before the beginning of 'the relevant period', or where at any time in the relevant period, the property is not enjoyed to the entire exclusion or virtually to the entire exclusion, of the donor, and of any benefit to him. For gifts made during the donor's life time, the 'relevant period' is the seven year period leading up to the donor's death. The type of property just described is referred to as 'property subject to a reservation' (s 102(2) of the Finance Act 1986 (FA)). The effect of s 102(3) of the FA 1986 is that any property which is subject to a reservation at the time of the donor's death is treated as still being comprised in the donor's estate at the time of death. What this basically means is that, since the property is still part of the donor's estate, the value of the donor's estate would not have been reduced by the gift of that property, and, therefore, the gift would not be a transfer of value. Thus, if the gift to Save our Frogs and/or the *Staffordshire Bugle* were subject to a reservation, there would be no inheritance tax implications at all in respect thereof (at least, during the Baroness' life time). There is no indication that either of the donees concerned has not *bona fide* assumed possession, but it is clear that the properties are not being enjoyed to the 'entire' exclusion of the Baroness, and of any benefit to her. Are they enjoyed 'virtually' to her entire exclusion? This concept of 'virtual' exclusion is usually taken as a *de minimis* rule, which means, according to the Inland Revenue's interpretation (RI 55, November 1993) that a gift does not fail in cases where the benefit to the donor is 'insignificant' in relation to the gifted property (that is, donors are not unreasonably prevented from having limited access to property which they have given away). Examples given in RI 55 include stays in the absence of the donee for not more than two weeks each year, and stays with the donee for less than one month each year. Invariably, this is a question of fact and degree. There is no indication that the Baroness' stays in either property amount to a significant period, and it would seem therefore that this *de minimis* rule would apply here. In any case, with respect to the gift to Save our Frogs, s 102(5) of the FA 1986 provides that the section does not apply to a gift which is an exempt transfer under s 23 of the IHTA 1984 – which we have concluded that this gift is. We would therefore conclude that the gift to Save our Frogs is an exempt transfer. With respect to the gift to the *Staffordshire Bugle*, the fact that the gift is not subject to a reservation under s 102 of the FA 1986 means that it is, after all, a disposition which reduces the value of the Baroness' estate – a transfer of value. This is a transfer which does not appear to be exempt under any provision of the IHTA 1984. It is also not a 'potentially exempt' transfer. This is defined in s 3A(1) as (in simple terms) a gift made by an individual to another individual or into certain types of trust. Clearly, the *Staffordshire Bugle*, being neither an individual nor a trust, does not fall within any of the permitted donees and therefore the gift to it is a chargeable transfer.

The value transferred to the *Staffordshire Bugle* will fall to be added to Baroness Kludge's cumulative total of chargeable transfers in the seven year period ending with this transfer (s 7(1)). We are told that the cumulative total currently stands at £140,000. The current transfer is to the value of £120,000, and it first might appear that this would take her cumulative total to £260,000. However, transferors are entitled to an annual exemption – a certain amount of tax-free transfers of value (see s 19(1) of the IHTA 1984 – in 1998–99, the annual exempt amount is £3,000). Assuming that the annual exemption is £3,000, we would need to deduct this amount from the sum of £120,000. This would leave a sum of £117,000. While it may appear that this is the figure to add to the cumulative total, again, another principle comes into play – 'grossing up'. In this context, s 5(3) of the IHTA 1984 provides that, in determining the value of a person's estate at any time, his liabilities at that time shall be taken into account. The liabilities concerned are specified in s 5(4), which provides that any liability of the transferor to inheritance tax (but not any other tax) on the value transferred will be taken into account. These provisions are to the effect that, in cases where the transferor is to bear the burden of inheritance tax on a gift, the initial transferred value is treated as net of inheritance tax. Where the transferor does not bear the burden of the tax (for example, in respect of deemed transfers that occur on the death of the transferor), then that value is gross. However, where the transferor is to bear the burden of the tax, the value originally transferred has to be grossed up at the transferor's marginal rates to determine the total amount by which her estate is depleted by the transfer. Since the primary responsibility for lifetime gifts falls normally on the transferor (s 199(1)), grossing up will, unless there is a clear indication that someone else is to bear the burden of the tax, be a feature of *inter vivos* transfers such as this, which are immediately chargeable. Grossing up in these situations is normally achieved by multiplying the value that was originally transferred (in most cases the value of the property itself) by a fraction determined by this formula:

$$\frac{100}{100 - R}$$

where R is the rate at which inheritance tax is charged on the transfer.

So assuming, as in this case, that we have a chargeable transfer of property worth £120,000, that the transferor has an annual exemption of £3,000, and that the gift is to be taxed at the rate of 20%, the total loss to her estate would be;

$$\frac{100}{100-20} \times £117,000 = £146,250$$

In cases where there is no tax due from the transferor on a chargeable transfer (either because the transferor's cumulative total is still within the nil rate band, or because the transferee is to bear the burden of the tax on the gift) grossing up is effectively displaced. In the present question, there is no indication that the *Staffordshire Bugle* is to bear the burden of the tax, and so we would assume that Baroness Kludge is to bear the burden (under s 119(1)), and that the £117,000 has to be grossed up. The issue however becomes a bit complicated in this case, because some of that amount will be taxed at a nil (0%) rate. Schedule 1 and s 7 of the IHTA 1984, which stipulate the rates of tax, provide for a certain amount (£215,000 in 1997–98 and £223,000 in 1998–99) to be taxed at the nil rate, and for amounts over that to be taxed at 40% (except that chargeable *inter vivos* transfers are taxed at half of 40% – that is, 20%). It is clear that tax at the nil rate is not going to reduce the value of the Baroness' estate, and so it is necessary to ascertain what actually does reduce it. In this case, assuming that the nil rate threshold is £223,000, tax will be due on;

(£140,000 + £117,000) – £223,000 =	£34,000
at 20%, the tax due =	£6,800
the gross transfer = £117,000 + £6,800 =	£123,800
the cumulative total = £140,000 + £123,800 =	£263,800

The gift to Lancelot can be disposed of more easily. It is clearly a transfer of value, and would be a chargeable transfer unless exempted in some way. While there are many full exemptions in the IHTA 1984, none of them seems applicable here. However, as we have just seen, there is a type of 'potential' exemption. Section 3A(1) provides for a type of transfer known as a potentially exempt transfer (PET). This is defined as a transfer of value, made by an individual on or after 18 March 1986, which would otherwise be a chargeable transfer, and which constitutes a gift to another individual, or certain specified trusts. The necessary conditions exist here, and thus the gift to Lancelot is a PET. The effect of the transfer being a PET is that it is not (immediately) chargeable. It is assumed by the IHTA that a PET will prove to be an exempt transfer (s 3A(5)), and a PET will indeed be an exempt transfer if the transferor does not die within seven years of making it (s 3A(4)). Thus, this gift will not attract any immediate inheritance tax consequences.

Next we address the gift of the Baroness' London house to her estranged husband (Baron Kludge), and the gift of £2,000 to his son, James. Again, both would appear to be transfers of value in that they are dispositions which reduce the value of Baroness Kludge's estate. The gift to Baron Kludge might be exempt under s 18(1) of the IHTA 1984 which provides that a transfer of value is exempt to the extent that the value transferred is attributable to property which becomes comprised in the estate of the transferor's spouse. The IHTA does not define the term 'spouse' but it also does not seem to ascribe any special meaning thereto. We may, therefore, assume that it will bear its ordinary meaning (the wife or husband of a person). This would seem to include 'estranged' spouses, since they would still be legally married until a decree of divorce becomes absolute (s 16 of the Matrimonial Causes Act 1973). Therefore, although the Baroness and her husband are estranged, she will still be entitled to this exemption for inter-spousal transfers. It was stated earlier that the gift of £2,000 to James Kludge would appear to be a transfer of value by virtue of being a disposition which reduces the value of the Baroness' estate. While this would normally be the situation in respect of gifts generally, this is not inevitable, and certain provisions may operate to produce a contrary conclusion. Relevant in this respect is s 11(1), which provides that a disposition by one party to a marriage in favour of a child of either party is not a transfer of value if it is (inter alia) for the maintenance, education or training of the child while the child is under the age of 18. In this case, some of the requirements are clearly satisfied – the £2,000 is a gift to a child of one party to the marriage, and the child is below the age of 18. The real question is the purpose of the gift – particularly, whether it was for James' maintenance, education or training. The answer to this is not obvious from the facts given, but perhaps one could assume that one main purpose of such a gift would be for the maintenance of the child. If so, then this would not be a transfer of value at all. If not, then the transfer would be a PET. It is submitted that s 11(1) applies here, and that the gift is, therefore, not a transfer of value.

The disposal of the Welsh mansion for £125,000 is obviously a 'disposition'. The fact that the mansion was sold for much less than it is worth means that Baroness Kludge's estate has been reduced by the amount of the undervalue. This then would mean that the sale is a disposition which causes a reduction on the value of her estate, and, by definition (under s 3(1) of the IHTA 1984) this would *prima facie* be a transfer of value. This first impression may however be negatived by s 10(1) of the IHTA 1984, which provides that a disposition is not a transfer of value if it is shown that it was not intended to confer a gratuitous benefit on any person, and if it was either made in a transaction at arm's length between unconnected persons, or was such as might be expected to be in such a transaction. This requires an examination of the motive or purpose of the transaction. In this case, it seems that the sale at an undervalue was prompted largely by forces beyond the Baroness' control (market forces), and not by any wish to confer a gratuitous benefit on the purchaser. The conclusion then is that the sale of the Welsh mansion is not a transfer of value.

In conclusion, most of Baroness Kludge's recent transactions would attract no inheritance tax consequences – either because they are exempt transfers (for example, the gift to her estranged husband) or because they are not transfers of value (for example, the sale of the Welsh mansion). One transaction (the gift of a country estate to the *Staffordshire Bugle*) is a chargeable transfer, and will attract an immediate charge to inheritance tax. It will also attract an additional charge (at 'death' rates) if the Baroness were to die within seven years of making the gift. One transfer (the gift to Lancelot) is a PET. This will be an exempt transfer unless the Baroness dies within seven years of making the gift.

Question 41

David died on 20 April 1998 when he was 65 years old. Prior to his death David carried out the following transactions, having made no previous chargeable transfers:

(a) in January 1997, he transferred his house, then worth £150,000, into the name of his daughter. At the same time, his daughter granted David a lease of the property for 10 years at a commercial rent;

(b) in August 1997, he exchanged a racehorse he owned for a horse owned by Anne. His horse was worth £60,000 and Anne's horse worth only £50,000, but David thought it had good potential. In fact, the horse broke its leg in its next race and had to be put down;

(c) David was an amateur artist and, in January 1998, he gave two large paintings to his sister, Sally. In his life time, he only sold a few paintings for no more than £500 each, but following his death, his work has become very popular, and Sally's paintings are now worth £50,000 each.

When he died, David left his remaining paintings to his mistress, Marcia. At the time of his death, these were collectively worth £100,000, but are now worth £300,000. David's residuary estate was worth £400,000. By his will, he left his residuary estate equally to his wife and his sister.

Advise his executors on the inheritance tax position.

Answer plan

Part (a)

You should consider:

• transfer of value to connected person – s 270 of the IHTA 1984:

  o potentially exempt transfer; reservation of benefit – s 102 of the FA 1986; *Nichols v IRC* (1975); contrast *Munro v Commissioner for Stamp Duties* (1934);

- o donee's enjoyment of gifted property to the entire exclusion of the donor – para 6 of Schedule 20 to the FA 1986;
- o disposition not intended to confer a gratuitous benefit – s 10 of the IHTA 1984;
- o death within two years after making a PET;
- computing the rate of inheritance tax.

Part (b)

Discuss transfer of value:

- potentially exempt transfer – ss 3 and 3(A) of the IHTA 1984;
- disposition not intended to confer a gratuitous benefit – s 10 of the IHTA 1984.

Part (c)

Sections 3 and 3(A) of the IHTA 1984 need to be considered here, as well as:

- annual exemption – s 19 of the IHTA 1984;
- small gifts exemption – s 20 of the IHTA 1984;
- sale of objects at market value – s 10 of the IHTA 1984;
- transfer on death – s 4 of the IHTA 1984;
- inter-spousal exemption – s 18 of the IHTA 1984;
- obligation to settle tax – ss 199 and 200 of the IHTA 1984.

Answer

Part (a)

There are a number of inheritance tax issues posed by the facts of this problem. The disposition of David's house worth £150,000 in January 1997, by way of gift *inter vivos* to his daughter, is a transfer of value to a connected person and is treated as a PET. The term 'connected person' is defined in s 270 of the IHTA 1984 by reference to the capital gains tax provision enacted in s 286 of the Taxation and Chargeable Gains Act 1992 (TCGA), David's daughter is a 'relative' as defined in s 286(8) of the TCGA 1992 and connected with David. The gift of the house to David's daughter becomes comprised in the daughter's estate and her estate is increased in value. Accordingly, David's transfer of value is potentially exempt.

On the same date, David's daughter granted David a lease of the property for 10 years at a commercial rent. This, *prima facie*, attracts the reservation of benefit provision within s 102 of the FA 1986. The disposition is treated as a gift and, during the 'relevant period' (period of seven years ending with the death of the donor), the property is not enjoyed to the entire exclusion of the donor and any benefit to him by contract or otherwise: see *Nichols v IRC* (1975); and contrast *Munro v Commissioner for Stamp Duties* (1934). The issue dealt with in these cases concerns the identification of the subject matter of the gift, that is:

> ... whether the subject matter of the gift was the beneficial interest in the estate shorn of the benefit of the rights and interests of the donor under the lease, or whether the gift was of the whole beneficial interest in the property. [*Per* Goff J in *Nichols v IRC*.]

The point here is whether the gift by David to his daughter is the beneficial interest in the house with an interest reserved by David in respect of the lease for 10 years within s 102 of the FA 1986, or whether the subject matter of the gift is the remainder interest in the house excluding the right created by the lease. The effect of the gift falling within s 102 of the FA 1986 is that the property is treated as continuing to form part of David's estate at the time of his death. Certain benefits enjoyed by David are ignored in considering whether David reserved any benefits 'by way of contract or otherwise'. These include an interest in land where retention or assumption by David of actual occupation of the land had been acquired for full consideration in money or money's worth: Schedule 20, para 6 of the FA 1986. David acquired a lease to the property for 10 years at a commercial rent. He is in actual occupation of the land for full consideration.

Accordingly, it is possible to substantiate an argument that David's occupation will not be within the reservation of benefit principles. Furthermore, since the lease was taken at a commercial rent, this does not involve a reduction in David's estate vis à vis the lease and does not constitute a transfer of value. David's executors ought to have no difficulty in proving that David had no gratuitous intention (subjective test: see *IRC v Spencer-Nairn* (1991)) notwithstanding that the transaction was between connected persons: s 10 of the IHTA 1984.

The effect is that David had made a transfer of value of a limited proportion of the value of his house, namely, the freehold reversion in his house, that is, his freehold house as reduced by the value of the lease. This transfer of value is potentially exempt. But David dies within two years after making the disposition. Accordingly, the PET becomes chargeable at the time of the original disposition. The rate of inheritance tax is ascertained by reference to David's cumulative total on the date of the disposition.

Part (b)

The exchange of David's racehorse worth £60,000 with Anne's racehorse worth £50,000 is capable of being construed as a transfer of value of £10,000 and a PET, subject to exemptions and reliefs. In other words, the exchange reduces the value of David's estate by that amount: see s 3 of the IHTA 1984.

However, the disposition may not be a transfer of value if David's executors can prove that David had no gratuitous intention, that is, that David had made a bad bargain, in that he genuinely thought that the horse he acquired had good potential. In order to discharge this burden, the executors are required to establish the following:

- that David did not intend to confer any gratuitous benefit on Anne; and

- either that the exchange was made in a transaction at arm's length between unconnected persons; or that it was such as might be expected to be made in a transaction at arm's length between unconnected persons.

'Connected persons' is defined in s 270 of the IHTA 1984 by reference to s 286 of the TCGA 1992. As there is no information regarding Anne's status, we can only speculate as to whether she is connected with David or not.

Part (c)

Subject to exemptions and reliefs, the gifts by David in January 1998 of two large paintings to his sister involve PETs. We have no indication of the value of these objects at the time of disposition. The annual exemption of £3,000 is available to be offset against PETs, but only after other immediately chargeable transfers have been taken into consideration: s 19(3) of the IHTA 1984. In any event, the small gifts relief under s 20 may be used to reduce the value transferred.

In addition, David sold a few paintings for no more than £500 each. If these were sales at their market value, then the dispositions would not be transfers of value, as David would not have had a gratuitous intent: s 10 of the IHTA 1984.

Following David's death, his paintings have become very popular and, despite the escalation in the value of the paintings acquired by his sister, the value transferred by the PETs is 'frozen' at the date of the *inter vivos* dispositions. In other words, the PETs are valued on the date of the transfer (January 1998) and enter David's cumulative total on the date of the disposition. Inheritance tax is calculated by having regard to the rate in force on the date of death.

On David's death, a transfer of value is effected and inheritance tax is charged on the value of his estate immediately before death: s 4 of the IHTA 1984. Tax is chargeable on this notional value after deducting reliefs, in addition to chargeable transfers (including PETs) made by David in the preceding seven years before his death. Accordingly, the value of the remaining paintings (left to his mistress), which was £100,000 on the date of David's death, enters into his cumulative total. The increased value of the paintings following his death is ignored. One half of the residuary estate was transferred to David's widow. Section 18 of the IHTA 1984 enacts that transfers between spouses are exempt from inheritance tax. Thus, £200,000 of the residuary estate is exempt from inheritance tax. The remaining portion of £200,000 of the residuary estate enters the cumulative total and, after deducting reliefs, the amount of inheritance tax is calculated.

The primary liability to settle inheritance tax on David's estate lies on his personal representatives, whereas the primary liability to settle the tax on PETs made within seven years prior to death lies on the donees. The personal representatives may retain a secondary liability to settle the tax on PETs: see ss 199 and 200 of the IHTA 1984.

Question 42

Emily has a set of eight antique porcelain toy soldiers, out of which she donates two to Grams Galleries Ltd, a local art gallery which specialises in antique pottery. The whole set is worth £4,000, but each soldier on its own is worth £100. Her solicitors have also just informed her that a debt of £30,000 owed to her by Scrooge Ltd has become statute-barred, due to an oversight of one of their articled clerks two years ago, and that they are 'most sorry'. She is reluctant to sue the solicitors for negligence. Assuming that Emily has used up her annual exemption, advise her as to the inheritance tax implications of the donation and her statute-barred debt.

Answer plan

A number of issues arise in this question. First, the obvious question of the value that is transferred by the donation to Grams Galleries (defined as the amount by which the transferor's estate is diminished as a result of the transfer). In this respect, students often make the mistake of applying the 'related property' rules to a situation such as this, and it would be helpful to demonstrate an understanding of why those rules are not applicable here. Secondly, there is the (also obvious) question, whether the transfer is chargeable, exempt, or whether it is a PET. It is obviously not a PET since the transferee is not an individual – but is it exempt? (This would fall on whether Grams Galleries is a charity or otherwise exempt.) With respect to the statute-barred debt, the question is whether the omission to sue for the debt before it became statute-barred is a transfer of value, and whether a failure to sue the solicitors for negligence would also be a transfer of value.

Answer

The IHTA 1984 charges inheritance tax on the value transferred by chargeable transfers (s 1). Chargeable transfers are defined as transfers of value made by individuals, which are not exempt transfers (s 2(1)), and transfers of value are dispositions which result in the reduction in the value of the disponor's estate (s 3(1)). In this question, the 'donations' made by Emily would be dispositions within the meaning of the IHTA. There is no doubt that these dispositions result in the value of her estate being diminished. Consequently, one would conclude that she has made a transfer of value. Two questions then arise – the value which was actually was transferred, and, whether this transfer will attract a charge to inheritance tax.

It has been seen that s 1 of the IHTA provides that inheritance tax shall be charged on the value transferred by a chargeable transfer. On the question of value, s 160 provides that (unless otherwise provided by the Act) the value of any property shall be its open market value. This might appear at first blush to indicate that the value transferred by Emily is £200 (the price that the two donated toy soldiers would be expected to fetch in the open market). However, s 3(1) provides that the amount by which the transferor's estate is diminished as a result of the transfer is the value that is transferred. This indicates that the relevant issue is not the amount that Grams Galleries Ltd can obtain in exchange for the soldiers (£200), but rather the amount that Emily has lost by giving away the two items. The whole set of eight was worth £4,000 as a complete set, but when Emily gave away two of the eight piece set, she no longer had a complete set, but was rather left with six individual pieces worth £100 each. This means that before the donation, Emily's antique soldiers were worth £4,000, but after the gift, what remained was worth £600. Her estate has therefore lost £3,400 and that is the value that was (initially) transferred. It is important to note however, that if the transfer proves to be chargeable, and (as is usually the case) the transferor (Emily) is to bear the burden of the tax, then her estate will also be losing whatever tax is charged on the transfers, meaning that the original £3,400 will have to be grossed up at the relevant tax rates. This is the effect of s 5(4), which provides that, in determining the value of a transferor's estate immediately after a transfer, any liability of his to inheritance tax on the value transferred will be taken into account.

It may be helpful to refer briefly here to the 'related property' rules. Simply summarised, the rules (in s 161) stipulate that if any property is worth more, when aggregated together with any related property, than it is worth on its own, the property shall be valued as the appropriate portion of the value of that aggregate. This may first appear to be applicable in this case, since the donated toy soldiers are worth more when aggregated together with the remaining members of the eight-piece set than they are worth on their own. However the main issue as to the applicability of these rules is the meaning of 'related property'. In this respect, s 161(2) provides that property is related to the property comprised in a person's estate if it is comprised in the estate of the person's spouse, or has within the preceding five years been the property of a charity, held on charitable trusts, etc. From this definition, it is clear that the related property rules do not apply at all in this case.

Having determined the net transferred value (whether it ought to be grossed up will depend on the outcome of the discussion that follows), the next question is whether inheritance tax is chargeable on that value. The starting position in the Act is that unless a transfer of value is exempt, it is chargeable (s 2(1)). The question then is whether there is anything in the Act which exempts this type of transfer from an inheritance tax charge.

Part II of the IHTA 1984 provides for a number of exempt transfers. Section 20 provides an exemption for small 'gifts'. The section provides that transfers of value by outright gifts to any one person in one year are exempt if the values transferred by them do not exceed a certain specified small amount (in the 1998–99 year, this amount is £250). Unfortunately, although the donated toy soldiers are worth only £200 in the hands of Grams Galleries Ltd, this exemption does not apply here, because, as we have seen above, the value transferred is not the amount gained by the transferee but rather the loss to the transferor's estate (the net value of which in this case is £3,400).

Other possible exemptions are those in s 23, which exempts transfers to charities, and s 25, which concerns gifts for national purposes. Although Grams Galleries Ltd is an art gallery, there is nothing in the question to suggest that it has the status of a charity, and thus the s 23 exemption would seem not to be applicable. Section 25 exempts gifts to bodies mentioned in Schedule 3 to the Act. Schedule 3 does mention a number of specific national bodies, such as the National Gallery and the British Museum, but then adds:

> Any other similar national institution which exists wholly or mainly for the purpose of preserving for the public benefit a collection of scientific, historic or artistic interest and which is approved for the purposes of this Schedule by the Treasury.

Emily would face a number of problems if she tried to claim this exemption. The first is whether Grams Galleries Ltd is a 'national institution'. While that term is not defined in Schedule 3, it is doubtful whether 'Grams' can be so regarded. The second question is the purpose for which Grams exists. We have insufficient facts on that issue. The main problem however would centre on the question whether Grams has been approved by the Treasury for the purposes of Schedule 3. Again, there is no indication from the facts that this is the case. It may, therefore, be assumed that such approval does not exist. In the event, it is submitted that Emily would not be able to claim the exemption in s 25.

If the gift was made before 17 March 1998 and Grams Galleries Ltd were a non-profit institution, it would be possible for Emily to make a claim under s 26 (gifts for public benefit). This exemption is subject to a Treasury direction, but s 26(1) provides that the Treasury can make a direction after the transfer has taken place. Such a direction would depend on the Treasury being of the opinion that the antique toy soldiers are 'of national, scientific, historic or artistic interest' (s 26(2)(f)). This would seem to be rather unlikely. This exemption has been abolished in respect of gifts made after 17 March 1998: see s 143 of the IHTA 1984.

It would appear then that the transfers by Emily to Grams Galleries Ltd do not fall under any of the categories of exempt transfers. The final question is whether they would be PETs. This question can be dismissed quickly. According to s 3A(1), in order for a transfer to be potentially exempt, the transferee must be an individual or an accumulation and maintenance trust or a disabled trust. Grams Galleries Ltd is none of these, and thus the transfers to it are not potentially exempt.

We will now examine the question of the statute-barred debt. We have seen that a transfer of value is a disposition which results in a reduction in the value of the transferor's estate. There is no doubt that the value of Emily's estate has been reduced by the debt of £30,000 becoming statute-barred. The question is whether it was reduced as a result of a 'disposition'. The situation here arose because of a failure to sue Scrooge Ltd for the debt before the time when the debt would no longer be claimable. The term 'disposition' is not defined in the IHTA 1984. It would seem to cover situations in which a person actively passes property or an interest therein to another – but would it cover a failure to act? The clear answer to this question is 'yes'. In this respect, s 3(3) of the IHTA 1984 provides that where the a person's omission to exercise a right leads to a reduction in the value of that person's estate, and an increase in the value of another person's estate, the person who omitted to exercise the right shall be treated as having made a disposition at the time (or the latest time) when he could have exercised that right – unless it is shown that the omission was not deliberate. In this case, Emily's omission to exercise the right to sue for her debt has resulted in a decrease in her estate, and a corresponding increase in the estate of Scrooge Ltd. However, the omission was due to the fault of her solicitors, and so, as far as she is concerned, the omission was not deliberate. We would therefore conclude that the mere occasion of the debt becoming statute-barred is not a 'disposition' and, therefore, not a transfer of value.

Emily may have a cause of action in negligence against her solicitors in respect of this 'oversight' by their articled clerk, but we are told that she is reluctant to sue them. Would this also be an omission which results in her estate being reduced, and that of the solicitors being increased? If so, a failure on her part to take action against the solicitors would then possibly amount to a transfer of value. It is difficult to resolve this definitively. Section 3(3) of the IHTA 1984 speaks about omission to exercise a 'right'. A right to sue in negligence is of course a certain type of 'right' (perhaps, more of a 'liberty') but exercise of the 'right' is no guarantee in itself of success, and, indeed, may lead to great financial loss in terms of costs. Emily's estate may or may not be increased if she sued, and whether the solicitors' estates would be increased by her failure to sue them would depend on the result of Emily's claim – which cannot be known in advance. It would seem that 'right' in s 3(3) of the IHTA 1984 must mean much more than a mere liberty to commence an action which may or may not succeed (a liberty or 'right' which everybody actually possesses). It is therefore submitted that failure to sue the solicitors will not be the type of omission referred to in s 3(3) and will not, therefore, be a transfer of value.

In conclusion, it is submitted that the transfers to Grams Galleries Ltd, not being exempt or potentially exempt, are chargeable transfers. Emily has already used up her annual exemption and so the whole of the £3,400 net transfer will be chargeable. Depending on her cumulative total of transfers in the seven year period leading up to the transfer, the tax charged may be at the nil rate (if below the 0% rate threshold) or at 'life rates'. If her cumulative total (with or without these current transfers) exceeds the 0% threshold, then the value transferred will have to be grossed up to reflect the tax charged on the net transfers. It is also submitted that Emily's omission to sue on her debt before it became statute-barred, not being deliberate, is not a transfer of value, and that her failure to sue her solicitors for negligence will also not be a transfer of value. This would indicate that no inheritance tax liability will arise from those omissions.

Question 43

Francois and Michelle, both French nationals who have been living in London for the past five years, have been unhappily married for three years and are now arranging a divorce. They have agreed, as part of the settlement, that Francois' mansion in France (worth £650,000), and Francois' holding of £120,000 worth of shares in a London company, will be transferred to Michelle. Francois intends after the divorce is finalised to return to France but Michelle intends to continue living in London. Francois has agreed to pay any inheritance tax due on the proposed transfers. Advise him as to the inheritance tax implications of the proposed course of action.

Answer plan

This question involves a number of issues. First, the question of exemptions available for transfers between spouses; secondly, the question of excluded property; and, thirdly, perhaps, the issue of PETs.

Answer

Section 1 of the IHTA 1984 provides for a charge to inheritance tax on the value transferred by a chargeable transfer. The IHTA 1984 goes on to define a chargeable transfer as a transfer of value made by an individual, but which is not an exempt transfer (s 2(1)). In this respect, s 3(1) of the Act describes a transfer of value as a disposition which results in a reduction in the value of the disponor's estate. From the facts as presented, there is no doubt that if Francois were to transfer the French mansion and the London shares to his wife, each such transfer would amount to a 'disposition' under the IHTA 1984. As such dispositions would certainly result in the value of Francois' estate being reduced, the dispositions would fall to be regarded as transfers of value. The crucial question then is whether these transfers of value are chargeable transfers or not. The answer to this question depends on a number of factors.

The first point is the question of the couple's nationality. Does the fact that they are French nationals affect the liability to inheritance tax? There is nothing in the IHTA 1984 to suggest that a person's nationality is relevant to inheritance tax liability. This means that the couple's nationality is, of itself, of no consequence as far as the taxability of the transactions is concerned. It may, however (in addition to the fact that Francois intends after the divorce to return to France), be relevant in other respects. Section 3(2) of the IHTA 1984 provides that no account shall be taken of the value of 'excluded property' which ceases to form part of a person's estate as a result of a disposition; and s 5(1) provides that the estate of a person immediately before his death does not include excluded property. These provisions lead us to the question whether any of the properties to be disposed of is excluded property.

Section 6(1) defines excluded property to include property situated outside the UK, if the owner of the property is an individual who is not domiciled in the UK. What this means is that the French mansion would be excluded property and therefore free of inheritance tax if Francois is not domiciled in the UK. The issue of his domicile is not clear. As a French national who has recently come to live in the UK, he probably had a French domicile to begin with – his domicile of origin (*Udny v Udny* (1869)). A domicile of choice can, however, be obtained by being physically present in another country, with a settled intention to remain there permanently (*Buswell v IRC* (1974)). That intention cannot necessarily be inferred from Francois's coming to live in London (*Re Clore (Deceased) No 2* (1984)), and is possibly negatived by his intention to return to France after his divorce. It is therefore possible to conclude that Francois is still domiciled in France, and that the French mansion is excluded property, the transfer of which will not lead to an inheritance tax liability in the UK. However, the fact that Francois had been living in London for five years (two years before getting married) may signify that he had indeed acquired a new domicile in the UK (assuming that this could be seen as evidence of a settled intention to remain here permanently, which intention has only recently changed – but *Re Clore* indicates that there must be some concrete evidence of such intention) – in which case the French mansion would not be excluded property. If this were to be the case, then other issues might arise.

Both transfers may possibly qualify as exempt inter-spousal transfers. Section 18(1) of the IHTA 1984 provides that a transfer of value is exempt if the value transferred is attributable to property which becomes comprised in the estate of the transferor's spouse. Although the Act does not define the term 'spouse', it can be assumed that since the term does not seem to have any special or technical meaning for inheritance tax purposes, it would bear its ordinary meaning, that is, the wife or husband of an individual. If so, then the condition specified in s 18(1) would be satisfied if the transfers are made before the divorce decree is made absolute (see s 16 of the Matrimonial Causes Act 1973). This would *prima facie* indicate that both transfers would be completely exempt from inheritance tax. However the Act contains a monetary limitation on the exempt value if, immediately before the transfer, the transferor is domiciled in the UK but the transferor's spouse is not so domiciled (s 18(2) – in 1998–99, the limit is £55,000). The question then is whether the conditions for the limitation are satisfied. This again boils down to the question of the present domiciles of Francois and Michelle, but especially that of Michelle. Since Michelle intends to continue to live in London after the divorce, it may be presumed that she has acquired a domicile of choice in the UK. This would then mean that the second condition (that the transferor's spouse is not domiciled) is not fulfilled, and that the limit on the exempt amount does not apply. This would appear to be regardless of whether Francois is domiciled in the UK or not. However, it is possible to argue (perhaps not very convincingly) that Michelle's wish to remain in London does not necessarily evince an intention to remain permanently, in which case she might still be domiciled in France. This would then raise a question as to the first limb of the restriction – that the transferor *is* domiciled in the UK. If Francois were held to be non-domiciled (which would invariably be the case if one could hold that Michelle is non-domiciled), then the first limb of the restriction would not be fulfilled. This question would of course only be relevant in respect of the London shares, since, in this scenario, the French mansion would be excluded property. It does appear from the literal wording of s 18(2) that *both* conditions must be fulfilled before the restriction would apply. This would be anomalous – the limit would apply if the husband is domiciled but the wife is not; but it would not apply in respect of the London shares if both the husband and wife are not domiciled. While this is probably not the result that was intended, it does seem to be the result of the provisions as they exist.

In conclusion, much depends on the issue of domicile, which cannot be categorically decided from the facts. If Francois were to be taken to have acquired a domicile of choice in the UK, the French mansion would then not fall within the definition of excluded property, but might be covered by the exemption for inter-spousal transfers. It would also mean that he will be treated as being domiciled in the UK for inheritance tax purposes for up to three years after he has departed from the UK (s 267(1)). If he has not acquired a UK domicile, then the French mansion would be excluded property, and would fall outside the scope of the charge to inheritance tax. Either way, it appears that the transfer of the French mansion to Michelle would be free of inheritance tax. The former situation might be subject, in the event of Michelle being non-domiciled, to a limit on the exempt amount (provided that Francois *is* domiciled).

Finally, a question arises whether if the limit to the exempt amount is applicable in respect of the inter-spousal transfer rules, any amount in excess of the limit can be treated as a PET. This would appear to be the case from the wording of s 3A(1) which provides, *inter alia*, that a PET is one which is made by one individual to another individual, which would otherwise be a chargeable transfer. If so, it would seem that the proposed transfers by Francois would in any event prove to be exempt as long as Francois does not die within seven years of making them (s 3A(4)).

Question 44

In December 1997, Sam (who is domiciled in the UK) set up a discretionary trust for the benefit of his three nephews. The trust property consisted of shares worth £300,000. The trustees have an express power to apply capital and income as they see fit. His three nephews are Andy (aged 28), Bernard (aged 23) and Charles (aged 12).

Advise the trustees:

(1) on the general inheritance tax position of the trust; and

(2) on the inheritance tax consequences if they were to take the following steps:

(a) they now appoint £25,000 of capital to each of the three beneficiaries;

(b) they appoint £75,000 of capital to Charles on terms which provide that he will not be entitled to the capital until he attains the age of 25, but he will be entitled to the income from it;

(c) all the trustees move out of the UK and administer the trust from abroad.

Answer plan

Part (1)

For this part of your answer, the following points should be addressed:

- chargeable transfer on the creation of a discretionary trust;
- grossing up if tax paid by Sam, effect if the trustees paid the tax;
- effect if Sam dies within seven years after the creation of the trust;
- availability of business relief – s 105 of the IHTA 1984;
- '10 year anniversary'; 'exit' charges and depreciatory transactions; computation of the rate of tax.

Part (2)(a)

You need to consider:

- exit charge under s 65(1)(a) of the IHTA 1984;
- computation of the rate of tax.

Part (2)(b)

Under this part, you need to consider the following points:

- whether the trustees have created an interest in possession;
- has Charles a right or a power to income? See *IRC v Person*;
- payment of income to Charles without an interest in possession – s 65(5)(b) of the IHTA 1984;

- favoured treatment of accumulation and maintenance trust under s 71 of the IHTA 1984.

Part (2)(c)

Settlement remains subject to English law because Sam was domiciled in the UK on the date of the creation of the settlement and the trust property is situated in the UK. Chargeable transfers by trusts resident outside the UK entitles the Revenue to claim the tax from the beneficiaries and/or the settlor: s 201(1) of the IHTA 1984.

Answer

Part (1)
Creation of the trust

The discretionary trust (a trust without an interest in possession) set up by Sam in December 1997 of shares worth £300,000 creates a chargeable transfer which is not a PET. The effect of this creation is that the cumulative total of chargeable transfers made by the settlor are aggregated with the value transferred by the settlor (£300,000). If the settlor pays the tax it would be necessary to 'gross up' the net transfer in order to ascertain the value of the reduction in Sam's estate which was due to the transfer. If, on the other hand, the trustees pay the tax, no 'grossing up' is required because the transferor makes a transfer of an amount equivalent to the transfer of value into the settlement less the tax. The reduction in the value of Sam's estate will be the value transferred to the trustees, namely £300,000. The amount which will be added to Sam's cumulative total will vary with the circumstances as to whether he pays the tax or the trustees bear the tax. The effect in respect of settlements without an interest in possession is that Sam's cumulative total of chargeable transfers will comprise the cumulative total of the settlement for all purposes. Moreover, if Sam dies within seven years of the creation of the trust, PETs made by him within seven years prior to his death will become chargeable. This may result in increased tax being payable on the creation of the settlement and by the trustees during the subsistence of the settlement.

Business relief may be available subject to more information regarding the shares: s 105 of the IHTA 1984.

Subsistence of the trust

The trustees will be liable to inheritance tax every 10 years (periodic charge) for as long as the trust remains without an interest in possession. The '10 year anniversary' is the 10th anniversary of the date of the commencement of the settlement (that is, December 2007) and subsequent anniversaries at 10 yearly intervals (s 61(1) of the IHTA 1984). The chargeable amount is the value of the assets in the trust immediately before the 10 year anniversary, provided that no interest in possession is enjoyed by the objects of the trust. Tax is charged at 30% of the rate that existed when the settlement was made (effective rate): see s 64 of the IHTA 1984.

In addition, tax is charged on other occasions such as when property ceases to be relevant property (exit charge) and the trustees effect depreciatory transactions (s 64 of the IHTA 1984).

In these circumstances, tax is charged on the reduction in the value of the trust, subject to a number of exceptions laid down in s 65(4)–(9) of the IHTA 1984. If the trustees pay the tax from related property remaining in the settlement, 'grossing up' is required in order to ascertain the value transferred. The rate of tax will depend on whether the chargeable event takes place before the first 10 year anniversary or subsequent 10 year anniversaries. During the first 10 year anniversary, tax is charged at an 'appropriate fraction' of the effective rate on the relevant property. The appropriate fraction is the number of complete successive quarters in the period beginning with the commencement of the settlement and ending on the day before the chargeable event, divided by 40 and multiplied by 30% (s 68(2) of the IHTA 1984). The rate applicable in successive 10 yearly anniversaries is the appropriate fraction of the rate of the last periodic charge (s 69 of the IHTA 1984).

Part (2)(a)
The trustees appoint £25,000 of capital to each of the three beneficiaries. The effect is that this is a chargeable event involving the exit charge under s 65(1)(a) of the IHTA 1984, in that the appoint-

ed property ceases to be relevant property (see s 58(1) of the IHTA 1984).

The tax will be computed by reference to the following formula:

- ascertain the rate applicable to the trust on the creation of the settlement;
- ascertain the appropriate fraction, that is, the number of completed quarters immediately before the distribution, and multiply by 40;
- the rate of tax will be:

$$\text{number of completed quarters since commencement of settlement} \times \text{settlement rate} \times 30\% \times \text{chargeable transfer} \times 40$$

If the trustees pay the tax out of relevant property remaining in the settlement, they are required to 'gross up' the transfer in order to calculate the value transferred.

Part (2)(b)

The trustees appoint £75,000 of the capital to Charles contingently on attaining the age of 25, but granted him an 'entitlement' to the income. The difficult question which is raised by the problem is whether Charles has an interest in possession. The phrase has not been defined by statute but was considered by the House of Lords in *IRC v Pearson* (1980). An interest in possession means a present right to present enjoyment of the net income of the fund. Could it be said that Charles has a *right* to the trust income as it arises? This would depend on the extent of the trustees' power to accumulate the income. (Note that s 31 of the Trustee Act 1925 is subject to any contrary intention, and a power to accumulate the income is evidence of a contrary intention: see *Re Erskine ST* (1971).) If the trustees have a power to deprive Charles of the trust income as and when it arises, then Charles does not have a right to the income. If this is the case, Charles will have only a contingent right to the capital on attaining the age of 25 with a power only to receive the income. The head settlement trustees (subject to the depreciatory transactions rule in s 65(1)(b) of the

IHTA 1984) may not be liable to a charge to inheritance tax on the creation of sub-settlement because only a reversionary interest is created in favour of Charles. This reversionary interest is excluded property: see ss 47, 48 and 53.

Furthermore, the payment by the trustees of income to Charles without giving him an interest in possession does not constitute a chargeable transfer (s 65(5)(b) of the IHTA 1984). In other words, the payment of income to Charles as and when the trustees decide to do so does not give Charles an interest in possession. The transfer of £75,000 of capital to Charles, subject to the terms as detailed, may create an accumulation and maintenance settlement within s 71 of the IHTA 1984. This is defined as a settlement where:

(a) one or more persons will become entitled to an interest in possession or the settled property absolutely, on or before attaining a specified age not exceeding 25 years of age; and

(b) income is accumulated for the maintenance, education or benefit of a beneficiary and there is no interest in possession; and

(c) either not more than 25 years have elapsed since the trust was created or all the persons who are or have been beneficiaries have a common grandparent.

These conditions appear to be satisfied until Trevor attains the age of 18 (when he will acquire an interest in possession, subject to any contrary intention: s 31 of the Trustee Act 1925).

The consequences of such a settlement are:

- no tax is payable on the 10 year anniversary;
- inheritance tax is not payable on the creation of the trust as the transfer is potentially exempt;
- no inheritance tax is payable when capital is advanced to Charles;
- there is no inheritance tax payable when Charles becomes entitled to the property absolutely or obtains an interest in possession.

On the other hand, if 'entitlement to income' within the question means entitlement as of right then an interest in possession is created. A chargeable transfer (exit charge) will be effected by the trustees in that the property ceases to be 'relevant property'. The value transferred will depend on whether the head settlement trustees pay the tax or not.

Part (2)(c)

All the trustees move out of the UK and administer the trust from abroad. This does not involve a chargeable event but has the potential of creating an awkward situation for the settlor, Sam, and the beneficiaries. The settlement remains subject to English law, since the settlor was domiciled in the UK on the date of the creation of the settlement and the trust property is situated in the UK. If the trustees make chargeable transfers outside the UK and are not resident in the UK (see s 201(5) of the IHTA 1984), then, but for special provisions to the contrary, it would have been difficult for the Revenue to recover the tax from the trustees who are primarily liable to settle the amount with the Revenue. Accordingly, the Revenue is allowed to claim the tax from the beneficiaries and/or the settlor (s 201(1) of the IHTA 1984). The effect of this secondary liability in respect of tax remaining unpaid after it ought to have been paid is enacted in s 204(6) of the IHTA 1984.

Question 45

Grimm is considering setting up a trust for the benefit of his two adult children. He is, however, concerned about their lifestyle and spending habits and would prefer that no income from the trust is paid to them until he can observe 'a clear improvement in their attitude to life'. His friend Jane advises him that he should be careful to create a trust with an 'interest in possession'. He now seeks your advice as to the meaning and implication of this term. Advise him.

Answer plan

Since the term, 'interest in possession', arises in the context of the specific provisions relation to settlements, this question is really about the inheritance tax treatment of settlements, and should be approached as such. Whether such an interest exists in a settlement or not has a significant effect on inheritance tax liability both at the time of creation of the settlement, and in some cases, for the rest of the settlement's life. Thus, there is a need to discuss the various types of settlement and how each is treated by the inheritance tax legislation.

Answer

Grimm has received good advice from Jane – at least, in the context of the potential inheritance tax consequences of his proposed course of action. The term, 'interest in possession', is one which features prominently in the rules governing the taxation of settled property, in that the inheritance tax treatment of settled property varies widely, depending on whether someone has an interest in possession in that settled property. Generally speaking, the inheritance tax regime seems to favour settlements in which an interest in possession exists, and to actively penalise those in which such an interest does not exist. First, we will look at the meaning of the term itself.

'Interest in possession' is not defined in the IHTA 1984, but the meaning of the term has been the subject of judicial decisions. In *Pearson v IRC* (1980), the House of Lords has opportunity for detailed examination of the concept. The case involved three beneficiaries who were entitled to all the income arising under a settlement, but whose entitlement was subject to the trustees' power to accumulate the income. The question whether the existence of this power of accumulation was fatal to the existence of an interest in possession was answered in the affirmative. The present interest of the beneficiaries was qualified by the existence of the trustees' power of accumulation, so that the beneficiaries had no immediate right to anything. Rather, they only had a right to payment in the future, of any such income as the trustees did not cause to be accumulated. Such a right was not an interest in possession, which was held to mean 'a present right of present enjoyment' of the income (*per* Viscount Dilhorne). In *Moore and Osborne v IRC* (1984), Peter Gibson J referred to an interest in possession as an immediate entitlement, which for the time being is absolute, to income as it arises. Viscount Dilhorne drew a distinction in *Pearson v IRC* between the exercise of a power which prevents a present right of present enjoyment from arising, and the exercise of a power to terminate a present right of present enjoyment. In the former, there is no interest in possession. This was the situation in *Pearson* itself. In the latter, an interest in possession exists until the exercise of the power to terminate the right. So a revocable appointment to X for life would for example give X an interest in possession because X would be entitled to any income that arises until, when and if, the power of revocation is exercised.

However, in spite of the distinction drawn by Viscount Dilhorne in *Pearson* between the exercise of a power which prevents a present right of present enjoyment from arising, and the exercise of a power to terminate a present right of present enjoyment, the question whether an interest in possession exists depends on the *existence* of a power in someone else to deprive the beneficiary of trust income which has already arisen, and not on the *exercise* of the power. It should be noted that references to a person being entitled to income from the trust are references to the net income of the trust. This was the view of Viscount Dilhorne in *Pearson*. What this means is that the existence of a power in the trustees to divert some part of the gross income of the trust from the beneficiary is not necessarily fatal to the existence of an interest in possession. In this respect, the courts have drawn a distinction between a power in the trustees to apply part of the gross income in order to administer the trust (administrative powers) and powers to dispose of the net income (dispositive powers). An administrative power is a power the exercise of which is intended to preserve the estate for the benefit of both the income beneficiary and his successors – in short, they related to prudent management in the discharge of the trustees' duties to maintain the trust estate. Dispositive powers, on the other hand, are those which, if exercised, have the effect of diverting the income so that it accrues for the benefit of others (see Lord Keith in *Pearson v IRC* and Lord Kincraig in *Miller v IRC* (1987)). Only the latter would preclude an interest in possession.

In the light of the foregoing discussion, it is clear that the trust which Grimm proposes to set up for his children would, if he had his wish that no income is paid to them until their attitude improves, be one in which they do not have an interest in possession. Such a wish could only be realised if the trustees have some sort of power or discretion to withhold the trust income from the children, and as we have seen, the existence of such a power would deprive them of a present right of present enjoyment of the income. Grimm wishes to know the implications of creating a trust with an interest in possession. We will start by mentioning a general overriding principle. Expressed simply, the IHTA 1984 does not favour settlements in which there is no subsisting interest in possession. Generally speaking, the inheritance tax legislation divides settlements into three main types – first, settlements in which an interest in possession exists; secondly, settlements in which there is no interest in possession; and, thirdly, a special category of the second type above – settlements in which there is no interest in possession, but which are treated favourably by the Act.

First, should be considered at the treatment of settlements with an interest in possession. Section 49(1) provides that a person who is 'beneficially entitled to' an interest in possession in settled property will be treated as being beneficially entitled to the property in which the interest subsists. Where the interest is only in part of the property, then there is an apportionment as appropriate (s 50(1)). What this means is that the beneficiary is treated as owning the capital (or the appropriate part thereof) of the fund or the settled property itself and that therefore the value of that property will be comprised in his estate. Thus, the creation of a settlement wherein an individual has an interest in possession, during the life of the settlor, will, because the settled property is treated as being comprised in the beneficiary's estate, be a PET (see s 3A(2)). This attracts all the attendant consequences (for example, it will be exempt if the settlor does not die within seven years of setting up the settlement). On the other hand, if such a settlement is created on death, it will attract the normal death charges. When the beneficiary dies, the value of the settled property in which he has an interest in possession will form part of his estate which is deemed to be transferred on his death (s 4(1)). By ss 51 and 52, settlements with an interest in possession can also be liable to an 'exit charge' – where the beneficiary's interest in the settled property comes to end during his lifetime, this is treated by s 52(1) as if he had made a transfer of value equal to the value of the property in which he had the interest, and tax is charged accordingly.

With respect to settlements in which there is no interest in possession (typically, discretionary trusts and accumulation trusts – the type that Grimm seems to desire) the first point is that the creation of the settlement in which there is no 'qualifying' interest in possession will be a chargeable transfer (with the exception of certain favoured trusts). A 'qualifying' interest in possession is defined by s 59(1) as an interest to which an individual (or certain types of close company) is beneficially entitled. Property in settlements with no such interest will also (with certain exceptions) be 'relevant property' (s 58(1)) for the purposes of the '10 year anniversary charge', a charge levied at 10 year intervals on settlements which have 'relevant property' in them (ss 61, 64, and 66). This periodic charge continues for as long as there is relevant property in the settlement, no matter how long the period is, and is perhaps the most serious disadvantage of settlements without a qualifying interest in possession. In the midst of a 10 year anniversary, these settlements can also be subject to an 'exit charge' whenever any part of the settled property ceases to be relevant property (s 65(1)(a)). Thus, in the scenario envisaged by Grimm, if and when he does become satisfied that the attitudes of his children have improved and the trust income then becomes payable to them (that is, they have acquired an interest in possession), an exit charge might become payable on the amount by which the value of the relevant property has been reduced by this event (s 65(2)(a)). A similar charge would arise (grossed up if appropriate) where the trustees make a disposition (in a case which does not fall within the situation just mentioned), whereby the value of the relevant property is diminished (s 65(1)(b)). This would be the case, for example, if Grimm gave the trustees a discretion to make certain payments, from the trust income, to his children while he was still waiting for their attitudes to improve, and then the trustees exercise that discretion in making payments. Basically, Grimm's proposed trust would attract inheritance tax charges at almost every turn.

As indicated earlier, there are certain types of settlement in which there is no interest in possession, but which are treated in a different way from that just described. The main examples are: accumulation and maintenance trust; and disabled trusts. First, an *inter vivos* creation of either type of trust will be a PET (s 3A(1)). Secondly, property comprised in such settlements will not be relevant property for the purposes of the 10 year anniversary charge (s 58(1)(b)). There may, however, be an exit charge, where, for example, an accumulation and maintenance trust ceases to be one (s 71(3)).

Our advice to Grimm then is this – an interest in possession is one which gives a person a present right of present enjoyment of trust income. It is a 'qualifying' interest in possession when it belongs to an individual (for example, Grimm's children), or certain types of close company. Its main significance lies in the significantly different ways in which the inheritance tax legislation treats settlements in which such an interest subsists, and settlements in which no such interest subsists. Grimm should not create the type of trust which he proposes if he has a wish to avoid the adverse inheritance tax consequences that would attach, not only when he actually creates the trust, but also at each 10 year interval thereafter, and at the period when income eventually becomes payable to his children.

Question 46

Mary settles £500,000 on trust 'for Jim when be becomes a Catholic'. The trust also has a proviso that the trustees can pay sums to Jim 'if they are of the view that he is in serious financial difficulties'. Jim is 19 years old and is an atheist. Advise Mary as to the possible inheritance tax consequences that this trust would attract.

Answer plan

This question involves a discussion of the type of trust which has been created here, and of the inheritance tax consequences of that particular type of trust. Issues which arise include whether an interest in possession exists in this settlement, and, if not, whether it could be an accumulation and maintenance trust.

Answer

Section 1 of the IHTA 1984 charges inheritance tax on the value transferred by a chargeable transfer, which is defined by s 2(1) as a transfer of value that is not an exempt transfer. A transfer of value is defined by s 3(1) as a 'disposition' which results in a diminution in the value of the transferor's estate. 'Disposition' is not defined in the Act, but would seem to be wide enough to include a transfer of funds to trustees. By that token, the creation of the trust by Mary by disposition which reduces the value of her estate, and would consequently amount to a transfer of value as defined. Is this transfer of value a 'chargeable transfer'? The answer would be affirmative if this is not an exempt transfer. The main exemption in respect of trusts is in s 3A(1)(c) which defines a PET to include a gift into an accumulation and maintenance trust or a disabled trust.

Disabled trusts (referred to in the Act as 'trusts for disabled persons') are covered by ss 74 and 89. Sub-section (4) of each section defines 'disabled person' to include a person who is incapable, by reason of mental disorder, of managing his own affairs, and a person in receipt of an attendance or disability allowance (under specified social security legislation). There is no indication from the facts that Jim falls under any of these categories, and thus it could be taken that this trust is not a disabled trust.

The question then is whether this is an accumulation and maintenance trust. This type of trust is described in s 71 of the IHTA 1984. The first requirement is that one or more persons will, on or before attaining a specified age not exceeding 25, become beneficially entitled to the settled property, or to an interest in possession in it (s 71(1)). Does Mary's trust comply with this? The first noteworthy point is that there is no 'specified age' in this trust. In fact, the trust makes no reference at all to Jim's age. Secondly, even if there were a specified age, it could not be said that Jim 'will' on or before that age become beneficially entitled to the settled property. The money is put on trust for Jim 'when he becomes a Catholic'. While the word 'when' (in contrast with 'if') may seem to indicate inevitability, the fact that Jim is currently an atheist and may in fact never become a Catholic means that he may never become entitled to the settled property. Whether he will become entitled to an interest in possession in it depends on the meaning of 'interest in possession'. This is defined in *Pearson v IRC* (1980) as a present right to present enjoyment of the property. Although the trustees are given a discretion to make payments to Jim if they take the view that he is in serious financial difficulties, this is not the same thing as saying that he has or will have a right to the enjoyment of those sums. Indeed, the trustees may never exercise that discretion in his favour. The conclusion then is that the first requirement of an accumulation and maintenance trust is not satisfied, and there is no need to investigate the point any further. In the event, Mary's trust for Jim will not be a PET.

What then are the inheritance tax consequences of what now seems not to be a PET? First, the creation of the trust is itself a chargeable transfer, and will attract an immediate charge at 'life' rates. This is so because there is nothing that makes the creation of the trust an exempt transfer. What happens after the initial charge depends on a number of things. In most cases, matters will end here, unless Mary dies within seven years of the creation of the trust, in which case a supplementary charge at 'death' rates may arise. However, any trust is potentially a 'settlement' under the IHTA 1984, and if a trust falls within that description, there may be consequences lasting beyond the initial charge.

The inheritance tax legislation provides specific rules in respect of the treatment of 'settlements'. If this trust falls within that definition, then it would be subject to those rules. 'Settlement' is defined by s 43(2) to include a disposition of property whereby the property is for the time being held in trust for any person subject to a contingency, or held by trustees on trust with power to make payments out of income from the settled property at the discretion of the trustees or some other person. Mary's trust clearly falls within the former, if not also within the latter. There is a contingency involved here – Jim becoming a Catholic, and the trustees have a discretion to make payments to Jim. Therefore, this trust would be a 'settlement' for inheritance tax purposes, and, according to s 44, Mary would be the 'settlor'.

The inheritance tax treatment of this settlement will depend on whether the property comprised in it is 'relevant property' within the meaning of the IHTA 1984. Section 58(1) defines relevant property as (with certain exceptions which are inapplicable here) settled property in which no qualifying interest in possession subsists. A 'qualifying interest in possession' is one to which an individual (or certain types of company) is beneficially entitled (s 59(1)). We have seen earlier that *Pearson v IRC* (1980) decided that an interest in possession refers to a present right of present enjoyment, and that Jim does not have such an interest in the trust created by Mary for him. It does not appear that anyone else has such an interest and it therefore seems that this is a trust in which there is no qualifying interest in possession.

This means that the property comprised in the settlement would be 'relevant property' for the purposes of the Act. The main implication of this is that the trust becomes liable to the '10 year anniversary charge'. Section 64 of the IHTA 1984 provides that where immediately before a 10 year anniversary all or any part of the property comprised in a settlement is relevant property, tax shall be charged on the value of the relevant property (the tax is calculated in accordance with rules in ss 66 and 67). The '10 year anniversary' in this respect refers generally to the 10th anniversary of the date when the settlement commenced, and subsequent anniversaries at 10 year intervals (s 61(1)).

Between the 10 year intervals, there are a number of other possible charges in respect of this type of trust. First, the 'exit charge'. This arises on any event whereby any part of the settled property ceases to be relevant property (s 65(1)(a)). This would be the case, for example, where Jim suddenly becomes a Catholic and thereby acquires an interest in possession in the settled property. The second type of charge occurs when the trustees (in a case where the exit charge does not apply) make a disposition which results in a diminution of the value of the relevant property (s 65(1)(b)). The tax in both cases is charged on the amount (net or grossed up) by which the value of the relevant property is diminished (s 65(2)). Neither of these charges will arise if the relevant event happens within three months from the commencement of the settlement or a 10 year anniversary (s 65(4)).

In conclusion, Mary's trust would seem to be one of those settlements the creation of which is a chargeable transfer, and which consequently is also subject to 10 year anniversary and possible exit charges.

Question 47

What is the effect of s 31 of the Trustee Act 1925 on inheritance tax?

Answer plan

This question is really about the inheritance tax treatment of certain types of trust, in this case, accumulation and maintenance trusts. Section 31 of the Trustee Act 1925 converts trusts for infant beneficiaries into accumulation and maintenance trusts. This has certain implications for inheritance tax.

Answer

As its title would indicate, s 31 of the Trustee Act 1925 contains provisions relating to trusts – in this case, trusts in which any one of the beneficiaries is an infant and is unmarried. Trusts fall within the general ambit of the IHTA 1984, which is very much concerned with the tax consequences of 'dispositions' whereby the value of an individual's estate is diminished (s 3(1) of the IHTA 1984). The term 'disposition' is not defined in the Act, but would seem in normal usage to cover situations in which a person passes property to trustees. The reduction in the value of the transferor's estate that necessarily follows such an activity indicates that any gift into a trust by the settlor is a 'transfer of value', thereby potentially attracting inheritance tax consequences. In spite of the fact that trusts would normally fall within the scope of the tax, the inheritance tax legislation provides specific provisions for the taxation of trusts. The provisions are in the context of a scheme for the taxation of settlements. Generally, the legislation deals with three types of settlement – first, settlements in which there is a qualifying interest in possession; secondly, settlements in which there is no

285

Q & A ON REVENUE LAW

qualifying interest in possession; and, thirdly, certain settlements in which there is no qualifying interest in possession, but which are treated differently from the second type just referred to. Accumulation and maintenance trusts fall within this third category of 'favoured' trusts in which there is no qualifying interest in possession. The broad effect of s 31 of the Trustee Act 1925 is to convert by operation of law certain types of trust which would otherwise not have been accumulation and maintenance trusts into this type of trust. This then results in significant inheritance tax advantages. In order to ascertain exactly how s 31 achieves this result, it is necessary to examine the provisions of the IHTA, which define what amounts to an accumulation and maintenance trust.

The relevant provisions are in s 71 of the IHTA 1984 which contains a number of requirements. We discuss these in no particular order. First, it is required in s 71(1)(b) that no interest in possession subsists in the settled property. 'Interest in possession' was defined by the House of Lords in *Pearson v IRC* as a present right of present enjoyment of the trust income. Discretionary trusts and contingent trusts (where the contingency is not yet satisfied) do not normally (whether or not the beneficiary is an infant) give a present right of present enjoyment, and thus would normally satisfy this requirement of s 71(1)(b). A typical example of an appropriate situation is one in which an infant's interest is contingent on the attainment of an age which the infant has not yet attained. Secondly, it is required in s 71(1)(b) that the income from the settled property is to be accumulated if it is not applied for the maintenance, education or benefit of a beneficiary. Thirdly, it is required in s 71(1)(a) that one or more persons will on or before attaining a specified age not exceeding 25, become beneficially entitled to an interest in possession in the settled property.

Obviously, all three conditions can be met by a trust which specifically provides therefor. For example, property could be settled 'for X absolutely when she is 22' with a clear direction that the trustees should accumulate whatever income is not applied for her maintenance, education or benefit before she attains that age. Regardless of the age of X, the requirements of s 71(1) of the IHTA 1984 will be satisfied. But what if the trust deed specified 'for X absolutely when she is 40' and said nothing about accumulation? Whether s 71(1) will be satisfied or not will then depend on X's age. If X is 20, then the provisions are clearly not met, because the age at which she will acquire an interest in possession (40) is higher than the maximum (25) specified by s 71(1). But what if X is 15 years old? This is where s 31 of the Trustee Act 1925 comes in. As stated earlier, s 31 of the Trustee Act 1925 applies to trusts with infant beneficiaries. The section provides that where the infant beneficiary's interest is not reversionary, the trustees may, during the infancy of the beneficiary, apply income from the settled property for his maintenance, education or benefit (s 31(1)(i)). Section 31(1)(ii) provides that if the beneficiary has not acquired a vested interest in such income when he attains the age of 18, then the trustees shall pay the income to the beneficiary until he attains a vested interest, dies, or his interest fails. Section 31(2) provides that during the infancy of the beneficiary, the trustees shall accumulate the residue of the income. Therefore, the effect of s 31 of the Trustee Act 1925 is that an infant beneficiary obtains an interest in possession in the settled property when he attains the age of 18. Since this age is one that is specified (by s 31 of the Trustee Act) and is obviously below 25, and the beneficiary will, on attaining that age, be entitled to an interest in possession in the settled property, it follows that any trust to which s 31 applies will satisfy the conditions in s 71(1) of the IHTA 1984. Therefore, in the example above of a trust 'for X absolutely when she is 40', when X is 15 years old, s 31 of the Trustee Act gives X an interest in possession when she reaches the age of 18. In effect, s 31 comes to the assistance of the parties when an infant beneficiary's interest (on the terms of the trust) is contingent on attaining an age in excess of 25.

The question then is the significance of this intervention by s 31 as far as the inheritance tax consequences are concerned. If s 31 converts a trust into an accumulation and maintenance trust when it would not normally have been such a trust, the inheritance tax consequences of such conversion could be quite dramatic. We have discussed earlier the different types of settlement for inheritance tax purposes. A trust in which there is no qualifying interest in possession is treated rather harshly by the inheritance tax regime. First, gifts into such a trust would be chargeable transfers (that is, immediately chargeable at 'life' rates). Secondly, property in such a trust would be 'relevant property' for the purpose of the charges levied on the value of the relevant property at 10 year intervals during the life of the trust, or until it ceases to be such a trust. Avoidance of this '10 year anniversary' charge is perhaps the most significant difference that s 31 would make. Section 58(1)(b) of the IHTA 1984 excepts from the definition of 'relevant property' trusts to which s 71 of the IHTA 1984 apply. Another major consequence of the intervention of s 31 is that gifts into accumulation and maintenance trusts are PETs (s 3A(1)(c)). This avoids the immediate charge at life rates, and may even avoid a charge altogether if the transferor does not die within seven years of any such gift.

To summarise, the effect of s 31 of the Trustee Act 1925 is to convert certain trusts for infant beneficiaries into accumulation and maintenance trusts, even in cases where they would not normally qualify to be so described. This conversion then has the further effect of avoiding immediate charges on gifts into the trust (because the gifts will be potentially exempt) and also of avoiding the 10 year anniversary charges (because the property concerned will not be 'relevant property' for those purposes).

Question 48

Sheila, aged 53, is the managing director of a small trading company in which she owns shares worth £500, 000. She founded the business 12 years ago and feels that it is getting close to the time for another to take over the responsibility for running the business. Sheila would like to transfer the business to her daughter, Amy, who already works with her, by passing these shares to her. Sheila is considering three possible ways of transferring the business:

(a) she donates the shares to Amy immediately;

(b) she gives the shares to Amy when she retires, which is likely to be in January 1999 or at the latest December 1999;

(c) she makes a will leaving the shares to Amy when she dies.

Advise Sheila as to the capital gains tax and inheritance tax consequences of each option so that she can decide which is best.

Answer plan

Part (a)

In respect of capital gains tax, you need to consider:

• shares – chargeable asset s 21 of the Capital Gains Tax Act 1992 (CGTA);

• gift by Sheila to Amy – ss 17, 18 and 206 of the TCGA 1992;

• joins election and hold-over relief in respect of gifts of business assets under s 165 of the TCGA 1992.

With regard to inheritance tax, the following issues should be addressed:

• potentially exempt transfer under s 3(A) of the IHTA 1984;

• business property relief under ss 103–14 of the IHTA 1984;

• inheritance tax paid added to Amy's base cost for capital gains tax – s 165(10) of the TCGA 1992.

Part (b)

For capital gains tax, the following points need to be considered:

• retirement relief under s 163 and 164 of the TCGA 1992;

• quantification of the relief.

For inheritance tax, consider:

• potentially exempt transfer under s 3(A) of the IHTA 1984;

• business property relief – ss 103–14 of the IHTA 1984.

Part (c)

Regarding capital gains tax, issues to be addressed are:

• acquisition of property by personal representatives at market value on the date of Sheila's death;

- acquisition of uplift in the capital gains tax base when the legatee (Amy) acquires the assets from the personal representatives – s 62 of the TCGA 1992.

For inheritance tax, you will need to discuss:

- transfer of value on death – s 4 of the IHTA 1984;
- computation of rate of inheritance tax;
- valuation of quoted and unquoted shares;
- payment of tax by instalments – ss 227–28 of the IHTA 1984.

Answer

Part (a)

Capital gains tax

The shares owned by Sheila constitute a chargeable asset (see s 21 of the TCGA 1992). If Sheila donates the asset (shares) to Amy, her daughter, Sheila will be deemed to have effected a chargeable disposal under s 18 of the TCGA 1992 (a disposal between connected persons shall be treated as a disposal otherwise than at arm's length). Section 17 of the TCGA 1992 enacts that a gift constitutes a disposal otherwise than at arm's length. Under s 286 of the TCGA 1992, an individual (Sheila) is connected with a relative (as defined). The disposal proceeds shall be deemed to be the market value of the asset at the time of the disposal.

However, both parties may make a joint election under s 165 of the TCGA 1992 to postpone the liability to capital gains tax (hold over relief). The relevant conditions seem to be satisfied. A number of conditions are required to be satisfied – an individual makes a disposal otherwise than under a bargain at arm's length and the asset consists of unquoted shares or securities in a trading company. The effect of the claim is twofold, namely:

(a) Sheila's disposal proceeds shall be reduced by the 'held over' gain; and

(b) Amy's allowable expenditure shall be reduced by the 'held over' gain.

Inheritance tax

With regard to inheritance tax, the gift to Amy is a transfer of value and a PET (see s 3(A) of the IHTA 1984) with the effect that, if Sheila dies within seven years from the date of making the gift, the shares will become chargeable to inheritance tax on the market value of the shares on the date of the gift, subject to business property relief.

Business property relief is available, under ss 103–14 of the IHTA 1984, for transfers of value *inter vivos* or on death of an individual in respect of 'relevant business property' as defined. Such property includes shares in limited circumstances. The relief is granted by way of a 50% reduction in the value of the business property transferred. However, in order to qualify for relief, the property is required to have been owned by the transferor for at least two years immediately before the transfer. The inheritance tax paid will be added on to Amy's base cost for capital gains tax purposes and will have the effect of reducing the gain that may accrue to Amy on future disposal: s 165(10) of the TCGA 1992.

If Sheila lives for longer than seven years after the disposition, then, provided that the reservation of benefit provision is not applicable, no inheritance tax is payable. It is unclear whether there is a reservation of benefit by Sheila continuing to be a salaried Managing Director.

Part (b)

Capital gains tax

If Sheila donates the shares to Amy in January or December 1999, subject to retirement relief, Sheila will be deemed to have made a chargeable disposal to a connected person at a value equivalent to the market value of the shares on the date of the disposal (see ss 17, 18 and 286 of the TCGA 1992).

By virtue of ss 163 and 164 of the TCGA 1992, retirement relief may be available to Sheila as she would, at the time of the disposal, be aged not less than 50. Other conditions which are required to be fulfilled are:

(a) Sheila must have been a full time working director, that is, a director who is required to devote substantially the whole of her time to the service of the company in a managerial capacity;

(b) the company is required to be Sheila's trading company or the holding company of a trading group. (Note the special definitions of 'trading company', 'holding company' and 'trading group' in Schedule 6 to the TCGA 1992).

The relevant conditions must be satisfied throughout a period of at least one year ending with the date of disposal. The quantum of the relief is dependent on the period during which the relevant conditions are satisfied. The maximum relief is available if the conditions are satisfied for a period of 10 years. On the facts, it would appear that Sheila is entitled to the maximum relief. If Sheila makes the disposal to Amy in January 1999, the relief available to Sheila is 100% of the chargeable gain up to £250,000 plus 50% relief on gains exceeding £250,000, but not exceeding £1 m. If Sheila makes the disposal to Amy in December 1999, the relief will be reduced as follows:

- the first £200,000 of gains will attract 100% relief; and
- the surplus gains not exceeding £800,000 will attract 50% relief.

Section 140 of the FA 1998 has amended Schedule 6 to the TCGA 1992 with the effect that from 6 April 2003 retirement relief will be abolished. The last year of full retirement relief is 1998–99. In the interim period, the relief will be phased out by reducing the monetary limits by 20% per tax year starting in 1999–2000.

Inheritance tax

The gift of shares to Amy will constitute a PET which will be chargeable if Sheila fails to survive the gift by at least seven years (assuming that no reservation of benefit had been retained by Sheila). Business property relief may also be available (see above).

Part (c)

Capital gains tax

On Sheila's death, no deemed disposal is made, instead, her personal representatives are deemed to acquire Sheila's estate for a consideration equal to the market value of the assets on the date of death. Her legatee, Amy, will acquire this 'uplift' in the capital gains tax base when the personal representatives distribute the shares to her: s 62 of the TCGA 1992.

Inheritance tax

On Sheila's death, inheritance tax will be charged on her estate as if she had made a transfer of value of the whole of her estate immediately before her death: s 4 of the IHTA 1984.

Sheila's cumulative rate is found by aggregating all PETs made by her within seven years prior to her death and transfers which are immediately chargeable to inheritance tax.

The value to be placed on the shares will depend on whether the shares are quoted or unquoted. If the shares are quoted on the Stock Exchange, the value for inheritance tax purposes is the lower of two prices, namely, 'one quarter up' or the 'midway' price.

The market value of unquoted shares needs to be estimated. This will vary with the circumstances such as whether dividends were paid within the last three years and the market value of the assets of the company. Whether tax may be paid in 10 equal instalments will depend on the nature of the assets owned by Sheila immediately before her death. Unquoted shares attract such privileged treatment: see ss 227 and 228 of the IHTA 1984.

Question 49

Donald, a businessman, in June 1998, destroyed a valuable stamp from his collection. The stamp was purchased for £2,000 two years earlier. At the time of the destruction the market value of the stamp was £12,000. At this time, Donald's cumulative total for inheritance tax purposes was £230,000. In July 1998, Donald spent £23,250 on a five week luxury holiday cruise for his good friend, Dorothy. During 1997 and 1998, Donald bought 1,000 shares in public companies at a cost of £3,000 for each year and donated these to each of his four golfing partners at Christmas. The average value of these shares at the time of Donald's death is £5,000. Donald's income is in excess of £100,000 net per annum and he was told by the secretary of the golf club that, in view of his income, the regular gifts of shares are exempt from inheritance tax.

In August 1998, Donald gave his daughter a painting by Renoir worth £160,000 at the time. The value on the date of his death is £200,000. The painting hangs on Donald's sitting room wall.

At the time of his death in February 1999, Donald owned 45% of the shares in an unquoted investment company, Dominique Ltd. His widow, Sally, owns 20% of these shares. His executors have ascertained that the combined value of Donald's and Sally's shares is £650,000. By his will Donald transferred his shares in Dominique Ltd to his two children equally. His half share in the matrimonial home, worth £125,000, is transferred by will to his two children equally. The remainder of the estate worth £200,000 is transferred by his will to his widow:

(a) consider the capital gains tax and inheritance tax implications of the above transactions; and

(b) compute Donald's liability to inheritance tax.

Answer plan

The following plan, taking each issue in turn, should enable you to deal with the important issues:

The stamp:

- destruction of stamp, transfer of value;
- whether the stamp was insured or not;
- s 10 of the IHTA 1984 exemption;
- destruction, a disposal under s 24 of the TCGA 1992;
- insurance proceeds, disposal proceeds under s 22 of the TCGA 1992.

The cruise:

- immediately chargeable transfer;
- no liability to capital gains tax.

The donation of shares to friends:

- PET;
- disposals under s 17 of the TCGA 1992.

The gift of the painting:

- PET;
- gift subject to a reservation of benefit;
- disposal under s 17 of the TCGA 1992.

The unquoted shares:

- valuation as related property;
- deemed acquisition at market value by personal representative and legatee at death.

The house:

- chargeable transfer of half share transferred to son;
- market value uplift at death s 63 of the TCGA 1992.

Remainder transferred to spouse:

- exempt transfer;
- market value uplift.

Answer

Inheritance tax is charged on the value transferred by a chargeable transfer. Subject to provisions to the contrary, a 'chargeable transfer' is any transfer of value which reduces the estate of the transferor (see s 3(1) of the IHTA 1984). A transfer of value is any disposition which reduces the estate of the transferor. Although the expression 'disposition' is not statutorily defined, it includes any sale, exchange or gift or destruction of property.

The destruction of the stamp

In June 1998, Donald destroyed a valuable stamp from his stamp collection. The stamp was worth £12,000. The destruction *prima facie* amounts to a loss or reduction of an equivalent amount to

Donald's estate for inheritance tax purposes. Thus, the destruction of the stamp amounts to an immediately chargeable transfer, grossed up at the rate of 20%, and enters Donald's cumulative total of dispositions, subject to the limitation contained in s 10 of the IHTA 1984.

If the stamp was fully insured, the insurance proceeds will be brought into the estate with the result that no reduction in the value of the estate is apparent. If the destruction is purely accidental, it is open to Donald to argue that the disposition was not intended to confer any gratuitous benefit on anyone and therefore not chargeable under s 10 of the IHTA 1984. The burden of proof to establish that the transaction is within s 10 is placed on the transferor/destroyer. For this reason, the transfer will not be included in the computation.

Capital gains tax is charged on the chargeable gain accruing to a person on the disposal of an asset during a year of assessment (see s 1(1) of the TCGA 1992). A 'disposal' is not comprehensively defined in the legislation but s 24 of the TCGA 1992 enacts that a disposal takes place on the occasion of the 'entire loss, destruction or extinction of an asset'. If the asset was uninsured, a loss would accrue to Donald equivalent to the allowable expenditure (of £2,000). It should be noted that no indexation allowance is granted in respect of disposals taking place after 30 November 1993 which result in a loss (see s 53(2A) of the TCGA 1992). If the asset was insured, the insurance proceeds will be included as the disposal proceeds and a gain or loss will accrue to Donald (see s 22 of the TCGA 1992). Even if a gain accrues to Donald *vis à vis* the stamp, he will be entitled to use his annual exemption (of £6,800 for 1998–99 year of assessment) to reduce the amount of the chargeable gain. If part of the gain is chargeable to capital gains tax, the rate of tax is equivalent to Donald's marginal rate of income tax.

The cruise

In July 1998, Donald spent £23,250 in purchasing a holiday cruise for his friend, Dorothy. This expenditure does not constitute a PET because the amount of the gift is not comprised in, and does not increase the estate of Dorothy (see s 3A of the IHTA 1984). The expenditure constitutes an immediately chargeable transfer of £23,250 as reduced by his reliefs. Donald is entitled to £3,000 annual relief (s 19 of the IHTA 1984 plus any unutilised amount of this relief in the immediately preceding year) and £250 worth of gifts per person (s 20 of the IHTA 1984). After reliefs, the chargeable transfer amounts to £20,000. If Donald pays the inheritance tax, the net loss to the estate is the amount of the chargeable gift (£20,000) plus the amount of inheritance tax (1/4 x £20,000 or £5,000), that is, the net gift is grossed up by the amount of tax or the net loss to the estate is £25,000. Following this transfer Donald's cumulative net total is £230,000.

The amount spent on the cruise is not liable to capital gains tax because sterling is not treated as an asset (see s 21 of the TCGA 1992). Indeed, it is unrealistic to imagine a gain in such circumstances.

The donation of shares to friends

The purchase of 1,000 shares in public companies followed by the gifts to Donald's four friends at Christmas are potentially exempt transfers (PETs). The advice given by the secretary of the golf club is inaccurate. Section 21 of the IHTA 1984 creates a relief in respect of the normal expenditure out of income. This relief *inter alia* is only applicable in respect of transfers made out of *income*. The donation of the shares to Donald's four friends is of capital assets.

Section 3A of the IHTA 1984 defines a PET as a lifetime disposition made by an individual which *inter alia* becomes comprised in the estate of the transferee or increases the estate of the transferee. The effect of creating a PET is that if the donor dies later than seven years following the disposition, the value of the PET becomes exempt from inheritance tax. If, however, the donor dies within seven years of the transfer, the amount of the transfer enters the donor's cumulative total at the time of the transfer and additional inheritance tax becomes payable. Unfortunately, Donald dies within seven years of the transfer and tax is payable on the value transferred. The total value transferred in the two years is £6,000, but since the £3,000 value transferred in 1997 is exempt by virtue of Donald's annual exemption for 1997, only £3,000 of the aggregate sum is treated as a PET. This amount is fixed at the time of the transfer notwithstanding that the shares increase in value. Alternatively, if the shares decrease in value at the time of death, the lower value is adopted for inheritance tax purposes: see s 131 of the IHTA 1984. The additional inheritance tax in respect of these shares payable by Donald's executors following his death is £3,000 x 40% or £1,200.

The gifts of shares to Donald's four friends constitute disposals under s 17 of the TCGA 1992. The gain is the difference between the market value of these shares at the time of donation as reduced by the consideration paid for their acquisition (including the incidental costs of acquisition and disposal) and indexation allowance. Donald's annual relief (£6,500 for 1997–98 and £6,800 for 1998–99) is available to be offset against these gains.

The gift of the painting

The gift of the Renoir painting worth £160,000 is a transfer of value and, subject to the reservation of interest limitation, is a PET. The PET becomes liable to inheritance tax on the death of the transferor (which in fact takes place) within seven years.

In respect of a reservation of benefit, s 102(3) of the FA 1986 enacts that where an individual disposes of property by way of gift and either:

(a) possession and enjoyment of the property is not *bona fide* assumed by the donee at or before the beginning of the relevant period; or

(b) at any time in the relevant period the property is not enjoyed to the entire exclusion or virtually to the entire exclusion, of the donor and of any benefit to him by contract or otherwise,

the property concerned is referred to as 'property subject to a reservation'.

The relevant period is a period ending with the individual's death and commencing seven years before or on the date of the gift, if it is later.

The gift of the painting was made by Donald in August 1998, but the painting was found hanging on his sitting room wall at the time of his death. It would appear that full possession and enjoyment had not been assumed by Donald's daughter during the relevant period. The gift is therefore subject to a reservation. In any event, the gift amounts to a PET. Either way, the value of the painting is taken into consideration at the time of Donald's death. The only difference between the two charging provisions concerns the value of the dispositions. As a PET, the value of the transfer at the time of the transfer is taken into account. This is £160,000. As a gift subject to a reservation, the value transferred is the value of the property at the time of death. This is £200,000. The reason for the latter rule is that the donor is deemed to remain entitled to the property immediately before his death. Inheritance tax on the painting will be £80,000 (that is, £200,000 x 40%).

The gift of the painting is treated as a disposal for capital gains tax purposes. The gain is computed as stated above and the rate of tax is Donald's marginal rate of income tax.

The unquoted shares

Donald died in February 1999 and by his will he transferred in favour of his children, his holding of 45% of the shares in Dominique Ltd, an unquoted investment company. Business property relief under ss 103–14 of the IHTA 1984 will not be available to Donald's executors because the company is an investment company.

The second issue concerns the valuation of the shares. The value of any property in a person's estate is found by taking related property into account if by so doing a higher value for the property would be obtained. Property is related to property in a person's estate if *inter alia* it is in the estate of his spouse, see s 161 of the IHTA 1984. Donald is the owner of 45% of shares and his wife, Sally, owns 20% of the shares in Dominique Ltd. Valued together, the holding is a controlling interest. The value of Donald's holding is taken as a proportion of the joint holding under the related property rules. This proportion is computed as follows: 45/65 x £650,000 or £450,000. This amount is bequeathed equally to his children and is liable to inheritance tax at the rate of 40% or £180,000.

Donald's half share in the matrimonial home is valued at £125,000 which is also devised equally to his children and is brought into account for inheritance tax purposes. The remainder of the estate of £200,000 is transferred to his widow. This transfer is exempt from inheritance tax (see s 18 of the IHTA 1984).

Capital gains tax is not payable on death. Instead, the executors and legatees obtain a free market value uplift in the capital gains base. The executors are deemed to *acquire* the assets of the deceased at market value on the date of death. Furthermore, the legatees are deemed to *acquire* the assets at the time of death and for the value at that time (see s 62 of the TCGA 1992). Accordingly, the children and Sally will acquire the relevant assets without liability to capital gains tax.

Computation of inheritance tax		Cumulative net total	
			£230,000
Transfer in July 1998		£23,250	
Deduct annual exemption 1998–99	£3,000		
Small gift	£ 250	£ 3,250	
		£20,000	£ 20,000
		£250,000	
Inheritance tax payable	£5,000		
PET of shares			£ 3,000
Inheritance tax payable	£1,200		

Value of estate at date of death

45% of shares in Dominique Ltd		£450,000	
Inheritance tax payable	£180,000		
Half share in home		£125,000	
Inheritance tax payable	£ 50,000		
Value of painting		£200,000	
Inheritance tax payable	£ 80,000	£775,000	£775,000

£1,028,000

Inheritance tax due on £775,000 at 40% £310,000

Question 50

Howard is aged 58 and seeks your assistance in drawing up his will. He is married to Mary. They have one child, Natalie, aged 14. Howard manages his trading company called Howard's Electronics Ltd. His pre-tax profits for the last accounting period were in excess of £500,000. Howard's main assets are his house valued at £200,000 which is vested in his sole name, income bearing bonds producing £5,000 per annum and shares in public companies worth £10,000. His wife, Mary is content to stay at home. She has few assets, jewellery worth £15,000 and a sports car worth £20,000.

Howard's main objectives are to enjoy his assets for as long as he can, to make provision for Mary should he die first and that his property should ultimately go to Natalie. He is also concerned about the future of his business should he die shortly. In particular, he wants to know whether the business will have to be sold in order to pay inheritance tax. He wishes to donate £10,000 to Oxfam either now or by his will.

Advise Howard on how he may arrange his affairs in order to achieve his objectives and keep inheritance tax to a minimum.

Answer plan

Your answer needs to consider the following matters:

* inter-relationship of the taxes;
* equalisation of estates;
* transfer of house to Howard and Mary as tenants in common;
* testamentary clause granting the survivor of Howard and Mary a licence to occupy the house but with a direct transfer of the deceased's interest to Natalie;
* survivorship clause;
* business property relief;
* retirement relief;
* 'gift aid';
* charitable covenants;

- s 23 of the IHTA 1984 exemption;
- PET's under s 3A of the IHTA 1984;
- 'back to back' arrangements.

Answer

Estate planning is an important activity that ought to be undertaken by the average taxpayer. Planning may take the form of *inter vivos* transactions designed to mitigate Howard's tax liability during his lifetime and on death. The ultimate goal of the tax planner is to ensure that Howard retains a larger proportion of his income and gains than he would have done if the plan had not been put into force. To be effective, tax planning must take into account Howard's overall tax liability, since the reduction of liability to one form of taxation may give rise to an increased liability to some other form of taxation, for example, where the objective is to reduce inheritance tax liability, transfers may give rise to increased liability to capital gains tax.

Capital gains tax is not chargeable on death. On Howard's death, his executor acquires an uplift in the capital gains tax base at market value. The legatees are deemed to acquire the assets of the deceased at the time of death and at the market value at that time, but no disposal is deemed to be made. Moreover, disposals between spouses while they are living together are treated for capital gains tax purposes as giving rise to no gain and no loss, that is, the allowable expenditure of the disponer is acquired by the transferee. For inheritance tax purposes, spouses are treated as separate individuals. Gifts between them during lifetime or by will are exempt. At the same time, it is inadvisable for Howard to transfer all his assets *inter vivos* or by will to Mary because this will result in a larger inheritance tax liability on the death of Mary, should she survive Howard.

Choosing the correct type of will may result in substantial savings of inheritance tax. As the will operates on death estate planning through wills becomes restricted. During the lifetime of the testator (testatrix), a number of key issues ought to be borne in mind. First, the importance of mutuality in that the husband and wife should each make appropriate wills. Secondly, the need to draft wills with the maximum flexibility. This requires the keeping of records particularly as to transfers of value and the need to keep wills under regular review to reflect changing circumstances. Thirdly, in preparing a will, the revenue aspects are but one of the factors to be taken into consideration and must be subject to the family and other circumstances.

The house currently valued at £200,000 is vested in Howard's name. Subject to any instructions to the contrary, it would be advisable for Howard to transfer the house into the joint names of Mary and himself upon trust for themselves in equal shares. This transfer will not be subject to capital gains tax or inheritance tax as stated above and has the effect of equalising the estates of both parties. The advantage of equalisation of estates from the point of view of inheritance tax is to ensure that Mary's inheritance tax threshold (of £223,000 for 1998–99) is not wasted.

Since Howard's objectives are to make provision for Mary, should he die first, and that his property should ultimately go to Natalie, it is recommended that Howard and Mary each make provision in their will to the effect that the survivor will be granted a licence to occupy the house for as long as he or she wishes and after that person's death (the survivor), the property will be transferred to Natalie. The value of the licence on the death of the occupying spouse should have little, if any, value. The effect of such clause in the will ultimately transfers the deceased's interest in the property directly to Natalie and ought to be wholly or partly exempt from inheritance tax. A survivorship clause which avoids the *commorientes* rule may be included in the will, requiring the surviving spouse to survive for a period of one month (or such other period as is appropriate) in order to avoid a double charge to inheritance tax. In this respect, s 92 of the IHTA 1984 provides that so long as the survivorship clause does not exceed six months there will be only a single inheritance tax charge.

Howard is aged 58 and runs his own company, Howard's Electronics Ltd. He is concerned about the future of his business. For inheritance tax purposes, business property relief (under s 103–14 of the IHTA 1984) may be available on a transfer made during Howard's lifetime or on death. The relief takes the form of a reduction of 'relevant business property' for the purpose of charging tax. The rate of reduction varies with the category of property concerned. There are two rates, 100% (effectively, an exemption) and 50%. In order to qualify, the property must normally be owned by the transferor for at least two years immediately before the transfer. It would be prudent for Howard to transfer part (to be determined by him after careful consideration) of the business to his daughter during his lifetime and the remainder of the business by will to Mary and Natalie. In this way, the business need not be sold in order to pay inheritance tax. Moreover, retirement relief from capital gains tax under ss 163–64 and Schedule 6 to the TCGA 1992 may be available to Howard. This relief is available if Howard has reached retirement age (50 for 1998–99) and makes a material disposal of business assets owned for a minimum period of one year prior to disposal. There is no necessity for Howard to retire in order to obtain the relief. The maximum amount of the relief is in respect of gains of up to £250,000 plus 50% of gains between £250,000 and £1 m, that is, gains of up to £625,000. This relief ensures that the *inter vivos* transfer of part of the business to Natalie will not require Howard to pay capital gains tax. Retirement relief is to be phased out over five years beginning with 1999–2000. The amount of gains eligible for relief is reduced each year by an equal sum of 20% and abolished entirely with effect from 6 April 2003. Howard has the potential to enjoy the maximum amount of relief during the year of assessment 1998–99.

Howard wishes to donate £10,000 to Oxfam either during his lifetime or by will. Whether the transfer is made *inter vivos* or by will the amount is exempt from income tax, capital gains tax and inheritance tax. There are a variety of ways in which the gift may be made during the lifetime of Howard. Section 25 of the FA 1990 introduced 'gift aid' in respect of single gifts of sums of not less than £250 to charities. Such sums are paid to the charity after deduction of income tax at the basic rate of tax and may be recovered from the Revenue by the charity. If Howard is a higher rate taxpayer, he is entitled to deduct the gross amount of the payment from his taxable income. Alternatively, Howard may execute a deed transferring a gross sum of £10,000 over a period of four years. The sums may be paid annually or in a lump sum, called a 'deposit covenant'. If the latter, the full amount (less the basic rate of tax) is 'deposited' with the charity which releases or withdraws one quarter of the specified sum per annum for charitable purposes. Under s 23 of the IHTA 1984, gifts to charities are exempt from inheritance tax without limit.

As a general rule, for inheritance tax purposes *inter vivos* gifts amount to potentially exempt transfers (PET's) which are disaggregated from the donor's estate, provided that he survives the gift for a period of seven years or more (see s 3A of the IHTA 1984). If such dispositions are to be made, they ought to be effected in respect of assets which are likely to increase in value. In Howard's case, this may take the form of a transfer (or several transfers) of shares in the public company to Natalie. Although capital gains tax is payable in respect of an *inter vivos* transfer at the market value of the asset at the time of the disposal, it is possible for Howard to use his annual exemption (of £6,800 for 1998–99) in order to offset the gain accruing on this disposal. Such transfer constitutes a PET. If Howard does not survive the disposal by longer than seven years, the transfer becomes chargeable at the value transferred at the time of the disposition, subject to taper relief if Howard survives for longer than three years. Alternatively, if Howard survives for seven years or more the transfer becomes exempt from inheritance tax.

Perhaps Howard may consider 'back to back' arrangements. These involve the purchase of annuities out of capital or income to enable him to take out one or more life policies written in trust for Natalie. The annuity payments are used to feed the premiums payable on the life policies. The gifts of the premiums may be exempt from inheritance tax if they fall within the normal expenditure out of income exemption under s 21 of the IHTA 1984. This arrangement is not treated as an associated operation if Howard is capable of passing a medical and the terms of the life assurance policy would have been the same even if the annuity had not been bought.

INDEX